THE PRIVATE
LIFE OF
EDWARD IV

THE PRIVATE LIFE OF EDWARD IV

JOHN ASHDOWN-HILL

AMBERLEY

This edition published 2017

Amberley Publishing
The Hill, Stroud
Gloucestershire, GL5 4EP

www.amberley-books.com

Copyright © John Ashdown-Hill, 2016, 2017

The right of John Ashdown-Hill to be identified
as the Author of this work has been asserted in
accordance with the Copyrights, Designs and
Patents Act 1988.

ISBN 978 1 4456 7132 1 (paperback)
ISBN 978 1 4456 5246 7 (ebook)

British Library Cataloguing in Publication Data.
A catalogue record for this book is available
from the British Library.

Typesetting and Origination by Amberley
Publishing.
Printed in the UK.

εἰ μὲν φράσω τἀληθές, οὐχὶ σ'εὐφρανῶ,
εἰ δ'εὐφρανῶ τί σ', οὐχὶ τἀληθὲς φράσω.

Ἀγάθων

(If I reveal the truth I shall not please you,
But pleasing you would not reveal the truth.

Agathon)

CONTENTS

LIST OF ILLUSTRATIONS

1. Edward IV's mother, Cecily Neville, Duchess of York. Redrawn by Geoffrey Wheeler after the Neville Book of Hours.
2. Edward IV's father, Richard, Duke of York. Redrawn by the author after BL MS Royal 15 E VI, fol. 3.
3. Edward IV's eldest sister, Anne of York, Duchess of Exeter. Nineteenth-century engraving of her funerary monument at St George's Chapel, Windsor.
4. Edward IV's paternal aunt, Isabel of York, Countess of Essex, from her funerary brass at Little Easton Church, Essex.
5. Edward IV's middle sister, Elizabeth of York, Duchess of Suffolk, from her alabaster tomb effigy at Wingfield Church, Suffolk.
6. Edward IV's youngest surviving sister, Margaret of York, Duchess of Burgundy: copy of her 1468 marriage portrait.
7. Jean II, King of France, great grandfather of both Charles VII and his queen. Copy of a contemporary portrait.
8. Charles VII, 'the Victorious', King of France, father of the first proposed brides of Edward, Earl of March. Nineteenth-century engraving after a fifteenth-century portrait.
9. Marie of Anjou, cousin and consort of Charles VII, and mother of the first proposed brides of Edward, Earl of March. Nineteenth–century engraving after a fifteenth-century portrait.
10. Jeanne of France, daughter of Charles VII, and later Duchess de Bourbon. Redrawn from her Book of Hours. Jeanne was the elder of the young Edward's potential French royal brides – the one favoured by his father, the Duke of York.
11. Madeleine of France, sister of Jeanne and later Princess of Viana. Redrawn from a contemporary portrait. Madeleine was the younger potential French royal bride – the one favoured for that role by her father, King Charles VII.

LIST OF MAPS

THE IMAGES AND ROYAL FAMILY BACKGROUND OF EDWARD IV

EDWARDUS QUARTUS[1]

Comforth al thristy, and drynke with gladnes,
Rejoyse with myrth, though ye have nat to spende.
The tyme is come to avoyden your distres.
Edward the Fourth the old wronges to amend
Is wele disposed in wille, and to defend
His lond and peple in dede with kynne and myght,
Goode lyf and longe I pray to God hym send,
And that Seynt George be with hym in his ryght!

Edward IV, who reigned, with one brief interruption, from 1461 until his death in 1483, was the first Yorkist King of England. He ruled England for twenty-two years during the second half of the fifteenth century. This was a troubled era, forming the main part of what is generally known as 'the Wars of the Roses'. Edward was the longest-reigning Yorkist king. However, the focus of this book is not upon his role as King of England. Instead it seeks to concentrate upon his alleged intimate personal relationships, and also upon the children he produced.

A good deal has been said about these points in the previous published accounts of Edward IV's reign as king. However, the present study approaches the story of the king's personal relationships in an entirely new way, in that it seeks to focus primarily upon surviving *contemporary* evidence. This means that it is based upon a specific search for sources which were written during Edward IV's own lifetime. Although consideration has also been given to any later source material, account has also been taken of the potential political context of the later writers, and of the slant which this may have produced upon the claims they put forward.

Most particularly this applies to the material which Thomas More wrote about Edward IV and his personal relationships in the sixteenth century, more than a quarter of a century after Edward's death. As earlier writers have sometimes already noted,[2] what emerges is the intriguing and somewhat perturbing fact that, in a number of cases, the claims made by Thomas More and other sources of the 'Tudor' period are not supported by genuine contemporary evidence. Indeed, their later claims are sometime *contradicted* by the surviving contemporary accounts.

Unfortunately, the picture which emerges from the surviving contemporary evidence is not always 100 per cent clear. Thus, some of the conclusions which are put forward in the present study have to be tentative. No claim will be made here that the hypotheses in question have been absolutely proved. However, it is important to emphasise that not a single theory is offered in the present study unless it is based upon some surviving evidence which has been clearly cited in the text.

Edward IV's family connections are interesting. His father was Richard of Cambridge, Duke of York. This made Edward a member of that branch of the medieval English royal family which was known as the house of York. Strangely, the statement that Edward IV was the son of Richard, Duke of York, was questioned in certain quarters during the king's own reign – and is still questioned by some modern historians. Clear evidence relating to this issue will be presented in chapters 3 and 4 (see below).

In terms of his siblings, Edward was the older brother of Elizabeth of York (senior), Duchess of Suffolk; of Margaret of York, Duchess of Burgundy; of George, Duke of Clarence; and of Richard, Duke of Gloucester (later King Richard III). In respect of his offspring, Edward was the father of the so-called 'princes in the Tower', and also the father of Elizabeth of York (junior), who later became the wife of Henry VII, the mother of Henry VIII and the ancestress of the present royal family. In fact, since his demise in April 1483 right down to the present day, with only two exceptions,[3] every subsequent English monarch has been a direct descendant of Edward IV.

While his private life has been more or less universally categorised as extremely lascivious, the facts – and the contemporary evidence – relating to this allegation have never really been documented or explored in detail. The present study will therefore investigate all of Edward IV's alleged sexual relationships. One key piece of potential evidence in this respect is where Edward IV spent his nights. For this reason the present work includes, for the first time, a detailed itinerary for the king based upon the surviving contemporary source material. The itinerary is divided between chapters 2, 6, 8, 11, 15, 18, 21, 24 and 26 of the book, and it offers the most complete record ever published of King Edward's movements, both in England and in the rest of Europe.

It is curious, given the number of his alleged liaisons, that while one of his living descendants still wears the crown today, the number of distinct and disparate lines of descent leading from Edward IV down to the present appears to be comparatively limited. If the allegations concerning his vast quantity of mistresses were authentic, one might have expected clear records of a far greater number of illegitimate children fathered by Edward IV – leading to numerous well-documented living lines of descent from that king. The truth about Edward IV's offspring will also therefore be explored in the greatest possible detail.

Edward IV was one of the last three kings of the medieval English royal family known today as 'the Plantagenets'. This is a phenomenon somewhat similar to that of the alleged medieval French royal surname 'Capet'. The name 'Capet' is applied by modern historians to all early medieval French royalty. However, we know that it astonished King Louis XVI in the late eighteenth century, when this 'surname' was applied to him and his immediate family by the French Revolutionary authorities. This was because although 'Capet' had been a kind of nickname used by Louis XVI's remote ancestor – the founder of the royal dynasty, King Hugh (*c.* 941–996) – it had never, in fact, consistently been used as an inherited surname by French royalty as a whole.

Likewise in England there is, in fact, no evidence that the appellation 'Plantagenet' was ever really used by most medieval English royalty. It is said that *Planta Genista* (the broom plant) had been employed as a heraldic emblem by the father of Henry II, King of England, namely Count Geoffrey of Anjou. However, there is only later evidence that a heraldic badge depicting a broom pod was used by some of his English descendants:

According to Brian Spencer in *Pilgrim Souvenirs & Secular Badges* chapter on Secular badges, page 293 & 295, initially the broom-pod was a French device, adopted in the French court as a royal badge and livery collar by 1378. Richard II used it in c.1395 to mark his alliance with Charles VI's daughter. The broom-pod design carried on in use during the 15th century and when Richard, Duke of York revived the use of the surname Plantagenet, then the punning reference to the Plantatgenets [*sic*] was realised (if not before), as the Latin name for the broom plant is 'planta genista'.[4]

In spite of the comparatively late introduction of the broom pod as a royal heraldic symbol in England, it does seem that the French nickname *Plantagenest* (later spelt *Plantagenêt*), which was derived from the Latin name of the broom plant, genuinely had been applied to Count Geoffrey.

> That Plantagenet was the cognomen of the father of King Henry the Second, Geoffrey Count of Anjou, who is also sometimes called *Pulcher*, or *le Bel*, there is ample testimony in the Chroniclers. He is called by both names by Gervase of Tilbury who was nearly a contemporary; and he is termed Plantagenest in the Chronicle of Geoffrey, monk of St. Martial at Limoge, and Prior of Vigeois, who wrote in 1183; in the *Chronicon Turonense*, compiled early in the thirteenth century; and in the *Opusc. de Origine Comitum Andegav.* throughout.[5]

In the seventeenth century, George Buck claimed that, in reality, the appellation had first been adopted about a hundred years earlier. According to Buck's version of the story, the name 'Plantagenet' was first applied to Count Geoffrey's *female*-line ancestor Fulk 'the Black', Count of Anjou, who was punished for a misdemeanour by being sent on pilgrimage to the shrine of the Holy Sepulchre in the Holy Land, and was scourged there, using broom branches.[6] If Buck is correct, then Count Geoffrey acquired the soubriquet from one of his female-line ancestors. It therefore seems curious that it subsequently came to be regarded as a surname (which is normally inherited in the male line). Buck goes on to argue that, despite the fact that controversy on the subject already existed in his day, Henry II and his descendants genuinely had used the name of Plantagenet. However, the authority which Buck cites for this claim comprises the listing of the monarchs in question in Master Brooke's slightly earlier *Genealogies of England*. Brooke's work hardly constitutes a primary source.

In reality, King Henry II of England – the son of Count Geoffrey of Anjou – never seems to have employed the name 'Plantagenet'. Instead, he was referred to as 'Henry Curtmantle (*Court-manteau*)', while his younger brother, Geoffrey, Count of Nantes, employed the appellation 'Martel'. There is also no real evidence that medieval English royalty employed the name 'Plantagenet' during the thirteenth and fourteenth centuries.

Yet, whatever the truth may be in respect of the use of the name 'Plantagenet' by the earlier generations, it seems certain that, some three and a half centuries after the house of Anjou had acquired the English throne, the nickname definitely was adopted as a surname by Richard, Duke of York, in the 1450s. In his article published in 1841, J. Gough Nichols, FSA, proved this point by citing the claim which Richard put to Parliament on 16 October 1460, in which he refers to himself as 'Richard Plantaginet commonly called

Duke of York' (*Rotuli Parliamentorum*, vol. 5, pp. 375, 377 and 378).[7] In fact, this action on the part of Edward IV's father seems to have constituted part of his claim to be the legitimate royal heir.

Ironically, in the following century the surname Plantagenet found itself formally applied by the so-called 'Tudor' dynasty to one of the illegitimate sons of Edward IV. Indeed, a peculiar modern argument now seems to assume that all medieval royal bastards would have been known by the surname of Plantagenet! The evidence in respect of those points will be examined in detail later (see below, chapter 28). Meanwhile, although no evidence exists that Edward IV himself *personally* used the name, he definitely applied it to at least one of his legitimate male relatives. The relevant record refers to the creation of Edward, the son of Richard, Duke of Gloucester (later Richard III), as the Earl of Salisbury. The boy is called by his uncle, the king, 'our dear nephew, Edward Plantagenet'.[8] Thus it is clear that Edward IV was familiar with the appellation. Probably, therefore, he would have been less amazed to find that the 'surname' Plantagenet is now applied by historians to himself and his entire family than King Louis XVI was when he first heard the French Revolutionaries calling him 'Louis Capet'.

In addition to the appellation 'Plantagenet', other terms which have been highlighted at various places in this introduction by the use of inverted commas include 'Wars of the Roses' and 'princes in the Tower'. Although Edward IV undoubtedly employed a rose – and possibly usually a white rose – as his chief heraldic badge, there is some doubt as to whether – or precisely when – his opponents employed the emblem of a red rose. However, I have dealt with that issue in another book, so it will not be explored again in detail here.[9] As for the so-called 'princes in the Tower', as this study progresses the point will emerge that it is questionable whether the two sons of Edward IV and Elizabeth Widville who are generally categorised in that way really were royal princes.

This question brings us back to the focal topic of this book, namely the sexual relationships of King Edward IV and the legal status of the offspring produced as a result of one of those relationships. Traditionally, the legal status of children depends on the legal status of the relationship itself. Thus the character of Edward IV – and its effect on English history – comprises a central element of this study. As we have seen, the traditional view of Edward is that he was highly promiscuous. It is also alleged that he failed to follow traditional royal practice in respect of his choice of a consort. This is based upon the widespread – but erroneous – belief that the standard practice in respect of English royal marriages was that the chosen consort was normally a foreign princess, who had been selected for political reasons.

The royal family to which modern historians generally apply the name 'Plantagenet' had mounted the English throne in 1154, in the person of King Henry II. The family then retained the throne until the death of Edward IV's younger brother, Richard III, at the battle of Bosworth, in 1485. Indeed, some members of the family survived into the sixteenth century as potential claimants to the crown. This royal dynasty was the one to which Edward IV belonged. Therefore, this study of Edward's private life will begin with a basic examination of the real evidence in respect of how his royal ancestors handled the questions of marriage and of illegitimacy. Hopefully this will clarify somewhat the actual background, in the context of which King Edward IV was (or should have been) operating. This is because, as has already been hinted, one notable feature of the reign of Edward IV is the problem surrounding his marriage policy. As we shall see, instead of making a politically arranged formal marriage with foreign royalty, Edward contracted alleged secret marriages with English widows. And in one way it is true that his conduct in this respect caused a major problem for the future of his dynasty.

The family tree below shows the main members of the English royal family from Henry II to Edward IV, and explores how they married. As can be seen, some of them married more than once.

As the tree shows, eighteen arranged royal marriages were made by those predecessors of Edward IV who are listed here. However, there were also eleven unarranged (personal choice) marriages. This suggests that for leading members of the royal family at this period there was just over a 60 per cent preference in favour of a suitably arranged royal marriage. But at the same time almost 40 per cent of the royal marriages noted here were based on personal choice. It is perhaps also worth mentioning the fact that, if a more extensive, complex and detailed family tree were examined, cases of marriage based on personal choice would prove to have been of even more frequent occurrence in the royal family, particularly during the fifteenth century.

Thus, while Edward IV's marriage decisions may have been regarded as inappropriate by some of his contemporaries, actually what the king did was in no sense a complete break with the royal precedents of his dynasty, despite the fact that his marital activity has often been represented in that way. For example, the founder of the dynasty, King Henry II, never contracted an arranged royal marriage. Instead, he chose his own consort, Eleanor of Aquitaine. She was not exactly a widow, but she was certainly not a virgin as she had formerly been the wife of Louis VII of France. Curiously, however, given that she was his chosen bride, Henry II then went on to prove unfaithful to Eleanor, and had a number of mistresses and illegitimate children.

More recently, Edward III's eldest son, the 'Black Prince', had also chosen his own bride – who was a widow – and had then proved sometimes unfaithful to her. As for the marital conduct of the Black Prince's younger brother, John of Gaunt, Duke of Lancaster, that had also been rather controversial and somewhat shocking. And John of Gaunt's younger grandsons, Humphrey, Duke of Gloucester, and John, Duke of Bedford, to some extent followed their grandfather's example (though they do not figure on this simplified family tree).

Another alleged feature of Edward IV is said to have been his relationship with various women to whom he was not married, and his consequent fathering of illegitimate offspring. If Edward IV did really behave in this way he would by no means have been the first 'Plantagenet' to do so. An examination of the same family tree which was used to examine royal marriage precedents – this time to explore the frequency of the generation of royal bastards – reveals a further set of interesting data. This suggests that the generation of bastards was by no means an everyday feature of medieval English royal life. Curiously, it also appears to suggest that those members of the royal family who insisted on avoiding arranged marriages and choosing their own partners were also potentially more likely to indulge in extramarital affairs, thereby producing some royal bastards. And this seems to be what is alleged in the case of Edward IV.

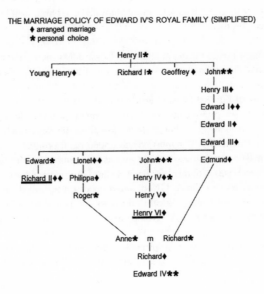

THE MARRIAGE POLICY OF EDWARD IV'S ROYAL FAMILY (SIMPLIFIED)
♦ arranged marriage
★ personal choice

About a century after his demise the following view of the reign of Edward IV (and its effect on his younger brother, Richard III) was published:

Though the vices of King Edward seemed not to add virtues to the condemned prince [Richard III], yet without question they do – making all his estimated ill actions of another nature. He [Richard] obtained his crown by fortune rather than by scheming ... for I think lust – or love if you prefer – could not more strongly have prevailed with the most licentious creature, breaking the bonds of friendship, discretion and politics. – and all to enjoy a woman [Elizabeth Widville] ... a widow & of his enemy, without bringing him either alliance or riches – props most pertinent to his newly enthroned royal house. In this respect he broke his alliance with his chief friend, the Earl of Warwick, whom he had sent to France to negotiate a marriage with the French king's niece [*sic* – Bona of Savoy], and who, having been deceived in this respect, then became his greatest enemy. But even more serious was his [Edward's] abominable abuse of God, for he had previously been betrothed (as his own mother constantly affirmed) to the Lady Elizabeth Lucy ... How soon the wrath of God followed his religious inconstancy is clearly demonstrated by his being driven from his throne into exile, the birth of his son in a sanctuary (having no other safe place available in his father's kingdom), and the misery of all his supporters. In which misery, who more truly followed him, who more faithfully aided him, than his now disgraced brother?[10]

The opening sentence focuses attention on Edward IV's 'vices', and it emerges fairly clearly thereafter that the vices in question have to do with Edward's alleged lust.

The view of Edward IV as vice-ridden in that respect is widespread, and Edward's alleged promiscuity has been presented in a very lively way by various historical novelists. For example, Josephine Tey says that Edward IV 'was – bar Charles II – our most wench-ridden royal product ... a six-foot hunk of male beauty'.[11] Sharon Penman has an opening scene in one of her books in which we encounter the young Richard out riding in the countryside with his elder brother Edward (Ned) and a maid-servant called Joan. In this scene, Edward and Joan sneak off to make love, leaving Richard to get lost. A taste of the encounter can be gleaned from this short quote:

Richard thought Joan was pleased to see Ned too. Her face was suddenly the colour of rose petals and she was looking at Ned sideways,

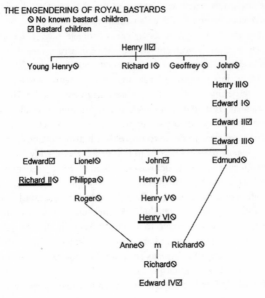

THE ENGENDERING OF ROYAL BASTARDS
⊘ No known bastard children
☑ Bastard children

filtering laughter through her lashes the way Richard had seen other girls do with Ned.

A few pages further into the novel, Joan has a predictable change of heart after having surrendered to Edward, and we find her tearful and ashamed in his presence. 'Much to Richard's surprise, Joan fled the solar as soon as Edward came through the doorway.'[12] Joan, of course, is a completely invented character – of necessity, because despite the fact that both historical novelists and serious historians have reported Edward IV as a great philanderer, actually we know nothing whatever concerning the names of any women who may have figured in his life as sexual partners prior to his accession to the throne. Thus historical novelists have been forced to use their imaginations and invent the girls depicted in their accounts of Edward's youth.

As for serious historians, they too seem generally to accept the view that his sexuality was a significant aspect of Edward IV's character. Keith Dockray reports that 'virtually all narrative sources allude to Edward IV's prodigious sexual appetite (with varying degrees of circumstantial details and judgement)'.[13] However, Dockray himself then goes on to mention only four roughly contemporary sources in respect of Edward IV and his sexual relationships. These are Gregory's Chronicle, the Crowland Chronicle, Domenico Mancini and Philippe de Commynes.

Of these original sources, Gregory's Chronicle merely reports, in the context of the announcement of Edward's marriage to 'Lorde Ryvers doughter ... Dame Elyzabethe, that was wyffe unto Syr John Grey', that 'men mervelyd that oure soverayne lorde was so longe with owte any wyffe, and were evyr ferde that he had be not chaste of hys levynge'.[14] This is quite a vague statement. Although it implies that contemporaries may have suspected that the young Edward had been up to various sexual activities, it produces not one scrap of clear evidence to prove this. It also mentions not one single name of a female partner apart from that of Elizabeth, Lady Grey (Elizabeth Widville). Of course, in spite of his lack of cited evidence, there might possibly have been some real basis for this chronicler's implied suggestion. Maybe his remark reflected rumours he had heard of Edward's relationship with Lady Eleanor Talbot, which, as we shall see later, unquestionably predated the announcement of his marriage to Elizabeth Widville. It may perhaps also have reflected another – and rather curious – liaison of Edward IV for which genuine contemporary evidence exists, but which has rarely been explored by historians (see below, chapter 9).

The Crowland Chronicle update (written a few years after Edward's death) says:

licet diebus suis cupiditatibus et luxui nimis intemperanter indulsisse credatur, in fide tamen catholicus summe ... fuit.[15]

The standard modern published translation of this Latin comment runs:

Although in his own day he was thought to have indulged too intemperately his own passions and desire for luxury he was nevertheless a catholic of the strongest faith.[16]

But the word *cupiditas* (*cupiditatibus*) does not necessarily imply sexual passions, and I should prefer to translate the comment thus:

Although in his day he was believed to indulge too extravagantly in ambitions and luxury, he was most strong in the Catholic faith.

Later, at the end of his assessment of Edward's reign, the chronicler adds:

I remain silent here [*only, of course, he does not!*] concerning what might have been discussed earlier in a more appropriate place, namely

> that men of every rank, condition and degree of experience in the
> kingdom marvelled that such a gross man so addicted to conviviality,
> vanity, drunkenness, extravagance and passion could have such a wide
> memory of the names and circumstances of almost all men.[17]

Although this remark certainly does not leave us with the impression that
the Crowland chronicler wholly approved of Edward IV, once again his
comments are vague and circumstantial. They offer no solid evidence of love
affairs.

It is curious that, in spite of his claim that he prefers to remain reticent,
the writer does advance a list of allegations against Edward. However, his
closest key word to the offering of an allegation of sexual immorality is the
one which is rendered in the published English translation as 'passion'. Once
again this is the Latin word *cupiditas*, which could equally well be rendered
into English as 'ambition' (see above). As he reveals later, the writer was very
well aware of the claim that Edward had been married to Lady Eleanor Talbot
(Lady Boteler). Indeed, he states specifically that after Edward IV's death it
was claimed that 'he had been precontracted to a certain Lady Eleanor Boteler
before he married Queen Elizabeth [Widville/Grey]'.[18] Yet nowhere does he
name any other alleged partner of the king.

In 1483, Domenico Mancini wrote:

> In food and drink he [Edward IV] was most immoderate; it was his
> habit, so I have learned [*which clearly implies that Mancini did not have
> personal knowledge of the matter, and is merely reporting hearsay*], to
> take an emetic for the delight of gorging his stomach once more. For
> this reason, and for the ease which was especially dear to him after
> his recovery of the crown, he had grown fat in the loins, whereas,
> previously, he had been not only tall but rather lean and very active. He
> was licentious [*libidinis*] in the extreme: moreover it was said that he
> had been most insolent to numerous women after he had seduced them,
> for as soon as he grew weary of dalliance, he gave up the ladies much
> against their will to other courtiers. He pursued with no discrimination
> the married and unmarried, the noble and lowly; however he took
> none by force. He overcame all by money and promises and, having
> conquered them he dismissed them.[19]

Other translations of the Latin word *libidinis* are possible, but in this instance
it does seem probable that Mancini was referring to licentiousness. Curiously,
however, he seems unable to supply the name of even one of the 'numerous
women' who fell victim to Edward's charms. Even his reference to Lady
Eleanor Talbot is oblique. He merely reports that it was claimed in 1483 that

'Edward ... when he took Elizabeth already had a legal alliance with another wife'.[20] Moreover, since he is writing of the period when Edward had grown fat, presumably his reference to licentiousness refers not to the early years of Edward IV's reign, but to the later years of the king's second reign (i.e. certainly after 1471 and probably after 1475). This was a period of his life when, as we shall see later, Edward definitely did have mistresses – something which may well have incensed Elizabeth Widville and her family (who are reported to have been Mancini's English informants).

Philippe de Commynes, who himself met Edward in the flesh on more than one occasion, reports that in the 1460s, prior to his dispute with his cousin, the Earl of Warwick, 'he was very young and the handsomest of the fine princes of his generation ... No man ever took more delight in his pleasures than he did, especially in the ladies, feasts, banquets, and hunts.'[21] However, his reference to 'the ladies' is vague. It does not necessarily imply sexual dalliance. Like both Mancini and the Crowland chronicler, Philippe de Commynes was specifically aware of, and refers to, the report of Edward's bigamy. However, he does not actually mention the name of the alleged first wife (Eleanor Talbot), reporting only that 'King Edward, being very enamoured of a certain English lady, promised to marry her, provided that he could sleep with her first, and she consented'.[22] He also names no other ladies associated with Edward IV except for Elizabeth Widville. Of her, he reports that 'later King Edward fell in love again and married the daughter of an English knight, Lord Rivers'.[23]

The other writers that Dockray cites as 'near-contemporary' are in fact nothing of the sort. Polydore Vergil wrote for Henry VII and Sir Thomas More wrote in the reign of Henry VIII. These two later writers do provide us with some additional names in respect of Edward IV's alleged relationships, though neither of them ever refers to Eleanor Talbot. This was thanks to the political correctness in respect of that specific relationship of Edward IV, which was very firmly imposed on the historical records in 1485 by Henry VII. However, Thomas More does mention Elizabeth Lucy. Indeed, as we shall see in greater detail later, for obvious reasons, he falsely asserts that Richard III alleged a pre-contract of marriage between Edward IV and *Elizabeth Lucy*, rather than between Edward IV and Eleanor Talbot.

We also hear from both More of 'Mistress Shore'. We have therefore now acquired a list of four names of ladies with whom, we are told, Edward IV had sexual relationships. These are Lady Eleanor Boteler (whose maiden name was Talbot), Elizabeth Lucy (whose maiden name is said to have been Wayte), Elizabeth Lady Grey (whose maiden name was Widville), and the lady who has gone down in history as 'Jane Shore', though her real first name, as we shall see, was actually Elizabeth, while her maiden name was Lambert.

Apart from a reference by Buck, early in the seventeenth century, to one Catherine de Clarington,[25] this completes the surviving list of Edward's alleged female paramours. No other ladies are anywhere named in connection with him. It is, to say the least, curious that if he was as debauched as later accounts would have us believe, more names have not been preserved in connection with that of Edward IV. Could it be that, rather like his grandson Henry VIII, Edward IV was therefore more of a serial monogamist than a polygamist?

It is also very curious that despite the fruitfulness of his union with Elizabeth Widville, very few other children of Edward IV are on record. Details have been preserved of a son, Arthur, and a daughter, whose name may possibly have been Elizabeth, both of whom have been ascribed to Elizabeth Wayte / Lucy. There is another daughter, Grace, whose mother is unnamed, but who is reported to have attended the funeral of Elizabeth Widville. And there are two other daughters, Isabel and (perhaps) Mary, on record – once again, with no named mother(s). Yet at least four bastard children have been imputed to Edward's younger brother, King Richard III. It seems curious that Richard – who has never been highlighted by historians in respect of his sexual peccadilloes – has been argued by some writers to have produced a potential sum total of bastard children more or less equal to that of his allegedly much more wanton elder brother!

At this point it might be helpful to consider why – and by whom – Edward IV was labelled a libertine if the allegation was not true. Like the besmirching of Richard III, and the airbrushing out of history of Eleanor Talbot, this may well be due – at least in part – to 'Tudor' propaganda.[26] Although he was married to Edward's daughter, Henry VII had no great love for the Yorkist kings, and it may have suited him to ensure that his father-in-law should be remembered as a profligate, debauched man. But it may also have been seen by Henry and his government as a helpful way of further undermining the fact of Edward's marriage to Eleanor Talbot. For, in spite of Henry's efforts, this was still remembered by various people, some of whom were in quite influential positions. If Edward was thought to have been in the habit of going to bed with all the women who came his way, one more woman, however highly born, was arguably of less account and could perhaps be the more easily dismissed.

Also, as has already been shown, the earliest accounts which suggest that in his later life Edward IV was licentious appear to be derived from Widville family sources. Interestingly, it might also have been in the interests of Elizabeth Widville, once she became aware of the king's earlier and (for her) dangerous relationship with Eleanor Talbot, to promote the story that her husband had always been on the look-out for all the possible mistresses, since for her, as also later for Henry VII, that story helped to undermine the legality of Edward IV's connection with Eleanor.

Anyone who wished to present Edward as a libertine was aided and abetted to some extent by the chance evolution of fifteenth-century fashion in respect of male clothing. Perhaps coincidentally (because the same tastes prevailed also on the mainland of Europe), by contrast with the fashions which came before and after, the reign of Edward IV coincided with a period of rather immodest tastes in clothing. This may have made it easy for anyone who wished to do so to tar the king with the same brush. Thus, for example, the contrast in character between Edward IV and his reputedly saintly predecessor, Henry VI, was emphasised by the change in the fashion of dress which roughly coincided with the new reign. Men's gowns, formerly long and all-enveloping, became suddenly very short. Churchmen complained that this new short garb, coupled with a tight hose which revealed what were described as men's 'privities', was scandalous. The Pope himself fulminated against the ridiculous new fashion in shoes which had toes so long that they had to be curled up around the legs. At the same time, for women the modest conical headdress gave way to the fantastic butterfly style, and women's dresses became very low-cut, revealing the bosom to such an extent that for the sake of maintaining some semblance of decency a flat triangle of fabric known as 'the piece' had to be inserted. From the 1480s, however, a return to more modest modes again prevailed: breeches began to envelope the upper part of men's legs, enclosing the tight tights and concealing the 'privities' once more. Women's dresses became less revealing and the butterfly gave way to the sober gable headdress.

Male costume during the reign of Edward IV.

PART 1
GROWING UP

2

1442–1458: ITINERARY

1442
APRIL
Born at Rouen[1]

1443 (age 1)
MAY
Rouen (his brother, Edmund, was born there)[2]

1444 (age 2)
SEPTEMBER
Rouen (his sister, Elizabeth, was born there)[3]

1445 (age 3)
APRIL
Rouen (planned marriage letter from his father to Charles VII)[4]

JUNE
Rouen (planned marriage letter from his father to Charles VII)[5]

OCTOBER
The York family returned to England from France[6]

1445/6
JANUARY
England (his sister, Anne, was married to the Duke of Exeter)

1446 (age 4)
MAY
England (his sister, Margaret, was born at Waltham Abbey)[7]

1449 (age 7)
OCTOBER
?Ireland (his brother, George, was born at Dublin Castle)[8]

1450 (age 8)
SEPTEMBER
The York family returned to England. Edward (aged 8) and Edmund (aged 7) were then established at Ludlow

1451 (age 9)
Based in Ludlow Castle?

1451/2
MARCH
Welsh border (Ludlow?) and said
to be marching on London[9]

1452 (age 10)
Based in Ludlow Castle?

1453 (age 11)
Based in Ludlow Castle?

1453/4
JANUARY
Predicted to be coming to London
with his father[10]

1454 (age 12)
APRIL
At Ludlow Castle with his brother
Edmund[11]

JUNE
At Ludlow Castle with his brother
Edmund[12]

1455 (age 13)
MAY
St Albans (at the battle – with his
father)[13]

1456–58 (age 14–16)
Based in Ludlow?

3

1442: PARENTS, SIBLINGS, GODPARENTS, AND OTHER FAMILY CONNECTIONS

It has been claimed that 'the Duke of York's main residence was Fotheringhay Castle near Peterborough',[1] but this is somewhat questionable. The Duke of York owned many properties, and Trim Castle in Ireland, Baynard's Castle in London, and Ludlow Castle on the Welsh border were also among his major residences at various times. However, the future King Edward IV was not born at any of these. Instead he is reported to have come into the world either in the small hours of the morning or in the early afternoon of either Friday 27 April or Saturday 28 April 1442, at the Castle of Rouen, which was then the headquarters of English government in Normandy – a government headed by his father. His birth on territory which did not form part of the realm of England might possibly have been one of the factors which later helped to produce groundless allegations that Edward was illegitimate (see below).

Most modern sources state blandly that Edward was born on 28 April, as though this were a fact, known for certain. This claim is based on the following statement from the *Annals* of William Worcester:

> 1442 Edward, King of England and France, the second son and heir of Richard, Duke of York, was born, on Monday [*sic*] 28 April after midnight in the second hour of the morning, at Rouen – who was conceived in the chamber next to the chapel in the Palace of Hatfield.[2]

Unfortunately, it is worth noting that Worcester's statement is undoubtedly *in*correct in respect of the day of the week to which it refers. 28 April 1442 was not a Monday but a Saturday. Moreover, elsewhere William Worcester recorded the birth date as 27 April:

> The Lord Edward was born, the second son of the most illustrious
> prince Richard &c, in the city of Rouen, on 27 day of the month of
> April, after midday, at 14.45, in the ongoing year of Our Lord 1442.[3]

Stratford, in his early twentieth-century biography of Edward IV, tried to
resolve this confusion by tentatively suggesting that 'the birth took place
at 2.45 a.m., which probably accounts for the different date'.[4] Sadly, his
attempted explanation merely muddles the two different dates and times.

It is therefore the case that, on the basis of the limited surviving
evidence, it cannot be asserted that 28 April was Edward's birth date.
Moreover, although the first record cited here (which refers to 28 April)
gives the hour of his birth as 02.00 or thereabouts (i.e. in the small hours
of the morning), the second record (which refers to 27 April) says that
Edward was born at 14.45 (in the afternoon). Thus, neither his precise
birthdate nor the time at which he came in to the world is known for
certain. The resulting uncertainty has a serious consequence. Attempts
have been made by modern historians to use Edward's alleged date
of birth to calculate when and where he was conceived – and also to
decide whether or not he was fathered by the Duke of York (see below:
Appendix). But such arguments are obviously ridiculous, given that
Edward IV's precise date of birth is unknown.

Only one tower of his birthplace, Rouen Castle, remains standing
today. That tower is highly unlikely to have been the part of the building
in which Edward's birth took place. It is also improbable that the
young Edward would have known that particular tower well during his
childhood, even though he apparently spent the early years of his life
at the castle (see Itinerary). This is because the surviving tower did not
constitute part of the normal residential section of the castle building in
the fifteenth century. In fact, it functioned as a prison tower. It was in that
tower, some years before the birth of Edward IV, that Joan of Arc had
been confined while undergoing her trial for sorcery, and while awaiting
her execution.

The account of Edward IV's birth penned by Mary Clive suggests that
Edward was not only born but had also been conceived in France. 'In May
1441 the Duke of York arrived in Rouen, the capital of Normandy, at the
head of an expeditionary force. His wife, Cecily, accompanied him, and in
the following spring, on 28 April 1442, she gave birth to a son in the castle
of Rouen. This was the future Edward IV'.[5] However, Clive's account is
at odds with the note (added slightly later than when the source was first
written, and in a different hand) which is contained in the text of William
Worcester's *Annals* (see above). This fifteenth-century note claims that

The Castle of Rouen as it might have looked in the fifteenth century.

Edward was conceived not in Normandy but in England – in a chamber next to the chapel at the Bishop of Ely's palace of Hatfield, in Hertfordshire.[6]

Possibly this sentence in Worcester's *Annals* was added in an attempt to undermine the rumours from France which later became current, and which suggested that King Edward IV (as he had by that time become) was illegitimate. This story, which possibly originated with – and was certainly propagated by – the French government, for political reasons, implied that Edward's mother, Cecily Neville, Duchess of York, had been unfaithful to her husband. The objective behind this account was the standard objective of all fifteenth-century French governments, namely to undermine in any way possible the current occupant of the English throne.

But the French story is contradicted by genuine pieces of evidence of considerable strength. First, there are the clear and explicit references in surviving letters written by the Duke of York himself, which refer specifically to Edward as his son and heir (see below, chapter 4). Also the illegitimacy story was very firmly denied in writing by Cecily Neville at the very end of her life, when her death was approaching. Her explicit denial of Edward's illegitimacy was recorded in her will. There she identified herself as 'Cecille wife unto the right noble prince Richard late Duke of Yorke, *fader unto the most christen prince my Lord and son King Edward iiij*[th]', and requested that once death had taken her, 'my body to be buried beside the body of my moost entierly best beloved Lord and housbond, *fader unto my said lorde and son*, and in his tumbe within the collegiate church of Fodringhay'.[7] Since her stark statement to the effect that Edward IV was the son of her husband was of no possible relevance to her own identity, she had obviously heard – and been deeply offended by – the story of her alleged marital misdemeanour. The elderly Cecily Neville was a deeply religious lady, and an oblate of the Benedictine religious order. It is therefore highly improbable that, with her death approaching, she would deliberately have penned a lie in respect of a subject to which she actually had absolutely no need to make reference in the context of her will.

Of course, as was suggested in the introduction (see above, chapter 1), the marriage of the Duke and Duchess of York had almost certainly been arranged. However, they seem to have genuinely come to love one another. Certainly the Duke of York consistently behaved as though he loved Cecily Neville, and was consistently faithful to her. Their children were numerous; the couple spent a great deal of time together, and there are no records of the duke ever having any mistresses.

Edward is most likely to have been born somewhere in the royal quarters of the Castle of Rouen (see the plan below). He was then baptised either at Rouen Cathedral or in the castle's chapel royal. There is no doubt that his younger brother, Edmund, and his younger sister, Elizabeth (both of whom were also born at Rouen in the following years), were baptised at the cathedral. But in the case of Edward there are conflicting accounts regarding his place of baptism, and there is no solid evidence to show that he was baptised in the cathedral. Scofield states that 'according to a note

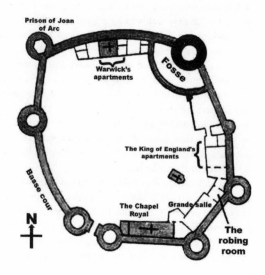

Plan of the Castle of Rouen.

left by antiquarian John Stow, the christening took place in the cathedral of Rouen'.[8] She gives no precise source for this statement, but her source was probably the earlier biographer, Laurence Stratford, who records that

> a note in MS in the British Museum speaks of his being christened in the Cathedral Church of Rouen, all the prelates and clergy being present 'in pontificalibus'. But against this must be set the fact that the Chapter Book of Rouen Cathedral has no entry of any such event, while permission for the reception and baptism at the Cathedral of his younger brother Edmund is recorded on May 18, 1443, as also that of his sister Elizabeth on September 22nd, 1444. There is an entry under the date of October 30th, 1442, giving permission to the Duke of York to use certain ornaments and vestments from the Cathedral 'to decorate the Chapel of the Castle of Rouen' for the celebration of the feast of All Saints. It is, therefore, reasonable to suppose that Edward was baptised in the Chapel of the Castle. His mother's brother, Richard, Earl of Salisbury, with Lord Scales and Lady Say, were his sponsors.[9]

Scofield notes that Stratford, 'having ascertained that there is no record of the christening in the chapter book of the cathedral, is of the opinion that Stow was mistaken and that Edward was baptised, not in the cathedral, but in the chapel of the castle'. However, she herself then goes on to argue that this 'evidence is of too negative a character to be of much value'.[10] Her case seems to be a good one. Obviously Stratford's implied conclusion that Edward may have been baptised in the chapel of the castle in *October* 1442 when the baby had been born in April is highly unlikely. Baptism at that period would never normally have been delayed for six months, and we can see from the evidence cited by Stratford that his younger brother, Edmund, was baptised at the cathedral on the day immediately following his birth in 1443, while their sister Elizabeth had her christening within ten days of her birth in 1444.[11] Nevertheless, in spite of that point – and Scofield's verdict – the general popular impression seems to have been that Edward's baptism probably did not take place in the cathedral.

Some historians have taken this to indicate that the little boy probably was illegitimate, and that his baptism was therefore not viewed as an important event by the Duke of York. (See below: Appendix.) However, even assuming that the baptism genuinely did not take place in the cathedral (which, as we have seen, is far from being absolutely certain), the real reason why the baby might perhaps have been baptised in the castle chapel would probably have been that baptism was taken very seriously in the fifteenth century. Thus, if a child showed any signs of weakness (s)he was baptised with all possible speed for the sake of his or her soul's salvation. Perhaps Edward seemed a slightly sickly child in the hours immediately following his birth, and for this reason his baptism may have been carried out immediately, and in the closest convenient religious location. After all, the Duke and Duchess of York might already have lost one son and heir – Edward's elder brother, Henry (see below).

Some writers also seem to have simply assumed that the place chosen for the baptism of an authentic child of the York couple would normally have been the nearest cathedral. As we have seen, it is true that Edward's younger brother, Edmund (later Earl of Rutland), and his younger sister, Elizabeth (later Duchess of Suffolk), were both baptised in Rouen Cathedral. Yet the choice of that location for those two subsequent baptisms can hardly have been political in its motivation. After all, Elizabeth was certainly not a potential York son and heir! Nor was she even the family's eldest daughter. Later the third daughter of the Duke and Duchess of York, Margaret (later Duchess of Burgundy), may well have been baptised at Waltham Abbey, where she was born. But the next son, George, who was born in Dublin Castle, was baptised neither in that castle's chapel, nor in the very nearby Dublin Cathedral of Christ Church, but at the city's more distant Dominican priory, which stood on the opposite side of the River Liffey to both the castle and the cathedral.[12] Obviously George's place of baptism must have been selected purely for religious motives of some kind. The York family is known to have had serious interests in the mendicant orders. It is therefore logical to assume that, wherever Edward IV was baptised, that location was also selected for religious rather than political reasons. Thus there is no reason to believe that the location chosen had any significance in respect of the later French political stories which cast doubt on Edward's legitimacy – but which became current only after he had been crowned. There is no evidence that such stories were current (even in France) during his childhood – or during the lifetime of Richard, Duke of York. If they had been, why would King Charles VII of France have seriously considered a possible marriage with Edward for one of his own royal daughters (see below, chapter 4)?

Edward was neither the first child nor the first son of the Duke and Duchess of York. His sister, Anne, and his brother, Henry, had both been born at the Palace at Hatfield, in 1439 and 1441 respectively. The following is a list of all the children of the York family, with their later titles supplied in parenthesis.[13] The children whose names are given in italics died young.

1. Anne (Exeter)	b. Hatfield (manor of the Bishop of Ely),[14] (?or possibly Fotheringhay Castle?), between 5 and 6 a.m. (or at 5 p.m.) on Monday 10 August 1439,[15] married January 1446, d. Sunday 14 January 1476.
1. *Henry (Harry)*	b. Hatfield (as above), 5 a.m., Friday 10 February 1441, d. before 1445.[16]
2. Edward (IV)	b. Rouen, (?)2.45 p.m., (?)Friday 27 April 1442,[17] became Earl of March 1445, d. early April 1483.
3. Edmund (Rutland)	b. Rouen, 7 p.m., Friday 17 May 1443,[18] created Earl of Rutland before 1454, d. Wednesday 31 December 1460.
2. Elizabeth (Suffolk)	b. Rouen, 2 p.m., Monday 21 September 1444,[19] married after 1453 and before 1458, d. 1503/4.
3. Margaret (Burgundy)	b. Waltham Abbey,[20] Tuesday 3 May 1446, married 1468, d. Thursday 23 November 1503.
4. *William*	b. Fotheringhay Castle, Friday 7 July 1447, d. before 1456.[21]
5. *John*	b. Neyte (manor of the Abbot of Westminster), Ebury ('Ey'), Westminster, Thursday 7 November 1448, baptised Chelsea, d. before 1456.
6. George (Clarence)	b. Dublin Castle, 12 noon, Tuesday 21 October 1449, d. Wednesday 18 February 1478.
7. *Thomas*	b. 1450/1451, d. before 1456.[22]
8. Richard (III) (Glos.)	b. Fotheringhay Castle (or possibly Berkhamsted Castle?), Monday 2 October 1452, d. Monday 22 August 1485.
4. *Ursula*	b. Sunday 20 July (Feast of St Margaret) 1455, d. before 1456.

It is possible that the eldest son, Henry, was still alive when Edward was born, and that he, at that stage, was the Duke of York's heir. However, it seems that Henry was always sickly, and he certainly died before 1445. Whether Henry died before Edward was born or afterwards, his known ill health may well have been the chief motivation for Edward's speedy baptism in the chapel royal of the castle at Rouen – if indeed that is what took place.

Baptism of a baby boy in the fifteenth century. The three figures holding the baby over the font are the two godfathers and the godmother.

Wherever the baptism took place, Edward, as a baby boy, would have required two godfathers and one godmother. Curiously – or perhaps significantly – the two of his godparents whose names remain on record proved to have family connections with Edward IV's two subsequent secret wives. Edward's godmother was Elizabeth Boteler, Lady Say, the sister of Lord Sudeley. Elizabeth Boteler married three husbands. From the first of these – Sir William Heron, Lord Say – she acquired the title of Lady Say. Her second husband was John Norbury (i), and her third husband was Sir John Montgomery. There were no children of her first marriage, but the offspring of her second and third marriages are shown in the family tree below.[23]

Through her brother, Ralph, Lord Sudeley, Elizabeth was the aunt of (Sir) Thomas Boteler who, seven or eight years later, was to become the first husband of Lady Eleanor Talbot.[24] Like her brother and her nephew,

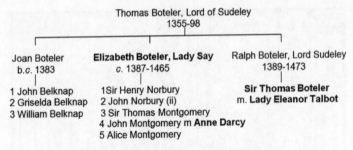

Thomas Boteler, Lord of Sudeley
1355-98

Joan Boteler	**Elizabeth Boteler, Lady Say**	Ralph Boteler, Lord Sudeley
b.c. 1383	c. 1387-1465	1389-1473
1 John Belknap	1 Sir Henry Norbury	**Sir Thomas Boteler**
2 Griselda Belknap	2 John Norbury (ii)	m. **Lady Eleanor Talbot**
3 William Belknap	3 Sir Thomas Montgomery	
	4 John Montgomery m **Anne Darcy**	
	5 Alice Montgomery	

The Family of Edward's godmother, Elizabeth Boteler, Lady Say.

Elizabeth was a direct descendant of the pre-Norman English royal house of Wessex.[25] Her nephew, Thomas Boteler, had been born in about 1421. He would have been about twenty-one years old at the time of Edward's baptism – when he may well have been serving in France, under his future father-in-law, John Talbot. Indeed, he may already have been betrothed to Eleanor (who was then aged six). It is even possible that Thomas Boteler attended Edward's baptism.

As for Lady Say's future daughter-in-law, Anne Montgomery (*née* Darcy), she would later prove to be a good friend of her cousin-by-marriage Eleanor Talbot, and also of Eleanor's sister, the Duchess of Norfolk. Indeed, Anne ultimately became closely connected with the deep religious devotion and commitment of those two Talbot ladies.

Lady Say's godmotherly role at the baby Edward's baptism in Rouen is clearly attested by a gift made to her in February 1464 by her godson, who had by then become King of England. In 1464 he commanded his chief butler that 'of our gift ye deliver incontinent upon the sight hereof a butt of tyre unto our right dear and entirely beloved godmother, Dame Elizabeth, Lady Say'.[26]

As for Edward's two godfathers, one of these was Thomas, Lord Scales. Unlike Lady Say, Lord Scales died before his godson succeeded to the English throne. However, a text is preserved which refers to Lord Scales in July 1460 as 'godfather of the said Earl of March'.[27] Subsequently the daughter and heiress of Lord Scales, Elizabeth, Baroness Scales, married Anthony Widville, Earl Rivers, the brother of Edward IV's second secret bride, Elizabeth Widville.

The identity of Edward's second godfather seems not to be on record. Stratford (see above) states that the man in question was the baby boy's maternal uncle, Richard, Earl of Salisbury. However, he cites no specific source for this information.

It was at the Castle of Rouen that the little boy, Edward, appears to have spent the first three and a half years of his life. Although his parents were also living there, like all aristocratic children of that period, Edward would not have been directly cared for by his mother. It was a local Norman woman who was employed as his nurse. Her name was Anne de Caux. We know her identity because her role as Edward IV's nurse was formally recorded later. Anne was awarded an annual pension of £20 by Edward IV for her services in 1474,[28] payment of which was later continued (or renewed) by Richard III.[29] Presumably Anne had, in due course, accompanied the York family back to England, and had thereafter remained resident in that foreign country.

There is a *Caux* in southern France (Gascogne), which is often assumed in family history to be the origin of every example of the name *de Caux* (or *Decaux*). However, a region known as the *Pays de Caux* also comprises the area of Normandy north of Rouen, around the ports of Le Havre and Dieppe. This coastal region of Normandy was presumably the geographic point of origin of Edward IV's nurse, Anne – and her surname.

Incidentally, the fact that Edward was brought up by a Norman nurse, in Rouen, means that he is almost certain to have grown up as a bilingual baby and boy. It is therefore not surprising that solid later evidence survives, proving that Edward IV was very well able to communicate in the French language. Philippe de Commynes, who met Edward on more than one occasion, after he had become King of England, reported that he spoke 'quite good French'.[30] Moreover, Commynes expressed absolute amazement at the quality of the French language used in a letter sent by Edward IV to Louis XI in 1475. Commynes said this letter was so impressive that 'I believe no Englishman could have had a hand in composing it!'.[31]

Edward's paternal ancestry was recorded, selectively, with one or two minor errors, but overall in a very interesting manner, by his contemporary William Worcester (*c.* 1415–*c.*1482) as follows:

> This Edward was the son of the aforesaid Richard Plantaginett, who was the son and heir of Richard Earl of Cambridge, who was the son and heir [*sic* – he was the *younger* son – but ultimate heir] of Edmund of Langley Duke of York and of Isabel, his wife, daughter and heir of Peter, the true and undoubted King of Castile and Leon. This Edward was the son of the aforesaid Richard Plantaginett, son of Anne, daughter of Roger Mortimer, son and heir of Philippa and of Edmund Earl of March, who was the son of Earl Roger, who was

the son of Earl [*sic*] Edmund,[32] who was the son of Roger first Earl of March, who was the son of Glwadus Ddu, who was the daughter and heir [*sic*] of Llewellyn, Prince of Wales, and the wife of Sir Ralph Mortimer, who was the son of Roger, who was the son of Hugh de Mortimer and his wife Matilda, daughter of William 'Longsword', who was the son and heir of Rollo, first Duke of the Normans. This Edward was Duke of Anjou through his father Richard Plantaginett, who was the son of Anne, who was the daughter of Roger, who was the son of Philippa, who was the daughter of Lionel, who was the son of King Edward III, who was the son of King Edward II, who was the son of Edward I, who was the son of Henry III, who was the son of John, who was the son [*sic*] of Richard,[33] who was the son of Henry II, who was the son of Geoffrey Plantaginett Count of Anjou, who was the son of Fulk, who was the son [*sic* – brother] of Geoffrey, who was the son of Fulk, who was the son of Raris(?),[34] who was the son of Fulk first Count of Anjou.[35]

Curiously, there is no focus on Edward's French royal ancestry. However, his descent from Edward III and the earlier Kings of England; from Pedro 'the Cruel' and the royal house of Castile and Leon; from the house of Anjou; from the house of Normandy; and (via the house of Mortimer) from Llewellyn, Prince of Wales, are all emphasised.

Maternal Line relatives (simplified)

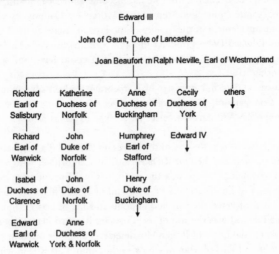

William Worcester makes no mention of Edward IV's maternal ancestry, but his mother was Cecily Neville, youngest daughter of Ralph Neville, Earl of Westmorland, by his second wife, Joan Beaufort. Joan was the daughter of John of Gaunt, Duke of Lancaster, by his long-term mistress and eventual third wife, Catherine de Roët. Catherine was a possible distant relative of John of Gaunt through his mother, Philippa of Hainault, for, like Philippa, she and her family came from the Low Countries. Her father was Sir Giles de Roët, known as 'Paon' ('the Peacock'). John of Gaunt was Catherine's second husband, for she had previously been married to Hugh Swynford.

Cecily Neville had been assigned to Richard, Duke of York, as a child bride by her parents, who were also the guardians of the young but wealthy royal duke. Although the couple probably married in 1424, their union was probably not a close relationship initially, for no child seems to have been conceived by Cecily until 1438.[36]

Friar Osberne Bokenham of the Augustinian priory of Clare in Suffolk characterised the childlessness of the couple as 'barreness' ('*annos steriles*') in the first of the two verses of his poem which lists the children of the York couple.

> Sir aftir the tyme of longe bareynesse,
> God first sent Anne, which signyfieth grace,
> In token that al her hertis hevynesse

R. Poſt annos ſteriles multos ſit primula proles
ANNA decora ſatis, ſed poſt hanc ſtirps probitatis
Naſcitur **HENRICUS**, cito quem virtutis amicus
CRISTUS in arce poli fecit regnare perhenni.
Prodiit **EDWARDUS** poſt hunc heres que futurus.
EDMUNDUS ſequitur, hinc **ELISABETH** generatur.
Poſt **MARGARETA**, **WILLELMUS** poſtera meta
Fit pro preſenti, donec ſua munera ventri
Det **DEUS** hinc matris ſolite ſignum pietatis.
MARGRET poſt proles hinc **WILLELMUS** que **JOHANNES**
Quos raptus ſeculo ſtatuit **DEUS** almus Olympo,
Inde **GEORGIUS** eſt natus, **THOMAS** que **RICARDUS**.
THOMAS in fata ſucceſſit forte beata.
Vltima iam matris proles fuit **VRSULA**, regis
Que ſummi voto celeſti iungitur agno.

The Latin text of Friar Oberne Bokenham's poem listing the children of the Duke and Duchess of York, as published by John Weever, in his book, *Antient Funeral Monuments*.

He as for bareynesse wold fro hem chace.
Harry, Edward, and Edmonde, eche in his place
Succedid; and after tweyn daughters cam
Elizabeth and Margarete, and afterward William.

John aftir William nexte borne was,
Which bothe be passid to goddis grace:
George was next, and after Thomas
Borne was, which sone aftir did pace
By the path of dethe to the hevenly place
Richard liveth yet: but last of alle
Was Ursula, to him whom God list calle.[37]

We have no way of knowing precisely when the marriage of the young Duke and Duchess of York was consummated. However, it was normal at that time for marriages of minors not to be consummated until the female partner had reached the age of either fourteen or sixteen – accounts vary.[38] Cecily Neville would have celebrated her fourteenth birthday in 1429, and 'there are indications (such as the indult to have their own altar) that Richard and Cecily shared a common household by the late summer of 1429'.[39] But Cecily did not reach the age of sixteen until 1431. The Duke of York's employment in France may help to explain why about seven more years then elapsed before Cecily conceived a child. Nevertheless, in spite of their lack of children during the early years of their marriage, it seems that the union of Richard and Cecily was eventually a very close one, and that their marriage was highly successful.

Despite the fact that, in the 1430s, while Richard was serving in France, he may have left Cecily behind in England, she later seems to have accompanied him more or less everywhere as a matter of course. Between 1439 and 1449 the Duke and Duchess of York had, on average, approximately one child a year. In 1445 (by which time the couple had four living children – two sons and two daughters) the Duke of York initiated negotiations for a marriage between their eldest surviving son, Edward, and one of the daughters of the increasingly victorious Charles VII of France. The story of the French marriage negotiations will be explored in detail in the next chapter. How far these negotiations progressed is somewhat unclear, but in the end they produced no result. Charles VII's daughters went on to find other husbands, and of course young Edward – the future Edward IV – later found other wives.

4

1445: THE DAUGHTERS OF FRANCE

Charles VII of France had married his second cousin Marie of Anjou (the paternal aunt of Henry VI's wife, Margaret of Anjou) on 18 December 1422. The couple shared a common ancestry, in that they were both great-grandchildren of King John II of France and his first wife Bonne of Bohemia (also known as Bonne of Luxembourg). In spite of the fact that Charles VII also had extramarital affairs, his marriage with Marie proved very productive. Marie bore her husband fourteen children, including one pair of twins. However, some of their children died very young, as tended to be the case, even in high-ranking families, in that period.

When Richard Duke of York began thinking of a potential bride for his young son and heir, Edward, the first possibility which occurred to him was that Edward should be betrothed to one of the daughters of King Charles. At that time the Duke of Suffolk was in France, seeking to arrange a marriage for King Henry VI with one of the nieces of the French queen. York therefore asked Suffolk to also make enquiries at the French court regarding the possibility of a marriage between young Edward of York and a French princess. Perhaps surprisingly (given the conflict between himself and the English in France – led by the Duke of York), Charles VII seemed very well disposed towards this proposal. 'He not only sent a gracious message to the duke by Suffolk, but on 19th February 1445, wrote to him from Nancy, expressing pleasure at the prospect of the marriage for which the duke asked.'[1]

When the French king's letter arrived, the Duke of York was busy entertaining Margaret of Anjou, who was then passing through Normandy on her way to England and her new husband, King Henry VI. But in April, Richard himself replied to Charles VII. He apologised for the delay, and promised to send a formal embassy in May to pursue the marriage plans for his son, Edward:

Most high, most excellent and most powerful prince, and most dread lord, I recommend me to you in such wise as most humbly I can and know.

And may it please you to know that by certain of your letters, which it has pleased you to send me, dated at Nencey in Lorraine, the xix. day of the month of February last past, touching the matter of the marriage of one of my three honoured ladies, your daughters, and of Edouart of York, my eldest son; and also by what my very dear and well-beloved cousin, the marquess and earl of Suffolk, has reported to me by mouth, I have learned that you are pleased to take the said marriage into consideration; and that when I should please to send my ambassadors to you to ...² the said matter, they would be welcome there.

Concerning the which thing, most high, most excellent, and most powerful prince, and most redoubted lord, I am much comforted and joyful, in consequence of the singular and true desire which I have to acquire your friendship and society; and with all my affection I thank you for it most humbly.

Your said letters by me received, I was immediately inclined to send my ambassadors to your highness, for the business; a thing which I could not do and accomplish so speedily as I could well have wished, in consequence of the arrival, on this side, of my lady the queen [*Margaret of Anjou*], whom, after that she was brought to and had arrived at the town of Pontoise, I have accompanied, as reason was, until she had embarked on the sea to go into England to the king, your nephew, and my sovereign lord. So I entreat you, most humbly, that of the delay of the mission of my said embassy to you, you would be pleased to have and hold me excused.

In order to declare more fully to you the causes of this said excuse, and other things touching the said matter under consideration, I send, at this present time, to you my well-beloved messires Richard Merbury, knight, and Jehan Ernoys, esquire, to whom, as concerns what they shall say and show to you at this time on my part upon the said matter, may it please you to yield full faith and credence, and to say or cause to say, and declare to them, the district in which you are, or shall be disposed to be, about the time of the fifteenth day of the month of May next following, at which time I am determined and entirely disposed to send my said embassy to your said highness, in order to treat, discuss, and conclude the business of the said marriage.

Most high, most excellent, and most powerful prince, and most dread lord, may it please you to send me and command your most noble will and pleasure as to one who is ready to give heed to the fulfilling of the same, as far as is at all possible. This knows the blessed Son of God, who have[3] you in His holy keeping, and give you good life and long.

Written at Rouen, the xviij. day of April [1445].
Your most humble kinsman.
The duke of York,
R. York.
Drosayne.

(Dorso) To the most high, most excellent, and most powerful prince, and most dread lord, the king.[4]

This time Charles VII responded with a clear proposal for agreeing to a marriage between his youngest daughter, Madeleine (born on 1 December 1443), and the young Edward. But as Madeleine was less than eighteen months old at the time, the Duke of York came up in his response with a different proposal.

Most high, most excellent, and most powerful prince, and most dread lord, I recommend myself to you very humbly.

And may it please you to know that I have received your gracious letters, dated at Heurres near Saint Michiel en Barroiz, the xiiij. day of the month of May lately past, presented to me by messieur Richard Merbury, knight, baillif of Gisors, and Jehan Harnoiz, esquire, baillif of Mante; and by them, and also by the report of the above-named, I have understood the good disposition in the which you are to further the conclusion of the marriage of one of my three most honorable ladies, your daughters[5], and my eldest son Edouart of York, with which I am perfectly rejoiced and consoled, and thank you therein; for I am well aware that my said eldest son could not be placed in and appointed to a more lofty position and connexion.

In your said letters Magdalene is named; but considering her very tender age, and that naturally and as speedily as age; will permit, I desire that issue should proceed of my said eldest son, seeing by the report of the said Merbury and Harnoiz that this my eldest son is of an age better adapted to and suitable for madam Jehanne de France, one of your said daughters, I have settled and fixed upon her, if it be the good pleasure of your highness to give heed thereunto. To which your highness and for this cause I send at this time, as an embassy, the reverend father in God the bishop of Bayeux, councillor of my lord the king, the said messire Richard Merbury, master Thomas Basin, doctor in canon and civil law, Jehan Declay, esquire, treasurer of the expenditure of my household, the said Jehan Hernoiz, and master Jehan de Drosayn, secretary to my said lord the king and to myself, to discuss and conclude upon the said matter, in which I have given them sufficient power upon my part. Whom, and five or four of them, may it please you of your grace to receive favorably, and to give as full faith and credence to what shall be said and told to you herein at this time on my part, as to myself, if I were there present; sending and intimating to me your most noble will and pleasure, that I may give heed to the accomplishment of the same according to my ability.

Most high, most excellent, and most powerful prince, and my dread lord I pray the Blessed Son of God that He would have you in his holy keeping, and give you good life and long.

Written at Rouen, the tenth day of June.
Your very humble kinsman, the Duke of York.
R. York.

(Dorso.) To the most high, most excellent, and most powerful prince and most dread lord the king.

[Then, in another hand,] Closed letters of the duke of York.[6]

The name 'Jehanne of France' is slightly confusing in terms of identity. Charles VII had a daughter usually referred to in England as 'Joan', who had been born on 4 May 1435. However there was also a younger daughter, who is generally referred to in English as 'Joanna'. Confusingly, both 'Joanna' and 'Joan' are named in modern French lists of Charles VII's children as 'Jeanne'.[7] Joanna was born (together with a twin sister, Marie) on 7 September 1438. Marie had died in 1439, but Joanna lived on until the day after Christmas 1446. Thus she was still alive when the Duke of York wrote his letter, and she may well have been the French princess whom he had in mind as a potential wife for his son and heir. In short, it is not precisely clear which of the two very similarly named daughters of Charles VII the Duke of York would have preferred.

It is, however, certain that York was suggesting a somewhat older daughter of the French king than the recently born Madeleine: a princess who would have been either seven years older than his own son and heir, or three and a half years older. Presumably what chiefly influenced the Duke of York in this direction was nervousness that an agreement for marriage with the very young Madeleine might go wrong if the little girl did not survive. It is therefore somewhat ironic that in actual fact Madeleine of France did survive, but the younger of the two Joans did not.

Charles VII's eldest surviving daughter in January and February 1444/5, when the Duke of York began his enquiries, was Radegonde of France, who had been born in August 1428. On 22 April 1430 she had been promised in marriage to Sigismund, heir to the archduchy of Austria. However, that marriage never materialised, because although Radegonde had been living when the Duke of York first began to explore the possibility of a French marriage for his son and heir, Edward, Earl of March, she fell ill and died in March 1444/5, before the duke wrote his earliest surviving letter on the subject of a French royal marriage for Edward.

The second surviving daughter of Charles VII and Marie of Anjou was Catherine, who had also been born in 1428. In 1440, at Blois, Catherine had been married to Charles, Count of Charolais – the future Charles the Bold, Duke of Burgundy, eventual brother-in-law of King Edward IV. At the time of the marriage, Catherine had been twelve years old, while her young husband was seven. However, the marriage was never consummated, because Catherine died six years later, in July 1446. But in any case, since she was already married, she would not have been available in 1444–45 as a potential bride for Edward, Earl of March.

The next surviving daughter of Charles and Marie was Yolande of France, who had been born in 1434. She was not committed to anyone in marriage in 1444–45, so the Duke of York might well have considered her as a possible bride for his son. Although her name is not mentioned in his surviving correspondence on the subject, as we have seen, York spoke of three available daughters of the French king. It may well have been that the three names he had in mind were Yolande, Jeanne and Madeleine. Maybe he had not fully grasped the fact that actually there were two unmarried French princesses bearing the name 'Jeanne'. As for Yolande, she later married Amadeus IX, Duke of Savoy, whose sister, Bona, we shall meet later, when she in her turn was put forward as a potential bride for King Edward IV of England.

After Yolande the only living daughters of the French royal couple were those whose names have already been cited as potential brides for

Edward, namely the elder and the younger Jeanne, and the very young Madeleine. The younger of the two Jeannes died in 1446, so in fact she would not have proved a good choice as Edward's French royal wife. As for the elder Jeanne, seven years later she married her cousin, Jean, future Duke of Bourbon. However, it seems that she too may have been a bad choice as a bride for Edward IV, because although she remained Bourbon's wife for thirty years (dying shortly before Edward IV), she produced no children.

As for the very young Madeleine, as well as being offered by her father as a possible wife for Edward Earl of March, she was also sought by the king of Hungary. But although they were betrothed for a time, the king died before they could actually be married. Thus, in the end, Madeleine married the king of Navarre, producing for him two children.

Portraits survive of Yolande, of the elder Jeanne, and of Madeleine. And of course we also have surviving portraits of their parents. As can been seen (plates 8 and 9), both Charles VII and his consort, Marie, had very French royal noses! Perhaps fortunately, none of their three younger daughters, Yolande, Jeanne (i) and Madeleine, seem to have inherited this feature from their parents. Images of Jeanne and of Madeleine are included here (see plates 10 and 11), and their noses were apparently of much more average dimensions. Thus from the point of view of their appearance, either Jeanne or Madeleine might have been a suitable Countess of March (and later queen consort of England).

But whichever daughter York had in mind as the ideal bride for his son and heir, Edward, apparently Charles VII would not be persuaded. Although the surviving letters make the plans for the marriage sound promising, actually nothing further was done, and the Duke of York simply seems to have abandoned his plans for a French royal marriage for Edward. Since the little boy had only been about three years old at the time of the negotiations between his father and King Charles VII, it is difficult to guess what (if anything) Edward himself knew of these possible plans for his future. Indeed, he probably never met any of the French princesses whom his father was thinking of as the boy's future consort. But apparently his father knew the daughters of Charles VII, since he refers to two of the available girls by name.

5

1445–1459: FROM FRANCE TO ENGLAND – AND IRELAND

In October 1445 the Duke and Duchess of York left France and returned to England with their four children, Anne, Edward, Edmund and Elizabeth. Richard's five-year appointment in France had come to an end. When Richard and Cecily sailed back to the English coast, another York child was already on the way, for Cecily was in her second month of pregnancy.

Three months after they arrived back in England, in January 1445/6, the couple's eldest daughter, Anne, then aged six and a half, was married to her cousin, the young Henry Holland, later second (or third) Duke of Exeter (1430–1475).[1] Anne's marriage may initially have meant that she was separated from the rest of her family. A bride of such a young age would not immediately have set up home with her husband, but would normally have lived under the care of her husband's parents until she reached the age of fourteen or sixteen (see above, chapter 3, note 38). Only then would consummation of the marriage have been permitted. In January 1445/6 John Holland, the second Holland Duke of Exeter (and Henry's father), was still alive, and although Henry's mother was dead, he had a stepmother, Lady Anne Montacute. But in July 1447, following the death of John Holland, Richard, Duke of York, was appointed guardian of the new young Duke of Exeter. This new situation might well have brought Anne back to her parents' care, together with her young husband.

Back in his homeland, the Duke of York regularly attended royal council meetings from 1446 to 1448. Initially, Richard seems to have used the guest house at Waltham Abbey as his *pied-à-terre* when he needed to be in the London area. Indeed, his and Cecily's fifth child, Margaret of York (later Duchess of Burgundy), was born at Waltham

Abbey on Tuesday 3 May 1446.[2] In October 1446 Richard was granted the abbey and town of Waltham as a kind of acknowledgement of his frequent need to be in or near London on the king's business. Shortly afterwards, however, the death of his Lancastrian cousin and friend, Humphrey, Duke of Gloucester, on 23 February 1446/7, led to Richard's inheritance of an even better *pied-à-terre*, Baynard's Castle, in London. However, on 30 July 1447, for political reasons the Duke of York was given the appointment of lieutenant of Ireland.

Initially the Duke of York had his new Irish role fulfilled by a local deputy. But eventually he himself decided to take up the post in person. It has often been assumed that when the Duke and Duchess of York finally set sail across the Irish Sea to Dublin, their children would have been left behind in England. Indeed, there has been a tendency to assume that all the children remained in the nursery at Fotheringhay Castle. However, there is absolutely no evidence in support of this contention. What is more, as we have already seen, the four eldest surviving York children had all dwelt with their parents at Rouen in France. They had not been sent back to a York family nursery in England. There is therefore a strong French precedent for the suggestion that in 1449, when Richard and Cecily (who was now pregnant once again) finally sailed to Dublin, they would probably have taken their children with them.

This would mean that Edward, Edmund, Elizabeth and Margaret are all likely to have lived with their parents at Dublin Castle (where the sixth child, George, was born) and also at the York family castle of Trim in County Meath. But the home of Anne of York at this time is less clear. Since she was now married she may have been living with her

Baynard's Castle.

The entrance gate of Dublin Castle as it would have appeared in the fifteenth century.

young husband, the Duke of Exeter, and his stepmother. However, she was only ten years old – still too young for her marriage to have been consummated – so it is also possible that both she and her young husband were resident in the York household, given that the Duke of York was Henry Holland's guardian. But the fact that Henry Holland was granted livery of his land on 23 July 1450 could arguably be seen as meaning that he and his wife were then resident in England. Thus it remains unclear whether Anne of York accompanied the rest of her family to Ireland.

But the probability seems strong that the other York children did so. This is in spite of the fact that Edward was now seven years of age. Of course, the standard medieval tradition was that

> until the age of about seven, sons of noble families would receive training in manners and basic literacy from their mothers or other female relatives. Upon reaching seven years old, a boy would be sent to the castle, great house or other estate of another noble family. This would match the age at which apprenticeships or servants' employment would be entered into by young males from lower social classes.[3]

However, there is no evidence to show that Edward was ever sent to another noble household. It seems clear that later, when the York family returned to England, Edward and his brother Edmund were both placed under the custody of suitable family servants at one of the Duke of York's own residences, Ludlow Castle. However, this only appears to have taken place after the family's return from Ireland to England in 1450.

Two letters from Edward and Edmund to their father, written at
Ludlow, survive. These date from April and June 1454, when Edward
would have been twelve years old. The first of these letters greets the
Duke of York, and thanks him for news sent. It then continues

> also we thank your noblesse and good fatherhood of our green
> gowns now late sent unto us to our great comfort. Beseeching your
> good lordship to remember our porteux [prayerbooks]. And that
> we might have some fine bonnets sent unto us by the next sure
> messenger, for necessity so requireth. Our thus right noble lord
> and father please it your highness to wit that we have charged
> your servant William Smith bearer of these for to declare unto
> your nobility certain things on our behalf, namely concerning and
> touching the odious rule and demeaning of Richard Croft and his
> brother. Wherefore we beseech your gracious lordship and full noble
> fatherhood to hear him in exposition of the same and to his relation
> to give full faith and credence.[4]

The reference to the Croft brothers has previously been interpreted as
meaning that the Crofts had been behaving odiously to Edward and
Edmund.[5] However, that appears to be a misreading of the text. Richard
and Thomas Croft were the younger brothers of Sir Richard Croft
of Croft Castle, near Ludlow. They were in their late teens, and were
presumably completing their education in the household of the two York
princes at Ludlow. It sounds as though in reality the Croft brothers had
been treated in an unkind manner by certain members of the Ludlow
household, and that Edward and Edmund were protesting about this
to their father. Later, as king, Edward IV certainly seems to have had a
favourable view of the Crofts.[6]

The second surviving letter reads as follows:

> To the right hiegh and mighty Prince, oure most worschipfull and
> gretely redoubted lorde and fader, the Duke of Yorke, Protector and
> Defensor of Englonde.
>
> Ryght hiegh and mighty Prince, oure most worschipfull and
> gretely redoubted lorde and Fader, in as lowely wyse as any
> sonnes con or may we recomaunde us un to youre good
> lordeschip. And please hit youre hieghnesse to witte that we have
> received youre worschipful lettres yesterday by your servaunt
> William Cleton, beryng date at Yorke the xxix day of Maij, by
> the whiche William and by the relacion of John Milewatier we

conceive your worschipfull and victorious spede ageinest your enemyse, to ther grete shame, and to us the most comfortable tydinges that we desired to here. Where of we thonke Almyghty God of his yeftes, beseeching Hym hertely to geve yowe that grace and cotidian fortune here aftur to knowe your enemyse and to have the victory of them. And yef hit please your hieghnesse to knowe of oure welfare, at the making of this letter we were in good helith of bodis, thonked be God; beseeching your good and gracious Faderhode of youre daily blessing. And where ye comaunde us by your said lettres to attende specialy to oure lernyng in our yong age that schulde cause us to growe to honour and worschip in our olde age, Please hit your hieghnesse to witte that we have attended owre lernyng sith we come heder, and schall here aftur; by the whiche we trust to God youre gracious lordeschip and good Fadurhode schall be plaesid. Also we besche your good lordeschip that hit may please yowe to send us Harry Lovedeyne, grome of your kechyn, whos service is to us right ageable; and we will sende yow John Boyes to wayte on youre good Lordschip. Ryght hiegh and mighty Prince, our most worschipfull and gretely redoubted lorde and Fader, We besche Almyghty God yeve yowe as good lyfe and longe as youre owne Princely hert con best desire. Writen at your Castill of Lodelow the iij day of June.

Youre humble sonnes,
E. Marche,
E. Rutlond.[7]

Signatures of Edward, Earl of March, and his brother Edmund, Earl of Rutland, 3 June 1454.

What emerges from these two surviving letters – a tiny fragment of what was obviously a much fuller correspondence – is that Edward and Edmund respected their father and were respected by him. The letters also reveal certain gifts made, and the fact that when something made them unhappy about their Ludlow household the two young boys brought this openly to their father's attention. This shows that they were not in command of the situation at Ludlow, which is hardly surprising, given their age. However, they were free to express their opinions to their father.

At the time when these letters were written, Edward was about to enter his teens. This would have been the period of his life during which sex began to have a meaning for him. Maybe the exploration of sexual activity and the eventual loss of his virginity took place for Edward at Ludlow, on the Welsh border. We have no surviving evidence to show what took place in his case, but contemporary evidence relating to other upper-class lads and men in the second half of the fifteenth century may help us to imagine what may have happened.

The first case to consider concerns Edward IV's cousin, the twenty-year-old John Mowbray, 4th Duke of Norfolk. On Friday 24 May 1465, while John Mowbray was staying at his town house at Broken Wharf, on the north bank of the Thames just south of St Paul's Cathedral, his forty-five-year-old cousin John Howard financed the young duke's visit to a

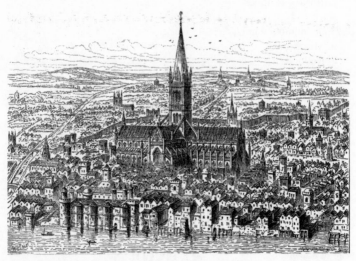

St Paul's Cathedral, Baynard's Castle and Broken Wharf.

brothel. John Mowbray was lent the sum of 20 shillings by Howard 'whan he lay at the stewe',[8] presumably just across the other side of the Thames, in Southwark. The interesting features of the transaction between Sir John Howard and the duke on 24 May are, first, the fact that Sir John clearly condoned and financed his young cousin's extramarital sexual activity; and second, that Howard himself seems to have accompanied his cousin on this occasion. This suggests that Howard himself was also frequenting the Southwark stews. Perhaps there was a special reason to account for that. At the period in question, Sir John Howard was still married to his first wife. But, sadly, that lady was suffering from an unknown illness which led to her death later that same year.[9] Sexual activity with her husband may therefore have become difficult for her. As for the young John Mowbray, he had been married to Elizabeth Talbot since both of them were children. But that marriage was principally a dynastic alliance. Apparently such an arranged marriage did not preclude the young Duke of Norfolk from finding other sexual outlets – with the backing and approval of his closest living senior male relative.

In John Howard's own case, a further possible hint exists that he may earlier have engaged in extramarital relationships at certain periods of his life. The evidence for this comprises an obscure reference in the surviving Paston correspondence to 'þe prest, Howardys sone' in April 1453.[10] This evidence is obviously vague, but one possible interpretation would be that an unnamed priest was John Howard's illegitimate son.

Nevertheless, it is certainly the case that John Howard appears to have condoned sexual activity outside marriage not only on the part of his young cousin, John Mowbray, but also on the part of his own teenaged sons. Thus, among his surviving household accounts, a list of the members of Sir John's household drawn up on 22 January 1466/7 mentions 'Richard, mast[er] Thomas' child'.[11] Master Thomas was Sir John's eldest son and heir, the future second Howard Duke of Norfolk and victor of the battle of Flodden. Thomas was of a very similar age to Edward IV, having been born in about 1443. Later, in 1472, he was to be married to his first wife, Elizabeth Tilney.[12] But in January 1466/7 Thomas was still unmarried, therefore the young Richard can only have been his illegitimate son. Since presumably the young boy had been born at least five years earlier, Thomas Howard would probably have been in his late teens when he fathered this bastard son.

It is just possible that Sir John Howard also offers an example of adult male support for the extramarital – or premarital – activity of a young Yorkist prince. Howard took an avuncular interest in the young Duke of Gloucester in the 1460s, and he may have condoned early sexual activity in Gloucester's case, as he had done with his own cousin and his own son. No specific evidence survives to prove this. However, Gloucester fathered at least two illegitimate children: a son, who was given John Howard's Christian name, and a daughter, Catherine. No record survives of the date of birth of either of these two children, but John was under the age of twenty-one in March 1485, and was therefore not born before 1465. Catherine married the Earl of Pembroke [Huntingdon] in 1484. She may have been fourteen or fifteen years old at the time of her wedding. Therefore both of the Duke of Gloucester's illegitimate children were probably engendered in the late 1460s.[13] Interestingly, this was a period when Howard had certainly begun to cultivate friendship with young Gloucester, and when the Duke of Gloucester is known to have visited Howard in Colchester and in Suffolk.[14]

At all events, in the fifteenth century, as at other times, boys were known to become sexually active during their teens. In the second half of the fifteenth century the various surviving Howard evidence further suggests that at least some upper-class households had no difficulty with that. Both the Howard evidence presented here, and the evidence relating to the illegitimate children of Edward IV's youngest surviving brother, Richard Duke of Gloucester (Richard III) shows that in such cases the birth of illegitimate children was acknowledged and the children were supported by the father.

This makes it somewhat significant that no records survive of any illegitimate children born to Edward in his teenaged years. Indeed, as we have already seen, Gregory's Chronicle reports that in 1464 'men mervelyd that oure soverayne lorde was so longe with owte any wyffe, and were evyr ferde that he had be not chaste of hys levynge'.[15] This clearly implies that as late as 1464 there was no direct awareness of any liaisons or illegitimate offspring of Edward IV. This strongly suggests that if Edward had lost his virginity by the time he came to the throne, he had not sired any illegitimate offspring as a result. As we shall see later, this view may also be supported by Edward's subsequent reactions to Eleanor Talbot and Elizabeth Widville. Could it be that, in his early twenties, Edward had some anxiety about his own ability to father a child? The other possibility would be that, as was once commonly the case in boarding schools and other male communities of the young, Edward's initial sexual experimentation was with other boys. This is also a theory which will be further explored later.

PART 2
FIRST WIFE, BOYFRIEND AND POSSIBLE BASTARD CHILD

6

1459–1461: ITINERARY

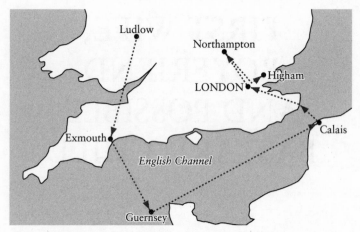

Movements of Edward, Earl of March, from September 1459 to August 1460

1459 (age 17)
SEPTEMBER
Ludlow Castle[1]

OCTOBER
Ludlow[2]
Devonshire (house of Joan, Lady
Dynham)[3]

Exmouth[4]
Guernsey[5]

NOVEMBER
landed Calais[6]

DECEMBER
Calais

1459/60
JANUARY
Calais[7]

FEBRUARY
Calais

MARCH
Calais

1460 (age 18)
APRIL
Calais

MAY
Calais

JUNE
Calais
Rochester and Dartford
('Dorceffort')[8]

JULY
entered London[9]
St Albans and 'Devistalle'
(Dunstable or Daventry?)[10]
Northampton (battle), London[11]

AUGUST
Higham, Suffolk[12]

SEPTEMBER
near Southwark[13]

Edward IV's movements from March to July 1461

OCTOBER
near Southwark (visiting
siblings there every day)[14]
Westminster[15]
St Paul's Cathedral (bearing
the king's train)[16]

DECEMBER
Gloucester[17]

1460/61
JANUARY
Welsh border (Ludlow?)

FEBRUARY
Mortimer's Cross; Burford (upon
Wolde) and London[18]

MARCH
London
REGNAL YEAR 1
London[19]
Bishopsgate / going north,
St Albans[20]
Barkway (Herts.) and Cambridge[21]
Nottingham

1461 (age 19; regnal year 1)
MARCH
Ferrybridge on the River Aire,
Towton, York[22]
Helperby, Northallerton (N.
Yorks) and Durham[23]

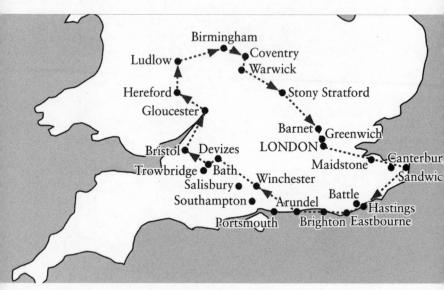

Edward IV's movements from August to December 1461

The Royal Manor House at Greenwich.

MAY
Newcastle-upon-Tyne, Durham, Middleham, York, Preston, Warrington (Lancs.), Manchester, Chester and Stafford[24]

JUNE
Lichfield and Coventry[25]
Coventry, Warwick, Daventry, Stony Stratford, Sheen, Lambeth, Westminster (coronation) and London[26]

JULY
Westminster[27]

AUGUST
Windsor Castle, Westminster, Sittingbourne, Canterbury, Sandwich, Ashford, Battle Abbey (Hastings), Lewes, Arundel and the manor of Bishop Waltham (Hants.)[28]

SEPTEMBER
Castle of Devizes and Bristol[29]
Bristol, Gloucester, Ross-on-Wye, Hereford, Ludlow Castle, Birmingham and Coventry[30]

OCTOBER
Warwick Castle, Daventry, Stony Stratford, Barnet, Greenwich and Westminster[31]

NOVEMBER
Westminster[32]

DECEMBER
Westminster[33]
Greenwich[34]

7

1460–1462: THE BEAUTIFUL ELEANOR

No one has ever questioned the existence of a relationship between Edward IV and Lady Eleanor Talbot. The only debates have been regarding Eleanor's social background and morality, and the nature of her relationship with the king and its precise dates. Intriguingly, Eleanor, who was of royal and noble descent, has been socially maligned by generations of historians. After a century of government-imposed silence in respect of her name, for four centuries aspersions were cast upon her birth, her ancestry and her morals. However, it has now been proved beyond any possible doubt that Eleanor's family background was aristocratic – precisely as stated in the 1484 act of Parliament which acknowledged her as Edward IV's legitimate wife.[1] As we shall see later, Eleanor's personal morality is also now established beyond any reasonable doubt.

There are therefore strong reasons for questioning the commonly held belief that Eleanor was merely Edward IV's mistress. Nevertheless, most writers have discounted the claim that Eleanor was married to Edward IV. Their conclusion is chiefly based on two assumptions. First, it is claimed that Richard III's later use of Eleanor's marriage story was merely a wicked and ambitious lie, employed by Richard for his own political advantage. Interestingly, however, the famous nineteenth-century historian, James Gairdner, stated that there was no justification for assuming that.[2] The second assumption is that the later actions of Henry VII in respect of Eleanor's marriage claim were completely pure and disinterested. Thus, many historians have naïvely followed the official government line which was firmly enforced by threats of severe punishment by King Henry VII in the autumn of 1485.

Yet Henry's action was very obviously political. It comprised the means which enabled him to present his intended bride, Elizabeth of York, as the Yorkist heiress to the throne of England. Henry's claim to this effect is very clearly documented by his contemporary writer, John Rous, who reported that the new king 'at once took to wife the celebrated Lady Elizabeth, daughter and *heiress* of Edward IV'.[3] This establishes beyond any possible doubt the fact that Henry VII had the strongest possible political reasons for attempting, in every way he could, to silence any mention of the possible marriage of Edward IV to Eleanor Talbot. Indeed, Henry VII himself stated that he wished to ensure that Eleanor's claim to be Edward IV's wife 'maie be for ever out of remembraunce and allso forgot',[4] because of course, if Eleanor Talbot had been Edward IV's true wife, then Henry VII's *own* wife, Elizabeth of York – the eldest daughter of Edward IV and Elizabeth Widville, and the mother of the 'Tudor' dynasty – was merely a royal bastard with absolutely no claim to the throne.

Nevertheless, the fact remains that in 1485 Henry VII presented not a single shred of evidence to prove that the Talbot marriage had never taken place. On the other hand, two years earlier Bishop Robert Stillington definitely had presented his personal evidence to the three estates of the realm to back his claim that he had married Edward and Eleanor. On that basis, backed by the clear evidence of Eleanor's strong religious faith and high birth (which would have made her unlikely to take on the role of a mistress), the present study accepts that a secret

The fifteenth-century priest and chronicler, John Rous.

marriage between Edward and Eleanor did indeed take place. As for the dates of the relationship between the couple, the new evidence published here in the itinerary of Edward IV (see above) will be used to try to pin down precisely when the couple could have been together.

The fullest and most detailed published account of Eleanor and her family background can be found in the present author's earlier work, *Eleanor, the Secret Queen*.[5] It is not possible to repeat all that information here. However, the first edition of that book contained an error in respect of the place and precise date of Eleanor's marriage to Edward.[6] On the basis of a record in the Patent Rolls, I had previously deduced that they had probably met and married in the Norwich area (where Eleanor later lived), early in 1461. My more recent and very detailed research on Edward IV's movements confirms that the marriage probably did take place early in 1461, but the new evidence now suggests that the location was not in the vicinity of Norwich, but at one of Eleanor's own Warwickshire manors.[7] We shall therefore begin by exploring how, when and where the relationship between Edward and Eleanor came into being.

Eleanor Talbot might possibly have known Edward in childhood, because their respective fathers' served together in France. She was probably born early in 1436,[8] and was of quite a high-ranking family background. Her parents were John, Lord Talbot, Count of Clermont, and his second wife, Lady Margaret Beauchamp (the eldest daughter and senior co-heiress of Richard Beauchamp, Earl of Warwick).

Eleanor Talbot's descent from Edward I

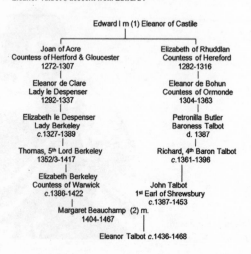

Edward I m (1) Eleanor of Castile

Joan of Acre
Countess of Hertford & Gloucester
1272-1307

Elizabeth of Rhuddlan
Countess of Hereford
1282-1316

Eleanor de Clare
Lady le Despenser
1292-1337

Eleanor de Bohun
Countess of Ormonde
1304-1363

Elizabeth le Despenser
Lady Berkeley
c.1327-1389

Petronilla Butler
Baroness Talbot
d. 1387

Thomas, 5th Lord Berkeley
1352/3-1417

Richard, 4th Baron Talbot
c.1361-1396

Elizabeth Berkeley
Countess of Warwick
c.1386-1422

John Talbot
1st Earl of Shrewsbury
c.1387-1453

Margaret Beauchamp (2) m.
1404-1467

Eleanor Talbot c.1436-1468

Both of Eleanor's parents were of royal descent, from King Edward I (see above).[9] Thus she was distantly related to Edward IV. However, Eleanor's blood relationship to the young king was not sufficiently close to constitute any kind of impediment to their marriage. Certainly the couple would not have required a papal dispensation. In the fifteenth century 'marriage was prohibited between persons sharing any common ancestor (or "stock") up to the level of great great grandparent'.[10] By their shortest lines of descent from Edward I, that king was Eleanor's 4x great-grandfather (on her father's side), and Edward IV's 6x great-grandfather. In fact, Edward and Eleanor were slightly more closely related via their common descent from Roger Mortimer, 1st Earl of March (see below). But even in that line of descent their closest relationship was too remote to require a papal dispensation. Roger Mortimer was Edward's 4x great-grandfather and Eleanor's 3x great-grandfather.

Thus, once Eleanor's first husband had died, she and Edward IV would have been perfectly free to contract matrimony if they so wished. Two of her first cousins, Isabel and Anne Neville, subsequently married the two younger brothers of Edward IV. Through their common Neville descent, these cousins of Eleanor Talbot were more closely related to their royal husbands than Eleanor was to Edward. Thus the Neville girls did require papal dispensations to authorise their unions. Ultimately, one of Eleanor's two cousins – Anne Neville – became the queen consort of England. Therefore Eleanor can certainly be considered to have been of potentially queenly birth. Her royal

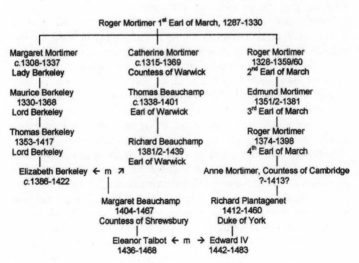

The common descent of Edward IV and Eleanor Talbot from Roger Mortimer.

and aristocratic family background makes it highly unlikely that she would cheerfully have accepted the dubious honour of becoming Edward IV's mistress. Even the less well-born Elizabeth Widville firmly rejected such a role a few years later, and insisted upon a marriage with the king.

Like Elizabeth Widville, Eleanor would have had absolutely no reason to compromise in this respect. After all, like Elizabeth Widville, she was a widow. As for Edward, when his relationship with Eleanor commenced he was still unmarried. If he loved and wanted her, nothing stood in the way of a marriage. At this period it was quite a common practice for upper-class widows to contract second marriages.[11] There were also precedents for English royal marriages with a widow.[12]

Not long after Eleanor's birth her father's service had been further acknowledged and rewarded by Henry VI with the grant of the English Earldom of Shrewsbury. Thanks to her mother, Eleanor was well educated. She was also brought up with a strong and orthodox religious streak to her character. It is not impossible that the young Eleanor may have travelled to France on some occasion with her mother and some of her siblings, to visit her father. If so, she might possibly have encountered in Rouen the young Edward, Earl of March, son of her father's colleague and commander, the Duke of York. However, there is no solid evidence to show that Edward and Eleanor first met in France, and Eleanor seems probably to have been brought up mostly (and perhaps exclusively) in England, under the guardianship of her mother.

Nevertheless, her childhood was probably fairly mobile, since the Talbot family held a chain of manors, 'from Marbury in South Cheshire through Whitchurch in North Shropshire, Corfham near Ludlow in South Shropshire, Credenhill near Hereford and Goodrich on the Wye in South Herefordshire to Painswick on the Cotswolds' edge in South Gloucestershire'.[13] The location of the Talbot manors is intriguing, given the fact that from about 1450 the young Edward seems to have been based in the same region, at Ludlow Castle. At first sight, this appears to suggest another possibility for an early meeting between Edward and Eleanor.

However, towards the end of 1449 or early in 1450 – at about the time when Edward seems to have been sent to live at Ludlow Castle – the thirteen-year-old Eleanor found herself married to the twenty-eight-year-old Thomas Boteler, son and heir of Ralph, Lord of Sudeley. From that point she presumably lived for just over three years at the Boteler family home of Sudeley Castle in Gloucestershire. Of course, Sudeley was not located at a huge distance from Ludlow. However, Eleanor was no longer available since she was now committed in marriage. Her residence at Sudeley would have lasted until 1453, when she and her husband presumably consummated their union (since Eleanor had then passed her sixteenth birthday), and were granted three homes of their own. These were Boteler family manors in Warwickshire: at Burton Dassett, Fenny Compton and Griff.

For about ten years Eleanor had remained a married woman. It was during this period of time that the young Edward progressed from childhood to adolescence, and that he presumably became sexually aware. Eleanor's marriage came to an end with her husband's death in 1459. The young widowed Eleanor initially remained in residence in the Warwickshire manors which had been granted to her and Thomas Boteler upon their marriage. The known movements of Edward Earl of March show that there would only have been quite limited opportunities for him to have met her in 1459 or 1460. Nevertheless, two such opportunities can now be highlighted. These will be explored in a moment.

Meanwhile, what did Eleanor look like when Edward met her and was attracted to her? The skeleton in Norwich which may be Eleanor's is that of a healthy young woman, who in life stood some five feet six inches tall.[14] Although an image of her once formed part of her mother's London tomb, that was lost as a result of the destruction of St Paul's Cathedral in the Great Fire of London. Thus there are now no surviving contemporary portraits of Eleanor. But contemporary images do exist of her parents, her sister and one of her nieces. Portraits of her father and of her sister are included in the illustrations. Her father, her sister, and her niece, Elizabeth Talbot of Lisle, all seem to have had dark brown hair and brown eyes. It is therefore probable that Eleanor, too, was a brunette. The Talbots as a whole, at this time, had rather prominent noses, and that feature Eleanor may also have shared. Facial reconstructions produced around the skull in Norwich which may be Eleanor's evoke a profile remarkably similar to surviving portraits of John Talbot, 1st Earl of Shrewsbury, to Elizabeth Talbot, Duchess of Norfolk, and to the recent facial reconstruction of Eleanor's niece, Anne Mowbray (see illustrations).

Eleanor's younger sister was described in 1468: '*la duchesse de Norfolck, une moult belle dame d'Angleterre*' ('the Duchess of Norfolk a very beautiful English lady').[15] These words were written by Olivier de la Marche in his memoirs; he had met Elizabeth Talbot in Flanders while she was accompanying Edward's sister, Margaret of York, on her Burgundian marriage trip. As for Eleanor herself, her impact on Edward IV strongly suggests that, like her younger sister, she too must have been very attractive.

Edward IV was nineteen years of age when he ascended the throne, and was not yet married at that time. The young king was six feet two inches in height, and had brown hair.[16] At this young age he was still of athletic build. Later, however, he would run to fat. There is some evidence to suggest that Edward may initially have been attracted by women a little older than himself. Both Eleanor Talbot and Elizabeth Widville fit into this category. Possibly he also preferred brunettes. In spite of a persistent legend that she was fair, one portrait of Elizabeth Widville at Queen's College, Cambridge appears to show dark auburn hair under the front edge of her headdress. As we have already seen, Edward may have lost his virginity prior to 1460, but if so, the identity of his early sexual partner (or partners) is not recorded.

During his teens Edward, then Earl of March, appears to have spent most of his time on the Welsh border, until October 1459. He then travelled southwards through Devonshire to Calais. Later, when he returned to England, in the early summer of 1460, Edward initially spent his time in the south and east of England. Thus his first opportunity for a meeting with the lovely Eleanor Talbot as a young widow would have occurred in November 1460. Then, as Edward travelled from London to the Welsh border, he would have passed close to Eleanor's Boteler family manors in Warwickshire. There seems to be absolutely no doubt that Edward found Eleanor attractive. It also appears certain that she responded to his advances. Initially her response was to decline Edward the sexual contact which he was seeking. But later – once his advances became couched in a form which was morally acceptable to her – her answer changed.

As can be seen from the itinerary, it is also possible that Eleanor may have met Edward after the battle of Mortimer's Cross towards the end of the second week of February 1460/1. This would have been just before the start of the penitential season of Lent. At that point Edward would again have found himself in the vicinity of her Warwickshire manors while travelling slowly from the Welsh border on his way to London and the throne. Either November 1460 or February 1460/1 – or both – could therefore have been the key occasion(s) on which Edward sought to seduce Eleanor by enticing her into his bed. As we have seen, prior to these two dates, even if Edward had known the girl, or had perhaps seen her from a distance, she would have been inaccessible to him.

However, it cannot have been in November 1460 or in February 1460/1 that Edward contracted a secret marriage with Eleanor Talbot. This is because the marriage was celebrated for them by Canon Robert Stillington. He was a young priest and an expert in canon law – but in 1460 he was in the service of the government of the Lancastrian king, Henry VI. It was apparently only after the proclamation of the young Earl of March as King Edward IV, in London, in March 1460/1, that Canon Stillington entered the service of the new Yorkist sovereign. Therefore, even though in November 1460 and in February 1460/1

Edward may have sought (successfully) to entice Eleanor into his arms – and (unsuccessfully) to entice her into his bed – their relationship cannot have been consolidated on either of those occasions.

According to the later report provided by Bishop Stillington (as the Canon of 1461 subsequently found himself promoted, on the incentive of King Edward IV), he himself officiated at the king's wedding with Eleanor, who had refused to give herself to Edward outside the relationship of a marriage as required and approved by the Church. This story has a rather familiar ring to it. A very similar account exists of Edward's later relationship with Elizabeth Widville. But regarding Edward's relationship with Eleanor, Philippe de Commynes reports a slightly different version. Commynes claims that Edward 'promised to marry her provided that he could sleep with her first *and she consented.*'[17] [The king] had made this promise in the bishop [of Bath]'s presence. And having done so he slept with her.'[18]

Nevertheless, Commynes' account is demonstrably slightly inaccurate in at least one respect. He refers to Stillington as a bishop. As we have seen, Stillington had not yet become the Bishop of Bath and Wells in 1461. He only received this appointment late in 1464 or early in 1465 – very soon after the king publicly announced his marriage to Elizabeth Widville. Indeed, his promotion may very well have been part of a royal bribe for keeping quiet about Edward IV's earlier entanglement with Eleanor. At all events, the precise wording of Commynes' account of Edward's relationship with Eleanor Talbot was written in hindsight, and is therefore slightly misleading.

Under fifteenth-century canon law, a promise of marriage (preferably before a witness), followed by sexual intercourse, did indeed constitute a valid marriage, and no further ceremony was required. Thus, even if Commynes' account of what took place was perfectly accurate, the marriage between Edward and Eleanor would have been valid, and Stillington need not actually have administered vows to them in his priestly office. Secret marriages were quite common practice in the later Middle Ages, and were universally accepted as valid even though they were not recommended by the church. Indeed, other examples of such secret marriage are recorded and / or alleged, even within the fifteenth-century English royal family. Such secret marriages merely required an exchange of promises to marry on the part of the contracting couple, followed by sexual intercourse. No witnesses – and no priestly celebrants – were essential. However, marriages of this kind could later prove difficult to authenticate. Indeed, numerous matrimonial disputes resulted from such complicated situations.[19]

Unfortunately modern historians have often made serious mistakes in their attempted explanations of the alleged relationship between Edward IV and Eleanor Talbot as a result of their total misunderstanding of the word 'precontract'. This word was certainly employed (by people who *did* understand what it meant) in the Act of Parliament of 1484 that acknowledged the marriage between Edward and Eleanor as valid. Unfortunately, however, many modern writers mistake 'precontract' as synonymous with 'betrothal'. Thus they have concluded that the relationship between Edward and Eleanor was something which fell short of being a genuine marriage. This is blatant nonsense. The meaning of the word 'precontract' was always exclusively retrospective. No couple could ever *make* a 'precontract'. They could only make a *marriage* (either in public or in secret). However, if one of the contracting parties subsequently committed bigamy, then the term 'PRE-contract' could be employed retrospectively, in relation to the second, bigamous – and therefore illegal – marriage, to refer to the *first* – and valid – marriage.

Although one form of secret marriage required only the couple to be present, make mutual vows, and then have intercourse, that does not seem to have been what occurred in the case of Edward IV and Eleanor Talbot. Reportedly there was at least one witness present at their marriage. He was the aforementioned Canon (later Bishop) Stillington, a priest who was an expert in canon law, and who would therefore have been able to evaluate very precisely the significance of the event. His presence indicates clearly that whatever words were exchanged between Edward IV and Eleanor cannot possibly have consisted only of spontaneous promises uttered on the spur of the moment. If Edward had simply been attempting to persuade Eleanor to come to bed with him he would hardly have arranged for a priest to witness his seduction.

In other words, the presence of a witness – particularly a clerical witness – comprises very strong evidence that a formal exchange of vows took place between Edward and Eleanor. Such an event must have been planned in advance. This witness later stated very publicly – and ultimately at considerable cost to himself – that Edward was married to Eleanor. The logical conclusion appears to be that the alleged secret marriage between Edward and Eleanor was no mere casual uttering of unmeant promises on the part of a king eager merely for sexual fulfilment. If the marriage took place it must have been a serious, if private, exchange of marriage vows – very similar to the simple, private ceremony later alleged to have been secretly conducted between Edward IV and Elizabeth Widville.

In terms of the chronology, we have seen that Edward may have met and been attracted to Eleanor at one of her Warwickshire manors in November 1460 and in February 1460/1. Later, at the start of the second week of June 1461, while travelling between Warwick and Daventry, Edward IV – who had meanwhile been proclaimed king of England – once again passed close by Eleanor's manors of Fenny Compton and Burton Dassett. The first of these manors had been granted to Eleanor absolutely by her former father-in-law, Lord Sudeley, following the death of Sir Thomas Boteler. As for the second of the two manors, that one was held by Eleanor for life, as part of her jointure. Therefore, if a formal secret marriage between Edward and Eleanor did indeed take place, the most likely date for it can now be pinpointed as Monday 8 June 1461.[20] The secret marriage was probably very quietly celebrated at one of Eleanor's Warwickshire manors – just as Edward's later secret marriage with Elizabeth Widville was privately celebrated at the Widville family manor in Northamptonshire. More than a year had now passed since Sir Thomas Boteler's death, and by June 1461 Eleanor would have been out of mourning for five or six months.

What happened afterwards is not clear. It appears unlikely that Edward would have taken Eleanor to London with him – though he might have had her smuggled to Windsor Castle, where he resided in August 1461. Possibly Eleanor joined him at Bristol or Gloucester, in September. Also Edward once again spent some time in the vicinity of Eleanor's Warwickshire manors at the beginning of October (see Itinerary). Nevertheless, it appears that agreed secrecy was initially seen as an essential element of the partnership. There are three possible reasons for this. The first is that Edward may have feared the reactions of his family. The second, that he may have been tricking and deceiving Eleanor. But the third intriguing possibility is that Edward may have been following an old tradition by coupling first and waiting to see whether or not the lady proved fruitful. As we have seen, there is no evidence that Edward himself had already fathered any children. Maybe he was waiting to see what would happen. If Eleanor had become pregnant, perhaps he would then have acknowledged their marriage. Indeed, as we shall see later, this may have been precisely how he handled things in his subsequent secret marriage with Elizabeth Widville.

Curiously, Eleanor's story and that of Elizabeth Widville have a number of common features. Both women were widows from Lancastrian backgrounds, both were attractive, both were a little older than the king. And in both cases, apparently, Edward's solution was the same. He went through a clandestine form of marriage and initially kept the affair quiet. Only the final outcomes differed. However, one key distinction between Eleanor Talbot (whose contract with the king was never publicly honoured during their lifetimes) and Elizabeth Widville (who ensured that she was crowned in Westminster Abbey) was the latter's proven fecundity, which Edward is said to have considered a great point in her favour.

There is a much later rumour, reported by George Buck, that a child had been born to the king by Eleanor Talbot.[21] Buck does not report the sex of this alleged child, or say what became of it. However, there is absolutely no contemporary evidence that such a person ever existed. Moreover, there are excellent reasons for doubting the story. Obviously such a child could later have claimed to be heir to the throne, as Charles II's son by Lucy Walter, James, Duke of Monmouth, did in the seventeenth century. But no such person ever advanced a claim to the English throne. Moreover, the wording of Richard III's Act of Parliament of 1484, which validated Edward's marriage to Eleanor, explicitly rules out the possibility that she bore him a child. For it states explicitly that 'it appeareth evidently, and followeth, that all th'issue and children of the said king beene bastards, and unable to inherite or to clayme anything by inheritance, by the lawe and custome of England'.[22]

Despite Buck's seventeenth-century speculation that she may have produced a royal baby, in reality it seems unlikely that Eleanor ever conceived by either of her husbands. Moreover, as we shall see later, her sister, the Duchess of Norfolk, also seems to have had some difficulty in conceiving. It is therefore possible that Eleanor was unable to bear a child. Perhaps it was because of her apparent barrenness that Edward's love for Eleanor gradually cooled. However, there is also the possibility that Eleanor herself ultimately decided, for reasons of her own, that marriage with Edward was not what she wanted.

Nevertheless, evidence certainly survives which suggests that Eleanor had certain claims upon the king. There is some evidence that he gave her property. Eleanor acquired in the 1460s at least one estate – the manor of Oare-under-Savernake – which seems to have comprised royal land.[23] And later, when Eleanor died, Edward IV's government appears to have taken deliberate steps to avoid any investigation of her tenure of this property.[24] There is also other surviving evidence which suggests that Edward treated Eleanor and her feelings with a degree of respect.

Towards the end of 1461, when the peers of the realm had been summoned to attend Edward IV's first parliament, Ralph Boteler, Lord of Sudeley, was an old man whose health was questionable. The loss of his son, Thomas Boteler, which had deprived him of his only direct heir, had probably been a shock to him. His former daughter-in-law, Eleanor Talbot, who undoubtedly maintained a good relationship with Lord Sudeley, must have been well aware of his uncertain health. It seems probable that she therefore exerted her influence on Edward IV to ensure that the king treated the old man in a kindly way. As a result, on 26 February 1461/2, Edward IV granted the elderly man

exemption for life … on account of his debility and age, from personal attendance in council or Parliament, and from being made collector, assessor or taxer of tenths, fifteenths or other subsidies, commissioner, justice of the peace, constable, bailiff or other minister of the king, or trier, arrayer or leader of men-at-arms, archers or hobelers. And he shall not be compelled to leave his dwelling for war.[25]

It was probably also Eleanor who, three months later, on 30 May 1462, persuaded the king to grant Lord Sudeley 'four bucks in summer and six does in winter within the king's park of Woodstock'.[26]

The chief piece of evidence which supports this suggestion that it was Eleanor Talbot who was behind Edward IV's early kindness towards Lord Sudeley comprises the fact that, once the intimacy between Eleanor and the king had come to an end, the relationship between the young king and her former father-in-law also changed. Ralph's royal exemption from attendance at meetings and from royal appointments became, in effect, null and void. Thereafter, Lord Sudeley once again found himself expected to take part in royal commissions. This change in his situation dates from the end of 1462,[27] thereby highlighting the approximate date at which the intimate relationship between Edward IV and Eleanor Talbot must have come to an end. It must also be significant that subsequently Edward IV's treatment of Lord Sudeley altered even more dramatically. In February 1469 the king was to break the old man completely and confiscate all his property. However, that only occurred eight months after Eleanor's death.

Meanwhile, although both parties always appear to have kept their relationship a secret, it seems that there may, nevertheless, have been some whispering about it. These whispers, which were reported later by both Mancini[28] and Vergil,[29] did not *name* Eleanor Talbot. Instead, they spoke of a relationship between the king and a person connected with the Earl of Warwick. In this context Eleanor's maternal descent from the Beauchamp family is significant. So too is the fact that the most important surviving member of Eleanor's family in terms of the national political situation in the early 1460s was undoubtedly her uncle by marriage, Richard Neville, Earl of Warwick. It is therefore perhaps unsurprising that, while the little-known Eleanor was not named personally, she was referred to via her close relationship to 'Warwick the Kingmaker'.

8

1461–1464: ITINERARY

Once Edward had become king of England the chief sources of information as to his whereabouts are the surviving documents which were issued by him or his secretaries. But it needs to be noted that sometimes – particularly when the documents in question were issued at Westminster – they do not necessarily prove that the king himself was in that location at the time. The existence of a document issued at Westminster (or elsewhere) at a time when other documents bearing the royal seal were being issued in a different place probably implies that the document in question was issued not by the king himself but by his staff, acting on his behalf. Nevertheless, at a time when all the surviving documents bearing the royal seal were being issued at (for example) Leicester Castle, that almost certainly means that the king himself was then staying there.

1461/2
JANUARY
Greenwich, the City of
London, Greenwich, Rochester,
Sittingbourne, Canterbury and
Westminster[1]

FEBRUARY
Westminster[2]
The city of London and Ware
(Herts)[3]

MARCH
The University of Cambridge and
the Tower of Cambridge
REGNAL YEAR 2
The University of Cambridge and
Huntingdon[4]
Peterborough, Peterborough
Abbey and Stamford[5]
Cambridge[6]
Grantham and Stamford[7]
Newark[8]
Lincoln[9]

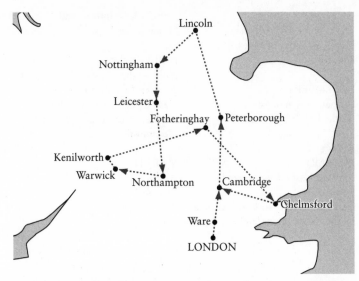

Edward IV's movements from February 1461/2 to August 1462

Newark and Eastwell
(Leics.)[10]
Southwell (Notts.)[11]

1462 (age 20; regnal year 2)
Nottingham[12]

APRIL
Derby and Burton upon
Trent[13]
Lichfield (Castle) and Leicester
Castle[14]

MAY
Leicester Castle[15]
Burton upon Trent[16]
Leicester Castle[17]

JUNE
Leicester Castle[18]

JULY
Leicester Castle[19]
Town of Northampton[20]
Warwick Castle, Kenilworth
Castle, Daventry and
Fotheringhay Castle[21]

AUGUST
Fotheringhay Castle, Chelmsford,
Cambridge, Greenwich, Ware and
Fotheringhay Castle[22]

SEPTEMBER
Fotheringhay Castle, the Tower of
London, the City of London, and
Westminster[23]
The manor of The More (near
Rickmansworth, Herts)[24]
Luton and the City of
London[25]

OCTOBER
Westminster, Fotheringhay
Castle, Grantham, Newark
and York[26]

DECEMBER
Durham (the monastery
[Cathedral Priory?] and city)[27]

1462/3
JANUARY
Alnwick Castle (surrendered to
Edward IV)[28]
Durham, Ripon, York, Doncaster,
Blythe (Northumberland),

Stamford, Grantham and
Fotheringhay Castle[29]

FEBRUARY
Fotheringhay Castle, Westminster,
Som'ych (= Somerych –
place unidentified), Hertford
(Castle), Syon (near Sheen) and
Westminster[30]

MARCH
Westminster[31]
REGNAL YEAR 3
Westminster[32]

Edward IV's movements from July 1463 to March 1463/4

1463 (age 21; regnal year 3)
Westminster[33]

APRIL
Westminster[34]
Monastery of Bello (not
identified.)[35]
Windsor Castle and Westminster[36]

MAY
Westminster[37]

JUNE
Westminster[38]

JULY
Westminster and
Northampton[39]

AUGUST
Northampton, Fotheringhay
Castle and City & Tower of
London[40]

SEPTEMBER
Coventry, York, Northampton,
Middleham, Beverley and
Kingston-upon-Hull[41]

OCTOBER
York and Pontefract Castle[42]

NOVEMBER
Pontefract Castle[43]

DECEMBER
York and Pontefract Castle[44]

1463/4
JANUARY
Pontefract Castle[45]
Nottingham[46]
Northampton[47]
Coventry[48]

FEBRUARY
Gloucester[49]
Kimbolton[50]
Huntingdon[51]
Cambridgeshire[52]
Waltham (Essex / Herts. border)[53]

MARCH
Westminster[54]

9

1462–1463: 'THE KING LOVED HIM WELL'

It seems that the next curious relationship of Edward IV was neither with a young girl nor with a widow. It was his alleged liaison with his second cousin, Henry Beaufort, Duke of Somerset (born 1436, executed 1464). It would potentially be easy to apply to this relationship a modern word such as 'gay' or 'homosexual'. However, the popular tendency to attempt to pigeon-hole people in black-and-white terms such as 'homosexual' or 'heterosexual' (or 'gay' or 'straight') is rather misleading. Human and other sexuality is not black and white, but exists in shades of grey. Although 'late medieval knightly masculinity was defined by sexual object choice, that choice being what we today would call heterosexual ... it did not have to be exclusive. ... For a man, to have a heterosexual relationship was to gain status in relation to other men by dominating a woman; whatever same-sex relationships he may have formed were not part of this game,'[1] but that is not to say that such relationships did not exist.

Terminology such as 'gay' or homosexual' will also be avoided here for two further reasons. The first is that such items of vocabulary did not exist in the fifteenth century with their modern meanings. Indeed, the term *homosexual* was only invented in the late nineteenth century. As for the word *gay*, that only acquired its sexual meaning in the second half of the twentieth century. Previously, nineteenth-century men who had relationships with others of the same sex had been referred to in roundabout ways, for example as 'Margeries'. Earlier, from the sixteenth to the early nineteenth centuries, such men were known as 'Mollies'.[2] However, Lord Alfred Douglas, who was in love with Oscar Wilde in 1891, expressed clearly the problem of language in respect of such a relationship when he described it as 'the love that dare not speak its name'.[3] Though the slant of his phrase is different, in some ways it recalls Edward III's fourteenth-century mention of 'the too horrible vice that is not to be named'.[4] King Edward III was probably referring to the specific vice of which his father has been accused, namely engaging in anal intercourse with a member of the same sex (see below).

The third reason for avoiding a word such as 'homosexual' is that even in the modern world the use of such a term is actually imprecise. For example, it is debatable, in the twenty-first century, whether describing a man as 'homosexual' necessarily implies that he has sex of some kind with another man (or other men). It might simply mean that he feels attracted to another man (or other men). It is also debatable whether the use of modern terms such as 'gay' or 'homosexual' suggests that the person so described is consistently and exclusively attracted to people of the same sex. It might simply mean that the individual is *sometimes* attracted to persons of the same sex – but possibly also sometimes attracted to members of the opposite sex. Thus, describing Edward IV as 'gay' or 'homosexual' would be both anachronistic and imprecise.

Nevertheless, there is little doubt that an intimate relationship did, for a time, exist between Edward IV and the Duke of Somerset, and that this relationship was perceived by contemporaries to be notably different in some way from Edward's well-known friendships with other men, such as Lord Hastings or Sir John Howard. The existence of possible male-to-male relationships was certainly recognised in Europe as a whole, and specifically in England, in the fifteenth century. Records exist of a late fourteenth-century London and Oxford resident whose name was John Rykener but who preferred to call himself 'Eleanor', wearing female clothing and having sex as the passive partner with various men, including a number of Oxford University students.[5] Later, in 1491, Richard Edmund, Fellow of Merton College, Oxford, was accused of 'the sin against nature', and found himself expelled – though he was allowed to remain until Christmas.[6] In these and other cases there are specific medieval references to both anal and oral intercourse between men. However, there are also references to close and loving male-to-male relationships which did not necessarily involve sexual activity.

It is therefore important, before attempting to explore the relationship which existed between Edward IV and Henry, Duke of Somerset, to establish how society viewed relationships between persons of the same sex at that time. This is a period of history which is 'commonly associated with brutal sexual repression'.[7] However, that appears to be erroneous and misleading. 'From the sixth until the early eleventh century, homosexuals were in fact treated no more harshly than couples who practised contraception.'[8] In the later Middle Ages in Europe the castigation of male-to-male sex increased. Nevertheless, in fifteenth-century England a relationship between two men, even if it involved regular sexual practice between them, never constituted a criminal offence. The criminality of such relationships was only introduced (or invented) in the sixteenth century, by Edward IV's grandson, King Henry VIII. In Europe as a whole, the sixteenth-century 'waves of prosecutions of homosexuals seem to be closely correlated with waves of persecution of witches ... For reasons which are still obscure, however, England escaped the worst excesses of these attacks on both sodomy and witchcraft, towards which a more pragmatic attitude seems normally to have prevailed.'[9]

Although all sexual activity outside marriage – whether with members of the same sex or members of the opposite sex – was always viewed as sinful by the Church, and was certainly not encouraged in the later Middle Ages, curiously 'university authorities did not enforce, much less the students adopt the teachings of the church about celibacy and chastity ... [and] of course homosexual activity was present too'.[10] In fact the Church readily acknowledged the existence of activities involving two members of the same sex, which even sometimes involved its priests, monks and friars. Thus, in the period with which we are dealing here, a relationship between two men was apparently seen neither as a crime nor as the kind of sin which automatically required grave earthly punishment. Since such relationships were known to exist, provided they did not include some specific aspect which was perceived as creating a problem of some kind they were not, apparently, seen as in any way threatening to society.

One way in which such a relationship could potentially be seen as threatening appears to be revealed by the relationship which had existed earlier between King Edward II and Piers Gaveston. The relationship between those two men was evidently viewed with hostility by their contemporary society, and it may be helpful to try to understand why that might have happened. Since the even earlier relationship between Richard I and the king of France had not been seen as a major problem, and the relationship between Edward IV and Henry, Duke of Somerset, was not apparently widely perceived as a major problem, it might be helpful to pinpoint how those two relationships differed from that of Edward II. The obvious point which emerges relates to the social status of the persons involved. Richard I (who, when his relationship with Philippe-Auguste commenced, was Duke of Aquitaine and a younger son of the reigning English sovereign, Henry II), and his partner, King Philippe-Auguste, were both royal princes, of very similar social status. Similarly, Edward IV and Henry, Duke of Somerset, were both members of the English ruling family, and of very similar social status. However, the relationship between Edward II and Piers Gaveston had been socially unequal. What is more, an earlier feature of European culture – for example amongst the Vikings – had been to view the active partner of a male homosexual relationship without hostility, while the passive male partner was perceived very unfavourably. Thus, in the case of Edward II and Gaveston, a man of mediocre birth (Gaveston) was suddenly perceived to be exercising influence and possibly control over the reigning monarch, who, despite his higher social status, was apparently perceived as the passive partner. That appears to be the reason why the relationship was so severely frowned upon – and why it is said that Edward II was killed by inserting a hot poker into his anus.

> Geoffrey le Baker describes how Edward's captors 'passed a red-hot soldering iron through a trumpet-like instrument ... into his anus, through the intestines and into his wind-pipe'; Ralph Higden refers to his having been 'slain with a hot broche [spit] put through the secret place posterielle [posterior]'. ... there are contemporary examples of anus to mouth impalement being used to punish sinners guilty of sodomy, in depictions of hell in Italian Last Judgement frescos. The branding of Nicholas' buttocks with a red-hot coulter (the blade of a plough share) in Chaucer's 'Miller's Tale' likewise has sexual connotations.[11]

If the later relationship between Edward IV and Somerset was perceived as sexual, it seems probable that Edward IV was not considered to be the passive partner. Evidence of this – in terms of the documentation of attempts to punish Somerset, but not the king – will be presented shortly (see below). However, it appears that the relationship of King Edward with the Duke of Somerset was never perceived or interpreted as involving any kind of gross social inequality. It is important, therefore, to establish clearly the family relationship which existed between Edward IV and Henry. They were second cousins, as the family tree below shows.

Curiously, Henry Beaufort was not only a second cousin of Edward IV himself, but was also the first cousin of the young king's spouse, the beautiful Eleanor Talbot. Henry's mother, Lady Eleanor Beauchamp, Duchess of Somerset, was the younger sister of Eleanor Talbot's mother, Lady Margaret Beauchamp, Countess of Shrewsbury. Indeed, it is possible that Henry's mother was one of Eleanor Talbot's godmothers,

THE RELATIONSHIP OF EDWARD IV AND HENRY, DUKE OF SOMERSET

John of Gaunt, Duke of Lancaster m 3 Catherine de Roët

John Beaufort	Joan Beaufort
Earl of Somerset	Countess of Westmorland
Edmund Beaufort	Cecily Neville
Duke of Somerset	Duchess of York
Henry Beaufort	Edward IV
Duke of Somerset	

and thus the source of her niece's Christian name. Given their close family connection, it seems that Eleanor Talbot must have been aware of her cousin Henry's intimate involvement with her royal consort. From her point of view, this unacceptable development may have been the key factor which led to her abandonment of her own relationship with the king, and her commitment to a religious life (see below, chapter 13).

Henry Beaufort, who had been born on 26 January 1435/6, seems to have been just a few months older than his cousin Eleanor. He may well have shared her dark hair colouring. Undoubtedly he also shared her attractive appearance. For example, the Burgundian chronicler Georges Chastellain – who presumably saw '*le duc de Sombresset*'[12] while he was living in the Low Countries in 1459, and again later, when he was in France – described him as 'a very great lord, and one of the most handsome young knights in the English kingdom'.[13] Henry's good looks were clearly significant, for they would explain why the young Edward IV – who had already been strongly attracted to the lovely Eleanor Talbot – now also found Eleanor's handsome first cousin Henry Beaufort, Duke of Somerset, exceedingly attractive.

It is also quite clear that the close blood relationship between Henry and his Talbot first cousins was always recognised, political differences notwithstanding. For example, in the summer of 1468, when Henry's brother was living in exile in the Low Countries, his cousin Elizabeth Talbot, Duchess of Norfolk, was a leading member of the English party which accompanied Edward IV's youngest sister, Margaret, to Flanders for the celebration of her marriage to Charles the Bold, Duke of Burgundy. Servants of the Duchess of Norfolk, acting perhaps on behalf of their mistress, apparently made contact in Flanders with Elizabeth (and Eleanor)'s exiled cousin. For when

Eleanor Beauchamp, Duchess of Somerset, the mother of Henry Beaufort, and the maternal aunt of Eleanor Talbot, as originally depicted in the Lady chapel window of the church in Warwick (F. Sandford, *A Genealogical History of the Kings and Queens of England*, London 1707, p. 332).

the Duchess of Norfolk with others returned into England, in whose company were two young gentlemen, that one named John Poyntz, and that other William Alsford, the which were arrested because, in the time of the 'foresaid marriage, they had familiar communication with the Duke of Somerset and his 'complices there, in the which they were both detected of treason.[14]

It seems obvious that Edward IV was not exclusively attracted to persons of the same sex. Although he had other male friends, his relationships with them were never described by contemporaries in the same way as his relationship with the Duke of Somerset. Edward has also already been shown to have made a considerable effort to win his way into bed with Eleanor Talbot, and we shall shortly be exploring his relationships with other members of the opposite sex.

As for Henry, Duke of Somerset, his sexual predilection is less clear. He is said to have fathered one single bastard son by a girl called Joan

THE RELATIONSHIP OF ELEANOR TALBOT AND HENRY, DUKE OF SOMERSET

Richard Beauchamp, Earl of Warwick m Elizabeth Berkeley

Margaret Beauchamp
Countess of Shrewsbury

Eleanor Talbot
Lady Boteler

Eleanor Beauchamp
Duchess of Somerset

Henry Beaufort
Duke of Somerset

Hill.[15] However, Henry never married. Indeed, he sometimes took extraordinarily forceful measures to avoid being pushed into an arranged marriage (see below). What is more, as we shall see at the end of this chapter, he may also have had an earlier same-sex relationship with a royal relative on the European mainland. Therefore even if the relationship between Edward IV and Henry was something of a novel experience for the former, it was probably the preferred kind of relationship in the case of the latter.

It is not absolutely certain when Edward and Henry first met. Henry Beaufort was a godson of King Henry VI, and had occasionally attended his godfather's court in the 1450s. It is therefore just possible that Edward may have seen him early in 1454, when Edward was approaching his twelfth birthday, and when Henry was just eighteen. At this time Edward may briefly have been with his father in London (see Itinerary). There is no evidence to prove that such an earlier meeting between Edward and Henry ever occurred. But on 22 May 1455, at the first battle of St Albans, both Edward and Henry are reported to have been present, so they may have seen each other – at a distance – on that occasion, when Henry was seriously injured, fighting at the side of his father (who was killed). Henry had to be carried away from the scene of the fighting in a cart.[16]

At all events, the two young men definitely met around the feast of Christmas 1462. Gregory's Chronicle tells us that thereafter, in 1463, Edward and Henry regularly slept together, and that the king loved the Duke of Somerset. The account of their meeting and the ensuing relationship is recorded as follows:

> Then King Edward ... made him[self] ready towards the north with any lords, gentlemen, and commons with him. And there he laid siege to Alnwick Castle,[17] and to the Castle of Bamburgh, and to Dunstanburgh. Bamburgh and Dunstanburgh were held by Sir Ralph Percy and Sir Henry Beaufort, the former Duke of Somerset, and the castle of Alnwick [was held by] Lord Hungerford. And Bamburgh and Dunstanburgh were yielded by Sir Ralph Percy and Sir Henry Beaufort, former Duke of Somerset, to the king's will, on the condition that the said Ralph Percy should have the keeping of the two castles, Bamburgh and Dunstanburgh. The said Sir Ralph Percy and Sir Henry Beaufort, former Duke of Somerset, swore to be true and faithful as true liegemen unto our king and sovereign lord Edward IV. And they came to Durham, and took the oath there before our king. And the king gave them his livery and great rewards.

And then the aforesaid Ralph Percy went back again to Northumberland and had the keeping of the said two castles under the terms of the appointment. And the said Sir Henry Beaufort remained with the king, and rode with him to London. And the king made very much of him; so much that he lodged with the king in his own bed many nights, and sometimes rode hunting behind the king, the king having about him not more than six horses maximum, of which three were of the Duke of Somerset's men. The king loved him well, but the duke thought treason behind fair cheer and words, as it appeared.[18]

The Duke of Somerset surrended Bamburgh Castle on Christmas Eve 1462, and it was following his surrender that he then met Edward IV. Obviously that meeting had a great impact on the two young men, for 'the Yorkist king restored Somerset to favour with a speed that shocked contemporaries'.[19] Peace was made between them, and Henry was even allowed to join the Earl of Warwick and his forces in the still-ongoing siege of Alnwick Castle.[20] As we shall see shortly, the conclusion of Gregory's Chronicle was that the Duke of Somerset was deceiving Edward throughout their relationship and was actually always his enemy is based purely on later evidence and on hindsight. There is actually no contemporary evidence to show that Somerset was deceiving the king during the months of their intimacy.

The key words of the description of the relationship from Gregory's Chronicle (above) states that Somerset lived with the king, that the king made much of him, and that they shared the same bed on many occasions. This is rather reminiscent of a much earlier report of the similar relationship between Edward IV's forebear, Richard I, and King Philippe-Auguste of France. That earlier relationship had been described as follows:

Richard, duke of Aquitaine, son of the king of England, remained with Philip, the king of France, who so honoured him for so long that they ate every day at the same table and from the same dish, and at night their beds did not separate them. And the king of France loved him as his own soul; and they loved each other so much that the king of England [Henry II] was absolutely astonished at the vehement love between them and marvelled at what it could mean.[21]

Thus it is by no means illogical to deduce, from the evidence provided by Gregory's Chronicle, that Edward IV and Henry Beaufort, Duke of

Somerset, may well have indulged for a time in some kind of sexual intimacy on a regular basis. But as was established earlier, this certainly does not mean that Edward IV should be categorised as what would nowadays be described as a 'gay' man. It is fairly well known that, from the sixteenth century until the not-so-distant past, similar situations as that which appears to have existed between Edward and Henry in 1463 were sometimes to be found in male boarding school dormitories, in universities, and also in military or naval contexts. 'In Oxford and Cambridge colleges in the sixteenth and seventeenth centuries it was normal practice for the tutor, who was usually a young bachelor in his middle twenties, to share his bedroom with several young students aged perhaps fifteen to eighteen.'[22] But of course, these would have been situations involving young men, many of whom subsequently went on to marry women and produce children.

Nevertheless, Edward IV's great love for Henry certainly produced some interesting results. It seems that Henry may sometimes have been rather too serious in character. Indeed, in some respects he was possibly rather a difficult man to deal with. Apparently he could be very quick-tempered on occasions. In Coventry, in October 1456, it had been necessary to physically restrain him in order to prevent him from attacking the Duke of York, and a month later he nearly came to blows with the Earl of Warwick in London.[23] Yet it seems that Edward IV, by his easy and loving manner and by his not infrequent granting of favours, was able to make the Duke of Somerset relax and even laugh. In the joust described below, the king seems to have overcome Henry's bad temper simply by asking him to be merry, together with offering him a small gift of some kind.

> Out of great love the king arranged a great joust at Westminster, that he [Henry] should experience some kind of chivalric sport after his great labour and heaviness. And with great insistence the king made him [Henry] put on his harness, and [he] rode in the list, but he would never cope with any man and no man could cope with him, till the king prayed him to be merry and sent him a token, and then he ran full justly and merrily, and his helm was a pitiful straw hat! And then every man marked him well.[24]

Presumably the joust was held during the month of March 1462/3, when the king was resident at the palace of Westminster (see Itinerary). The king was also resident at Westminster in the early summer of 1463, but it sounds as though the joust must have been held earlier in the period of his relationship with the Duke of Somerset. Jousting wearing a straw hat as one's 'helmet' must have been seen as very light-hearted behaviour. Probably it caused a good deal of laughter at the time, and clearly it was well remembered – and recorded – later.

The relationship between Edward and Henry, whatever its precise nature, appears to have commenced in about January 1462/3 and to have lasted at least six months. The two men remained together until July 1463 – and possibly a little longer:

On 10 March [Somerset] was granted a full pardon and the Westminster parliament, which sat from 29 April to 17 June 1463, reversed the attainder passed against him in 1461, allowing him to recover his landed estate. On 22 June an annuity of £222 was returned to him and shortly afterwards his younger brother Edmund Beaufort was released from the Tower. This dramatic reconciliation was followed with considerable interest on the continent; a letter to Louis XI of 1 July 1463 reported how Somerset was in close attendance on the king. Edward had made extraordinary efforts to win the duke's trust and allegiance: he hunted with him, arranged a tournament in his honour, and even shared a bed with him.[25]

However, it appears that, in the summer of 1463, Edward IV had to secrete Henry in one of his kingly castles in order to protect him from people who would have liked to kill him:

The kynge sone aftyr ... was purposyd to ryde into Yorke schyre and to the contray a boute, to see and understonde the dysposyscyon of the pepylle of the Northe. And toke with hym the Duke of Somersett, and ij c of hys men welle horsyd and welle i-harnaysyd. Ande the sayde Duke, Harry of Somersett, ande his men were made the Kyngys garde, for the Kyng hadde that duke in moche favyr and trustyd hym welle. But þe garde of hym was as men shulde put a lombe a monge wolvysse of malyscyus bestys; but Alle myghty God was the scheparde. And whenn the kynge departyd from London he toke hys way to Northehampton, and thedyr the kynge com a Syn Jamys day the Apostylle [25 July], ande that fals duke with hym.[26] And the comyns of the towne of Northehampton and of the schyre a-boute sawe that the fals duke and traytoure was so nyghe the Kyngys presens and was made hys garde. The comyns a rosse uppon that fals traytur thee Duke of Somersett, and wolde have slayne hym with yn the kyngys palys. And thenn the kynge with fayre speche

and grete defeculte savyde hys lyffe for that tyme, and that was
pytte, for the savynge of hys lyffe at that tyme causyd mony mannys
dethys son aftyr, as ye shalle heyre. And then the Duke [*sic* = King]
sende that fals Duke of Somersett in to a castelle of hys owne fulle
secretly, for save garde of hys the dukys lyffe, and the dukys men
unto Newe Castelle, to kepe the towne, and gave hem goode wages
fulle treuly payde.[27]

The attack upon the Duke of Somerset was unquestionably because
the men of Northampton strongly resented the relationship which
they perceived had come to exist between Edward IV and the Duke of
Somerset. In fact it was similar to what had happened earlier, in the
case of Edward II and Piers Gaveston. Since Somerset was attacked but
Edward IV was not, it also appears that Somerset was probably perceived
as the passive sexual partner. It sounds from a later report (see below) as
if the castle to which the Duke of Somerset was sent by Edward IV was
either in or near Wales. Possibly it may even have been that familiar home
of Edward's own youth, the castle of Ludlow.

This public attack on Somerset, together with the implication that he
was viewed as the passive sexual partner, may well have been what turned
him against his relationship with Edward. As we have seen, Somerset
appears to have been a very short-tempered man. Nevertheless, hitherto
he had apparently been genuinely very much influenced by Edward and
the king's affectionate conduct towards him – as we saw in the case of the
joust. At all events, it was apparently not until December 1463 (almost a
year after their relationship began) that Edward finally realised that the
Duke of Somerset was no longer his friend and was not to be trusted.
Edward was staying at the castle of Pontefract. At that point,

thys same yere a-boute Crystysmas that fals Duke of Somersett, with
owte any leve of the kyng, stale owte of Walys with a prevy mayny
towarde the Newecastelle, for he and hys men were confeteryde for
to have be-trayde the sayde Newecastelle.

... Ande thenn the kynge, owre soverayne lorde Edwar the iiij,
hadde knowleche of hys fals dysposyscyon of thys fals Duke Harry
of Somersett.[28]

Piquancy is added to this strange and interesting tale when one looks
at the chronology, for Henry Beaufort, who was born early in 1436,
was of almost exactly the same age as his cousin, Lady Eleanor Talbot,
Edward IV's earlier love, whom he may also have physically resembled in

some respects. Thus he was about six years older than the king. During the six or so months of their relationship in 1463 the young king was twenty-one years old and Henry Beaufort was twenty-seven.

Although, as we have seen, he reportedly fathered one illegitimate son at some stage, Henry Beaufort never married. 'In 1457 Queen Margaret of Anjou suggested a marriage between Somerset and his cousin Joan, sister of James II of Scotland, but the proposal came to nothing.'[29] Indeed, the Duke of Somerset himself seems to have done his best to undermine Margaret of Anjou's marriage project for him, by deliberately casting public aspersions upon the morality of the Scottish Queen Mother, Mary of Gueldres, the widow of James II, who was then acting as regent for her son, King James III, and who was thus the centre of power in Scotland:

In March [1462], the Duke of Somerset returned from Flanders in a carvell to Scotland. And the Queen of Scotland, held him in the highest degree of hatred, because he had revealed her carnal intercourse to the king of France, and she made the Lord of Halys[30] lie in wait to kill him.[31]

Thus, the attempted plan for his Scottish royal wedding came to nothing. When he died a year later, Henry's title was notionally inherited by his younger brother, Edmund. The sum of the surviving circumstantial evidence is therefore by no means inconsistent with the notion that Henry, at least, might possibly have preferred partners of the same sex.

This suggestion is further supported by the fact that, prior to his relationship with Edward IV, 'Somerset had also won the admiration of Charles, count of Charolais, the son and heir of Philip the Good, duke of Burgundy. The two met at Ardres on 12 August [1460]. Charolais entertained his guest with a lavish dinner and a firm friendship was forged.'[32] Charles the Bold, Count of Charolais, and later Duke of Burgundy, has also (in spite of his three marriages) been described as 'homosexual'. 'At any rate his illegitimate half-brother Baudouin and his associate Jehan de Chassa virtually accused him of buggery when they fled from his court at the end of 1470.'[33] Charles the Bold obviously had a sincere feeling of some kind for the Duke of Somerset, because in 1461–62, when the new French king, Louis XI, arrested Somerset, the English duke's life was saved by the Count of Charolais.[34] And as we have already seen, in spite of his marriage with Edward IV's sister, Margaret, Charles was also housing the Henry's brother in the Low Countries in 1468.

10

1460–1464: THE FIRST ROYAL BASTARDS?

Although there are surviving contemporary English sources from the reign of Edward IV which refer to the king's relationship with the Duke of Somerset, no such contemporary English sources have survived that mention his relationship with Eleanor Talbot, and cite her name. As we have seen, Mancini and Vergil later referred merely to an unnamed female connected with the Earl of Warwick. Henry VII subsequently did his best to destroy all record of the Act of Parliament which had posthumously recognised Eleanor's marriage to Edward, citing her married name and the title of her father. However, because of the secret nature of Edward's relationship with Eleanor, it may never have been mentioned in any strictly contemporary written documents.

Similarly, no contemporary sources survive which refer to Edward IV's relationships with other women. For example, although it has been claimed that 'according to the Patent Rolls for 4 December 1476, it was during this same year that [Mistress] Shore began her liaison with Edward IV, after his return from France',[1] in reality this is untrue. There are three possible explanations for the total lack of contemporary references to mistresses of Edward IV. It could be because the relationships in question were not seen as in any way important at the time. Or it could be because it was considered improper to refer to such relationships. However, it could simply be because there were hardly any such relationships, and such relationships as did exist were not long-term or in any way serious, so that in fact they failed to become matters of contemporary public knowledge.

Intriguingly, in this context, it is also the case that there is only *one* surviving piece of contemporary evidence that Edward IV ever personally acknowledged the existence of any bastard children. The source in question dates from the 1470s, and it mentions (though it does not name) just one single bastard son. This contemporary source will be quoted later (see below, chapter 20).

Thus, the earliest surviving English source which makes a detailed claim that Edward IV had mistresses is Sir Thomas More's *History of King Richard III*. According to his nephew, William Rastell, More is reputed to have written his *History of King Richard III* in 'about the yeare of our Lorde 1513'.[2] However, More's text only appeared in print much later, in the 1540s and 1550s. Thus we are dealing with a source which certainly postdates the reign of Edward IV by a minimum of thirty years, and which possibly does so by more than half a century. More's text is also a source which undoubtedly reflects the 'Tudor' political propaganda machine in respect of Richard III. Therefore it may also have been restructuring the image of Edward IV for political reasons.

More claims that Edward IV himself

> would say that he had three concubines, which in three divers properties diversely excelled: one the merriest, another the wiliest, the third the holiest harlot in his realm, as one whom no man could get out of church lightly to any place, but it were to his bed. The other two were somewhat greater personages, and nevertheless of their humility content to be nameless and to forebear the praise of those properties. But the merriest was ... Shore's wife'.[3]

Given the explicit reference to Mistress Shore (for details of whom see below, chapter 22), if Edward IV did genuinely make a remark of this nature, he could only have done so in the second half of his reign – in the 1470s or early 1480s.

It is generally assumed that the holy lady with whom Thomas More's later text alleges that Edward claimed a relationship was Eleanor Talbot. It is also generally assumed that the other high-ranking lady, who is described as very wily, was Elizabeth Lucy. The first interpretation is almost certainly correct. However, the second may well be a misinterpretation. As we shall see later, the person generally identified as Elizabeth Lucy was definitely not reported to be high-ranking in other surviving sources. Even more significantly, it is questionable whether such a person as Elizabeth Lucy ever really existed. The evidence in this respect will be presented shortly. Moreover, if Edward IV perceived no clear distinction between women with whom he contracted secret marriages and women with whom he simply had a sexual relationship (as the generally accepted reference to Eleanor Talbot in his alleged quote implies) then it may well be that the '*wily* harlot' to whom he reportedly referred was actually none other than Elizabeth Widville, Lady Grey. Indeed, in terms of time, such an interpretation would appear logical, implying that the list runs in reverse chronological order – with the merry Mistress Shore as the king's most recent alleged sexual partner, the wily Elizabeth Widville as the one in the middle, and the holy Eleanor Talbot as the earliest woman with whom the king had a significant relationship.

More also claimed that, when the king was arguing with his mother over whether or not he ought to acknowledge his relationship with Elizabeth Widville, he made the point 'that she is a widow and hath already children, [and] by God's blessed lady, I am a bachelor and have some too'.[4] If genuine, this alleged remark must presumably have been made in the autumn of 1464. It therefore implies that at that stage in his life, despite the fact that he had produced no children by Eleanor Talbot, Edward IV may nevertheless have succeeded in fathering children by some other woman (or women). If so, that might have been one of the factors which encouraged Edward to end his genitively unproductive relationship with Eleanor.

Apart from his references to 'Dame Elizabeth Grey' (Elizabeth Widville), Thomas More's first mention of the *name* of an alleged partner of the king refers to the summer of 1483 (when Edward IV was already dead). More states that at that point in time Richard, Duke of Gloucester (then Lord Protector of the Realm), decided that

> Doctor Shaa should in a sermon at St Paul's Cross signify to the people that neither King Edward himself nor the Duke of Clarence were lawfully begotten, nor were not the very children of the Duke of York, but gotten unlawfully by other persons by the adultery of the duchess, their mother; and that also Dame Elizabeth Lucy was verily the wife of King Edward, and so the prince and all his children bastards that were gotten upon the queen.[5]

This statement is blatantly untrue. There is not a shred of evidence that Richard, Duke of Gloucester, was ever behind the making of such claims. In respect of the alleged illegitimacy of his elder brothers, Richard's ongoing relationship with his mother, the dowager Duchess of York, makes such conduct on his part highly unlikely. It was the Duchess of York's London house (Baynard's Castle) which was Richard's headquarters during the difficult summer months of 1483 – the weeks which eventually led to the English crown being offered to Richard as the only living legitimate heir of his late brother, Edward IV. It is also clear that Cecily Neville had supported this move. Later, following his accession to the throne, Richard III continued to maintain close contact with his mother. For example, following the death of his queen consort, Anne Neville, and at a time when he was planning a new royal marriage with a Portuguese princess, Richard III went to visit his mother, who at that time was living in semi-retirement at Berkhamsted Castle in Hertfordshire. Richard paid a visit to his mother at Berkhamsted on Tuesday 17 May 1485.[6] No doubt he wished to keep her up to date regarding the progress of negotiations for his second marriage.

There is also absolutely no evidence that Thomas More's other claims regarding what was said in respect of the succession to the English throne in the summer of 1483 have any basis of truth. It is clear from other sources that the argument put forward in the summer of 1483 – not by Richard, Duke of Gloucester, but by the Bishop of Bath and Wells – to the royal council was simply that the marriage between Edward IV and Elizabeth Widville was invalid and that therefore all the children of that 'marriage' were illegitimate. This was the evidence which was submitted to the three estates of the realm – and later to a formal parliament – and which resulted in the crown being offered to Richard, Duke of Gloucester. Moreover, the exclusion from the royal inheritance of the line of George, Duke of Clarence, was very clearly stated by the three estates and Parliament to be due not to the duke's illegitimacy (which was never mentioned, and which no one had ever alleged), but to Edward IV's act of attainder against him. That was the legal process which had led to the execution of the Duke of Clarence, and to the consequent exclusion of his son, Edward, Earl of Warwick, from the royal inheritance.

It is also absolutely clear that the person named by Parliament as the legitimate wife of Edward IV was not 'Dame Elizabeth Lucy' but Eleanor Talbot, Lady Boteler. Thus, More's claim that Edward IV was said to have married a woman called Elizabeth Lucy was a pure piece of 'Tudor' fabrication. This lie was presumably deliberately invented as a piece of careful government planning – just in case people happened to recall (in spite of Henry VII's very careful subsequent attempts to write this fact out of history) that a claim in respect of the existence of an earlier marriage of Edward IV had been formally accepted by Parliament.

It is therefore the worrying case that the earliest surviving source which mentions the name of 'Dame Elizabeth Lucy' as a partner of King Edward IV appears to consist of nothing but mythology. Since the whole of Thomas More's paragraph which includes the earliest surviving record of this alleged lady's name is pure fabrication, it inevitably raises the question of whether the name 'Elizabeth Lucy' itself may perhaps also have been an invention – made not by More, but perhaps by Cardinal Morton, who was probably the source for the 'Tudor' propaganda which More was disseminating. This makes it questionable whether a woman called Elizabeth Lucy ever really existed – particularly since, in spite of careful research, no such person has ever actually been identified. Henceforth, therefore, unless any genuine evidence for her existence can be found, the name of 'Elizabeth Lucy' will always be cited in inverted commas in the present study, on the grounds that it appears to be nothing more than an invented pseudonym.

More also puts forward the claim that in the autumn of 1464 the dowager Duchess of York had sent for 'Elizabeth Lucy'.

> And albeit that she was by the king's mother and many other put in good comfort to affirm that she was ensured unto the king, yet when she was solemnly sworn to say the truth, she confessed that they were never ensured. Howbeit, she said his grace spoke so loving words unto her that verily she hoped he would have married her, and if it had not been for such kind words she would never have showed such kindness to him to let him so kindly get her with child.[7]

Since we saw clearly earlier that More's use of the name 'Elizabeth Lucy' as Edward's earlier marriage partner should actually have referred to Eleanor Talbot, the intriguing question now arises as to whether Cecily Neville, Duchess of York, had always been well aware of her son's secret marriage with Lady Eleanor. Did the dowager Duchess of York have an interview with *Eleanor* on this subject in the autumn of 1464?

However, More's story also contains another significant feature. It implies that, although 'Elizabeth Lucy' denied that she was married to the king, she had borne him a bastard child. There are many problems with this. In addition to the fact that More was earlier shown to be telling lies, the sixteenth-century English version of his text which is frequently quoted is a rather free vernacular translation of More's original Latin, which was more laconic. However, we nevertheless have a situation in which Edward IV is reported to have fathered more than one illegitimate child prior to 1464 – a situation, moreover, in which the mother of at least one of these alleged royal bastards is reported to have borne the name 'Elizabeth Lucy'.

The next significant source which refers to Edward IV's relationship with 'Elizabeth Lucy' is George Buck, whose *History of the Life and Reigne of Richard III* was written in 1619. Interestingly, in spite of the attempts of 'Tudor' political propaganda to write her out of history, Buck was clearly well aware of Edward IV's relationship with Eleanor Talbot. Although Buck made some errors in respect of Eleanor's maternal pedigree and life story, he obviously knew a good deal about her and her relationship with the king. It is therefore potentially credible that he may also have produced additional authentic information in respect of Edward IV's other heterosexual relationships.

Buck cites More's story of the claim, allegedly made by the Duchess of York in 1464, that Edward IV was contracted to 'Elizabeth Lucy'. According to this story, as we have seen, Cecily Neville 'urged his Contract with the Lady Elizabeth Lucie, and his having had a childe by her, (as she said;) and thought her self bound in conscience to charge him with'.[8]

But Buck goes on to say,

> The truth is, he was never contracted to her, though he loved her well, being of an affable and witty temper; nor did she ever alleadge the King was betrothed to her, but that he had entangled her by sweet and tempting language; And who knoweth not *Credula res amor est*? But true it is, he had a childe by her, which was the Bastard *Arthur*, called commonly (but unduly) *Arthur Plantagenet*, afterward made Viscount *Lisle* by *H.8* [Henry VIII].[9]

Buck states very plainly that, in his view, 'the Historians have much and foully erred'. But, having revealed the alleged name of her bastard son by the king, he then goes on to tell us that 'Elizabeth Lucy was the daughter of one *Wyat* of Southampton, a mean Gentleman (if he were one) and the wife of one *Lucy*, as mean a man as *Wyat*. True it is, the King kept her as his Concubine.'[10]

It definitely appears to have been the case – and the evidence will be reviewed later – that at some stage in his life, Edward IV fathered an illegitimate son called Arthur. It is also clearly the case that the mother of this son was a member of a family based in Hampshire, the surname of which was not Wyat but Wayte. However, there is no evidence whatever to show that Edward's girlfriend from the Wayte family bore the Christian name of Elizabeth. There is also no evidence that she ever bore the surname of Lucy. And there is no evidence that she produced more than one child by Edward IV. The king's only child who was clearly connected in his maternal line to the Wayte family was Edward's alleged son, Arthur.

Moreover, we have no clear surviving evidence of precisely when Arthur Wayte – later Arthur Plantagenet, Viscount Lisle – was born. The possible evidence in this respect will be considered later, in chapter 19, when the facts regarding the Wayte family, and Edward IV's possible relationship with one of its women, is examined in detail. For the moment, however, it is sufficient to say that there is absolutely no evidence to show that Arthur was born prior to 1464. Indeed, in due course we shall see that such an early birthdate for Arthur appears to be highly improbable.

There is therefore no clear evidence to support the claim that Edward IV had fathered illegitimate offspring prior to the autumn of 1464. However, it remains *possible* that he had done so, and that one such royal bastard may have been the illegitimate daughter whom Edward later married into the Lumley family (see below, chapter 28).

PART 3
THE SECOND MARRIAGE

1464–1465: ITINERARY

1464 (age 22; regnal year 4)
MARCH
Westminster[1]

APRIL
The City and Tower of
London, Westminster and
Dartford[2]
The Tower of London[3]
St Albans[4]
Stony Straftford[5]

MAY
Grafton Regis[6]
Northampton, Leicester Castle
and Nottingham[7]
York[8]

JUNE
York and Middleham[9]
Doncaster and Pontefract Castle[10]

JULY
Pontefract Castle, Doncaster,
Ashby(-de-la-Zouch) and Leicester[11]

AUGUST
Oakham Castle[12]
Stamford[13]
Fotheringhay Castle and the
manor of Woodstock[14]
Chichester[15]

SEPTEMBER
Penlee (Cornwall)[16]
Malmesbury Abbey[17]
Newbury[18]
Reading Abbey[19]

OCTOBER
Reading (town and abbey)[20]
High Wycombe[21]

NOVEMBER
Reading Abbey[22]
High Wycombe[23]
Sonning Eye[24]
Reading Abbey[25]

DECEMBER
Sonning Eye and the manor of
Eltham[26]

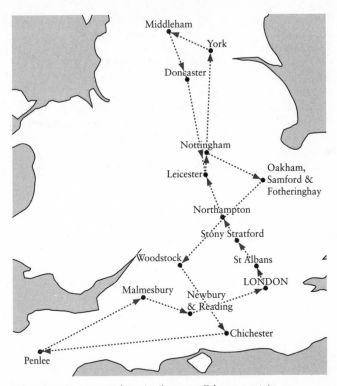

Edward IV's movements from April 1464 to February 1464/5

1464/5
JANUARY
Westminster[27]

FEBRUARY
Westminster[28]

MARCH
Westminster[29]
REGNAL YEAR 5
Westminster[30]

1465 (age 23; regnal year 5)
MARCH
Westminster[31]

APRIL
Sheen, Westminster and
Greenwich[32]
The manor of Sheen[33]

MAY
The manor of Greenwich[34]
The Tower of London,
Westminster and Greenwich[35]

JUNE
Greenwich[36]
Westminster[37]

JULY
Windsor Castle, Westminster,
Canterbury, Maidstone and
Westminster[38]

AUGUST
Syon and Windsor Castle[39]
Westminster[40]

SEPTEMBER
Pleshey Castle / the manor of
Pleshey (near Chelmsford),

Hertford Castle and
Westminster[41]

OCTOBER
Greenwich[42]

NOVEMBER
The manor of Greenwich[43]
Westminster[44]

DECEMBER
Westminster[45]

12

1463–1464:
BONA – *SAVOIR FAIRE*

Edward IV was no longer a virgin. We know that he had now had at least one girlfriend – the beautiful Lady Eleanor Talbot. It is just possible that he had had more than one girlfriend, though there is no real evidence to that effect. Moreover, he had had at least one boyfriend – Eleanor's cousin, the handsome Duke of Somerset. Nevertheless, the general view of him was that he had yet to enter into the kind of marriage which was normally expected of a king as the potential source of his son and heir.

There is a widespread popular myth that the normal English royal marriage was always with a foreign princess. This story was hopefully exploded by the present author in an earlier work, where it was shown that, since the Norman Conquest, only about 39 per cent of English monarchs have actually married foreign princes or princesses.[1] However, the fifteenth-century precedent in terms of the marriages of the English sovereigns of that period had generally followed the pattern set out in the myth. Thus, the queens consort of the three Lancastrian monarchs, Henry IV, Henry V and Henry VI, had been respectively Joan of Navarre, Catherine of France, and Margaret of Anjou. The first two of these royal brides had been daughters respectively of the king of Navarre and of the king of France, while the third was the daughter of a French prince of the blood royal, who was also the titular king of Naples and Jerusalem.

The dethroning of Henry VI had also resulted in the dethroning of his consort, the French princess Margaret of Anjou. In some circles it was therefore perceived as a potentially wise move to seek to re-establish a relationship with the French royal house of Valois by planning a suitable marriage for the new king of England. This was definitely the view taken by one of Edward IV's leading supporters, his maternal line cousin, Richard Neville, Earl of Warwick.

Ironically, Richard Neville was the uncle by marriage of Eleanor Talbot. His wife (and the source of his noble title), Anne Beauchamp, was the much younger half-sister of Eleanor's mother, Margaret Beauchamp, Countess of Shrewsbury. Both of them were daughters of Richard Beauchamp, Earl of Warwick. But Margaret and her husband, the 1st Earl of Shrewsbury, had contested the Beauchamp inheritance of her half-sister, Anne, and the latter's husband, Richard Neville. Thus the relationship between the two Beauchamp half-sisters and their families had not always been entirely amicable. Although there appears to have been some awareness that Edward IV may have been involved with one of the Earl of Warwick's female relatives (see above, chapter 7), in 1463–64 Richard Neville himself seems to have had no more specific knowledge of the precise nature of his niece's relationship with the king than did the general public.

Some people might wish to view Warwick's ignorance in this respect as potential proof that no real marriage existed between Eleanor and Edward. Actually, however, Warwick's lack of knowledge in this respect proves nothing, for, as we shall see shortly, he was equally ignorant of Edward's secret involvement with Elizabeth Widville. As far as Warwick knew, the king was still free to marry. Initially, therefore, he proposed a marriage between Edward and the Queen Mother of Scotland, Mary of Gueldres.

Mary of Gueldres had been born in 1434. She was therefore eight years older than Edward IV. Indeed, her age could potentially have been a factor which might have appealed to the young king. Both Eleanor Talbot and Elizabeth Widville seem to have been older than he was, Eleanor having been born probably in February or March 1435/6, and Elizabeth having been born in about 1437.

Mary of Gueldres was the daughter of Arnold, Duke of Gueldres. Her mother was a niece of the Valois prince Philip the Good, Duke of Burgundy, and Mary was brought up at her great-uncle's Burgundian court. In 1449 she had been married to King James II of Scotland, for whom she produced six children. However, she was widowed in 1460, when her husband was killed by the explosion of one of his own cannon at the siege of Roxburgh. The twenty-six-year-old Mary of Gueldres then became Queen Mother of Scotland, and the following year she was appointed by the Scottish Parliament to act as regent for her ten-year-old son, King James III. During her marriage with James II, Mary appears consistently to have been an excellent and loyal consort, and after her husband's death she did her best in the role of regent for their son, the new king.

Inevitably, however, Mary found herself caught up in the fighting for the crown which was going on in England. Following Henry VI's defeat, his wife, Margaret of Anjou (who was Queen Mary's distant cousin), sought refuge in Scotland, together with her son, Edward of Westminster. Mary of Gueldres received them both, in exchange for their promise to hand over to Scotland the town of Berwick. As we have already seen, Margaret of Anjou took what she saw as an advantage of this opportunity to propose a marriage alliance between the leader of her forces, Henry Beaufort, Duke of Somerset, and his cousin, King James III's aunt Princess Joan of Scotland. However, the Duke of Somerset made absolutely sure that this marriage would not take place by casting aspersions upon the morality of Mary of Gueldres while he was visiting the French court – an action on his part which not only ensured that he would not be forced into a marriage, but which also placed his life under threat in Scotland, because the Scottish Queen Mother was absolutely furious when she discovered what Somerset had been saying about her.

Macdougall states that 'stories that circulated in later generations, alleging that Queen Mary had been the mistress successively of Edmund [*sic*] Beaufort, duke of Somerset (*d.* 1471), and Adam Hepburn, without much doubt originated in confusion with another maligned queen mother, James I's widow, Joan'.[2] However, Macdougall refers to the wrong Duke of Somerset (Henry's younger brother, Edmund, who claimed that title after Henry's death). He also seems to be unaware of the questions regarding the sexuality of Henry, Duke of Somerset, and the motive which may therefore have pushed him to make Mary of Gueldres his enemy.

And although some writers have rather naïvely assumed that Somerset had been telling the truth about Mary of Gueldres,[3] in actual fact there is absolutely no evidence to show that the Scottish Queen Mother was living in an immoral relationship. Indeed the available evidence we have about her appears to suggest that she was a sincere religious lady. The only other source of criticism in respect of Mary was 'the queen's great rival, Bishop James Kennedy of St Andrews, who was pro-French and Lancastrian by conviction, [and who] tried to upset Mary's more realistic inclination towards Burgundy and the Yorkists, partly by besmirching the queen's name through accusations of causing divisions and bloodshed'.[4] But the bishop never raised questions about Mary's morality. It therefore seems clear that the Duke of Somerset invented that particular story for his own purpose – namely to avoid being forced into a marriage with a Scottish princess.

At all events the Earl of Warwick seems not to have thought that Mary of Gueldres was in any way immoral. In June 1462 he met Scottish representatives at Carlisle. At this point Margaret of Anjou and her party had left Scotland for France, and Mary of Gueldres was trying to take advantage of that situation in order to restore Scottish peace with Yorkist England. In Carlisle, Warwick put forward a completely new plan for Scottish marriage alliances. What he proposed was that the young King James III and his sister should marry respectively a sister and a brother of King Edward IV. He also made a more surprising proposal that the children's mother, Mary of Gueldres, should marry King Edward himself. Presumably Warwick's proposals were serious. It is even possible that he had sought Edward IV's approval for his suggestions.

But, like the earlier projects of his father to marry him to a French princess, the latest proposal of his cousin, Warwick, to arrange his marriage with the Queen Mother of Scotland, bore no fruit for Edward IV. Margaret of Anjou's return to the northern kingdom, with French supplies of men and money, made it impossible for Mary of Gueldres to pursue any of Warwick's royal marriage suggestions. As for the Earl of Warwick, he now had to direct his search for a diplomatic royal marriage for Edward IV elsewhere. A year or so after his Scottish proposal, he began actively seeking to promote the possibility of a diplomatic marriage between Edward IV and the closest thing he could find to a French princess.

By this time the reigning King of France was Louis XI, the son of Charles VII. He had mounted the French throne on the death of his father, in 1461. While his father had been alive the Dauphin Louis had tended to side with his cousins the Duke of Burgundy and the Count of Charolais against Charles VII. But now, of course, with his father's death, the situation had altered.

Louis' first wife had been Margaret of Scotland, but that marriage proved fruitless and unhappy, and the Dauphine Margaret had died childless in 1445. Six years later the Dauphin Louis had married for a second time. His new consort was Charlotte of Savoy. Since she was only nine years old at the time of their marriage, Louis' first child – a daughter, Anne – had only been born in 1461. The result of his marriage history was therefore that in 1463 King Louis XI did not really have a viable daughter available as a potential English royal consort for Edward IV. Nevertheless, despite his daughter's very young age, Louis XI had put Anne of France forward as a potential bride for Edward IV in the summer of 1463.

When Jean de Lannoy was sent to England by Louis XI in March 1463/4, he definitely brought proposals for a French royal marriage. As a French envoy Lannoy was not very kindly received at Dover, but the Earl of Warwick hastily sent members of his own household to escort Lannoy and his entourage to London, where he installed the French ambassador in the guesthouse at the London Blackfriars.

Anne of France (later regent of France) –
proposed as the bride of Edward IV
in 1463.

Lannoy's proposal was initially for Edward IV's marriage with the French king's little daughter. But Edward IV – for reasons which may have had nothing to do with the age of the proposed bride – definitely seems to have been dubious about the project. Eventually Louis XI himself also apparently decided that perhaps his daughter was too young to become the queen consort of England. As for Louis' sisters, the daughters of the late King Charles VII – some of whom had been actively considered as potential brides for the young Edward by his father, the Duke of York, many years earlier, in 1445 (see above, chapter 4) – they were all now married. Thus there was no true French princess of the immediate line of the blood royal available as Edward IV's potential consort.

For this reason King Louis began seeking other possible ways of promoting a marriage alliance between Edward and France. And since his own second bride – now the queen consort of France – was Charlotte of Savoy, and came from a large family, it was a daughter of the ducal house of Savoy whose name was now put forward as the possible English queen consort. This was a kind of approach which had been previously accepted in England – when King Henry VI had married a relative (in his case the niece) of the then queen of France (see above chapter 4). Moreover, just like both Marie and Margaret of Anjou, Charlotte of Savoy was a direct descendant of King John II of France and his first wife, Bonne of Bohemia (and Luxembourg). Thus, she and her sisters did carry French royal blood.

Charlotte of Savoy, the daughter of Louis, Duke of Savoy and Prince of Piedmont and his wife, Anne of Cyprus, had been born in 1441. Her only living elder sister, Marguerite, was already married. However, she also had three living younger sisters: Agnes, Maria and Bona. Attention

Charlotte de Savoie, femme de Louis XI, d'après un tableau d'environ 1470.
(Séré, *Le moyen âge et la Renaissance*, t. I.)

Charlotte of Savoy, Queen consort
of France.

was finally focussed on Bona. She had been born at Turin in August 1449. Thus in 1463 she was fourteen years of age. She was therefore a young but potentially viable royal bride for the twenty-one-year-old Edward IV. Moreover, she came from a very large family. Her parents had produced a total of nineteen children. Not all of these had survived. Nevertheless, her family background made Bona seem to be a potentially very promising queen consort for England in terms of her prospective fruitfulness.

The Earl of Warwick strongly backed the new proposal from France, and tried hard to persuade Edward IV to accept it. But 'the young monarch pleasantly, agilely, evaded Warwick's attempts to pin him down'.[5] In September 1464, at a council meeting in Reading, Warwick once again strove to bring Edward to the point of finally agreeing to the dynastic alliance with Bona. To his amazement and fury, however, the king's reply on this occasion was that the proposed French royal marriage would not be possible, because he was already married. Warwick was not the only person present who was shocked and astonished. And as the news spread, even those few people (such as Canon Stillington and perhaps the Duchess of Norfolk and the dowager Duchess of York) who may have been aware of the nature of Edward IV's attachment to Eleanor Talbot found themselves shocked – because the person Edward now named as his wife was not Eleanor, but Elizabeth Widville, Lady Grey.

13

1463–1464: *DEO DEVOTA*

By the summer of 1464 Edward IV had been involved in three relationships: with Eleanor Talbot, with Henry, Duke of Somerset, and with Elizabeth Widville (see below, chapter 14). At that stage, however, his relationships with the two *women* were not matters of public knowledge. Thus the only relationship of which most people would have been aware was that of the king with his Beaufort male cousin.

As we have seen, much later stories allege that by 1464 Edward had fathered a bastard child or children, but there is not a shred of solid contemporary evidence to back such a claim. There is also no solid evidence that by 1464 Edward IV had involved himself with any woman other than his two alleged wives. Since only undocumented later stories claim to reveal the identity of a woman with whom the young king had engaged in an extramarital affair – a woman who may never have existed in reality – the fact is that neither we nor his contemporaries know of the young king having a mistress (as opposed to a secret wife) prior to the end of 1464.

This complete lack of the name of even one mistress, combined with the complete lack of evidence of pre-1464 royal bastards, means that the genuine contemporary evidence, both in terms of girlfriends and in terms of children, strongly indicates that the image of Edward IV which has traditionally been presented is false, and that during the early years of his reign he did not engage in a vast and continuous sequence of love affairs. It also suggests that prior to 1464 both the young king himself and his subjects may have felt some concern about whether he would ever father an heir to the throne. In this context it now seems hardly surprising that, as we have already seen, the contemporary Gregory's Chronicle stated that 'men mervelyd that oure soverayne lorde was so longe with owte any wyffe, and were evyr ferde that he had be not chaste of hys levynge'.[1] However, it now seems that the feared lack of chastity may have referred to the public knowledge of Edward's same-sex relationship with his second cousin the Duke of Somerset.

As for his relationship with Eleanor Talbot, that had failed to produce a pregnancy. Since Eleanor had also failed to conceive during her earlier marriage to Sir Thomas Boteler, one possibility could be that she travelled to Norfolk in order to make a pilgrimage to the shrine of Our Lady of Walsingham. Her younger sister, Elizabeth, later sought divine intervention on her own behalf in similar circumstances (see below). Certainly Eleanor seems to have moved to Norfolk to live close to her sister, who was now the Duchess of that county. However, no solid evidence exists to show that Eleanor made a pilgrimage to the Walsingham shrine. It also seems that, for various reasons, she was now on the verge of deciding that she preferred to separate herself from the young king. Given their close family relationship, she must have been aware of Edward's involvement with her cousin, Henry Beaufort. Perhaps it was her knowledge of that partnership which helped to bring to an end her own intimacy with her sovereign.

Of course, neither Edward nor Eleanor sought to terminate their connection by means of an annulment. To take that course would have required formal acknowledgement of the existence of a marriage between them. It seems that both parties preferred to maintain silence. Indeed, George Buck later reported that Edward 'held them not his friends nor good subjects which mentioned' his connection with Eleanor.[2] As for the king's position, presumably it was that since his relationship with Eleanor was proving fruitless he wished to explore other possibilities for producing an heir.

Eleanor herself appears to have had her own reasons – which we shall explore in greater detail shortly – for maintaining a dignified silence in terms of the world at large. However, the members of her immediate family were not in the same position in relation to Eleanor as were members of the general public. It is probable therefore that close family members were aware of her contract with the king. The subsequent relationship of Elizabeth Talbot, Duchess of Norfolk, with her elder sister certainly seems to show evidence of a protective streak. The relationship of these two Talbot sisters was a very close one, which lasted well beyond Eleanor's grave. When Elizabeth was in her fifties, her elder sister, who had died thirty years earlier, was still very much on her mind. In the 1490s Elizabeth showed her concern for the good of Eleanor's soul by making an endowment which, by that time, she could ill afford, and which she was ultimately obliged to pay by instalments.

As for Eleanor herself, during her lifetime she never made any appeal to the Church courts to have her marriage with Edward IV established and publicly recognised. Had she wished to take action in this respect, a case heard by the Church courts would have been the correct procedure for her to follow. Indeed, it was a process which was by no means uncommon in medieval England. Records of appeals made for the recognition of an earlier, secret marriage (or 'pre-contract') do exist in a number of cases.[3] However, the proceedings of the Church courts were sometimes lengthy and stressful. Also, of course, none of the cases on record involved members of the royal family. It is therefore arguable that fighting her case in the Church courts never seemed to be a realistic option for Eleanor. Probably in one sense she felt obliged to accept the demise of her royal relationship. It was better for her simply to keep out of the public eye and live a quiet life in retirement. As we shall see shortly, there is also strong evidence that, for her own personal motives, this became Eleanor's preferred option.

As for Edward IV, once his active relationship with Eleanor had ended, he seems to have been grateful to her for her maintenance of a tactful silence. The king certainly treated her with consideration, and showed some regard for her wishes – for example, in respect of her friend and former father-in-law, Lord Sudeley.[4] Given her discretion, there is no indication that Edward IV himself ever perceived Eleanor herself as any kind of threat. However, the attitude taken subsequently by Eleanor's ultimate successor, Elizabeth Widville (once the latter had learned of Eleanor's relationship with the king), could well have been different. After all, as long as she remained alive, even a silent Eleanor constituted a serious potential threat both to Elizabeth herself and to her new royal progeny.

At all events, for whatever reason, it certainly seems to have been the case that, once her relationship with Edward IV had become inactive, in preference to remaining alone on her own manors in Warwickshire, Eleanor preferred to place herself under the protection of a powerful relative. As a result she apparently moved to the Eastern Counties, and to a house which belonged to her sister, the Duchess of Norfolk. This was East Hall, at Kenninghall in Norfolk, a property which formed part of the jointure which had been settled by the Mowbray family upon Eleanor's younger sister, Elizabeth Talbot, at the time of the latter's marriage to the 3rd Duke of Norfolk's son and heir.[5]

The house was a large and strong one. Had it survived it would probably today be referred to as a castle.[6] It was surrounded by a moat and by flint walls, within which lay a large courtyard containing stables, kennels, garderobes, a kitchen block and the main residential quarters, centred on a great hall with an adjacent solar block which contained more private family rooms, and a chapel.

Elizabeth Talbot's ownership of East Hall is testified by documentary evidence, and also by the marks which she later left on Kenninghall Church.[7] Elizabeth's own residence at the hall, and her work on the church, probably date from the 1470s and 1480s, when she was a widow. In the 1460s, however, it seems likely that the house was occupied by her sister, Eleanor. Indeed, as we shall see later, it appears probable that Eleanor also died there.[8]

One result of Eleanor's association with the village of Kenninghall may well have been her growing interest in the Carmelite religious order. Kenninghall had already produced two noted Carmelites, the late John Kenyngale, former chaplain to Edward IV's parents, prior of the White Friars in Norwich and Father Provincial of the Carmelite order in England until his death in 1451, and Peter Keningall, Prior of the Carmelite Priory in Oxford and noted preacher.[9] Eleanor may have met Prior Peter before she came to East Anglia, either during her own residence in Warwickshire or through her stepmother-in-law, the second Lady Sudeley, whose previous home, at Minster Lovell Hall, was not far from Oxford. The evolution of Eleanor's very strong Carmelite connection will be examined in detail shortly. First, however, let us review her other important patronage in the Eastern Counties – at the University of Cambridge.

During the 1460s Eleanor Talbot became an active patroness of Corpus Christi College, Cambridge. There, towards the end of 1461 or early in 1462, she endowed a priest-fellowship which is specifically designated in surviving records as being *ex fundatione Helionore Butler*.[10] The first priest appointed to this new fellowship was Thomas Cosyn, a Norfolk priest and scholar who subsequently succeeded to the mastership of the college. Cosyn clearly knew Eleanor well, and regarded her very highly. In 1496, when Corpus Christi College was updating Eleanor's fellowship foundation by means of a new agreement concluded with her surviving sister and executrix, Elizabeth Talbot, Thomas Cosyn (who was then the master of the college) recalled Eleanor in warm terms, referring to her sincere religious faith and to the close and friendly relationship which had existed between her and Corpus Christi. He also applied to his erstwhile patroness the word 'renowned'. Since Eleanor had lived very quietly, little would have justified the use of such a term during her lifetime. However, Thomas Cosyn employed it to describe her in 1496. No doubt he was recalling the Act of Parliament of 1484 which had acknowledged Eleanor as England's rightful queen consort, not to mention the fact that subsequently Henry VII had found himself compelled to do his level best to write Eleanor out of history!

It is possible that Eleanor's initial interest in Corpus Christi College was inherited. Her late uncle, Henry Beauchamp, Duke of Warwick, is also believed to have patronised Corpus Christi, and his arms were displayed in the College Hall.[11] It was in 1462 that Thomas Cosyn became the first priest appointed to Eleanor's newly founded fellowship at Corpus Christi College. His admission increased the number of the college fellows by one. His initial religious duties required him to keep the *obits* of the 1st Earl of Shrewsbury, and of Sir Thomas Boteler and his mother, while at the same time praying for the good estate of Eleanor herself, of her mother, the dowager Countess of Shrewsbury, and of Lord and Lady Sudeley. Provision would also have been made for his prayers for the living to be transformed into additional anniversary commemorations following their respective demises.

As her endowments at Corpus Christi College show, Eleanor's character was now developing in a special way. During her childhood, her religious beliefs had, of course, been inculcated under the guidance of her mother, Lady Shrewsbury. It appears that Eleanor's faith was never superficial. Indeed, this was a common family feature which Eleanor apparently shared with her mother, her brothers and her sister.[12] Eleanor's father is also reputed to have 'had an inborn sense of justice and fair play'.[13] Eleanor's personal faith apparently grew deeper and deeper with the passage of time.

Later, following the death of her husband, Elizabeth Talbot, Duchess of Norfolk, also developed her spiritual life very deeply. Elizabeth, together with her friend Anne Montgomery (*née* Darcy, cousin by marriage of Sir Thomas Boteler), did this chiefly under the guidance of the Franciscan order. Together with Anne and a small circle of other ladies, the dowager Duchess of Norfolk eventually formed a spiritual community associated with the prestigious Abbey of the Poor Clares ('the Minories') at Aldgate.[14]

Eleanor, on the other hand, seems to have elected to pursue her religious development under Carmelite guidance. As we have seen, this may have been a connection which initially arose through Eleanor's associations with the village of Kenninghall. Evidence for her strong Carmelite connection is supplied by Eleanor's seals, by the possible negotiations conducted on her behalf with the Whitefriars, and by her eventual burial at the Norwich Carmel (see below). In the case of the Duchess of Norfolk her degree of spiritual commitment was ultimately to be very profound, and there is no reason to doubt that this was also true

The Abbey of the Poor
Clares ('the Minories'),
Aldgate. Redrawn
from Anthonis van den
Wyngaerde's 'Panorama of
London', *circa* 1544.

in the case of Eleanor. It will scarcely be possible, therefore, to understand
the person Eleanor was to become in the last five years of her life, without
taking account of this spiritual development.

The Carmelite order had been founded in the twelfth century in the
Holy Land by a group of male Christian hermits who settled on Mount
Carmel, near the 'fountain of Elijah', and sought to live lives of religious
contemplation. There were no female members of the order at that time.
Subsequent Moslem victories forced the hermits to leave the Holy Land,
and they then settled in western Europe, where they established religious
houses.

Until the fifteenth century the Carmelite order remained essentially
male. There were no Carmelite nuns at that time. However, women could
be associated with the order – albeit without ceasing to be members of the
laity. Prior to the fifteenth century, the details of such female connections
were somewhat complex. It was in the second half of the fifteenth
century that changes took place. In October 1452 Pope Nicholas V
formally established the second and third orders of the Carmelites.
The new 'second order' was for Carmelite nuns, while the 'third order'
(members of which are called 'tertiaries') represented a formalised system
of association for those lay people who wished to join the Carmelites
without giving up their lay status. As for the 'first order', that, of course,
comprised the friars – the successors of the original hermits.

The changes introduced by Pope Nicholas spread across Europe slowly
over the next fifty years or so. Carmelite nuns failed to reach England
prior to the Reformation, so Eleanor cannot possibly have become a
Carmelite nun. Obviously, had she wished to become a nun she could

easily have chosen one of the other religious orders which had existing religious houses in England during her lifetime. Instead, however, she seems to have chosen to become a member of the Carmelite third order. Evidence for this survives in terms of her apparent use of the scapular (see below). Dr Thomas Cosyn's subsequent characterisation of his friend and patroness as *Deo devota* ('vowed to God')[15] clearly implies that she took religious vows of some kind, and this was something which tertiaries were (and are) required to do. But, significantly, profession as a tertiary was and is open to married people. Eleanor's association with the Carmelite third order would therefore have been entirely compatible with her married state – a state which would have precluded her from becoming a nun while Edward IV remained alive.

As a tertiary, Eleanor would have been committed to the daily recitation of the Divine Office according to the Carmelite usage. Following an earlier Carmelite tradition, it is also possible that she may have chosen to dwell in a fixed abode agreed with the Carmelite prior to whom she had made her oblation. Her interest in the Carmelites may have arisen initially as a response to their long-standing tradition of devotion to the Blessed Virgin. 'This promise of the special protection of Mary, together with the indulgences associated with the wearing of the scapular, would [probably] have outweighed any other motives for electing to become associated with [the Carmelites]'.[16] But both in its origin, and also as later reformed in the sixteenth century by St Teresa of Avila and St John of the Cross, the ethos of the Carmelite order comprises a strong contemplative and mystical element.

Contemplative Christianity undoubtedly flourished in late medieval England. 'Women saints and mystics proliferated in the thirteenth and fourteenth centuries ... [and] on the whole [they] did not come from the lower orders of society.'[17] Richard Rolle, Walter Hilton, the anonymous author of *The Cloud of Unknowing*, and Julian of Norwich all lived and wrote in England in the late fourteenth century, so their works of spiritual guidance may well have been accessible to Eleanor. For those people who, like Eleanor (and the present author), were chosen to receive it, the message of contemplative Christianity was – and is – very significant in its impact on lifestyle.

> You are well aware that, when you were in the Common state of the Christian life, living with your friends in the world, God, through his everlasting love ... would not allow you to live the kind of life that was so far away from him. In that most gracious way of his, he kindled your desire for himself, and bound you to him by the chain

of such longing, and thus led you to that more Special life, a servant among his own special servants. He did this that you might learn to be more especially his and to live more spiritually than ever you could have done in the common state of life.

And there is more: it appears that he is not content to leave you just there ... but in his own delightful and gracious way he has drawn you to this third stage, the Solitary. It is in this state that you will learn to take your first loving steps to the life of Perfection, the last stage of all.

... At this stage ... you must keep an eye on your enemy. You must not think yourself any holier or better because of the worthiness of your calling ... . You ought to be all the more humble and loving to your spiritual husband who is Almighty God, King of Kings and Lord of Lords and yet who has so humbly come down to your level, and so graciously chosen you out of his flock to be one of his 'specials' ...

So go on, I beg you, with all speed. Look forward, not backward. See what you still lack, not what you have already; for that is the quickest way of getting and keeping humility. Your whole life must now be one of longing, if you are to achieve perfection. And this longing must be in the depths of your will, put there by God with your consent. But a word of warning: he is a jealous lover, and will brook no rival; he will not work in your will if he has not sole charge; he does not ask for help, he asks for you.[18]

The author of *The Cloud of Unknowing* may well have been a friar – possibly even a Carmelite.

In the words of a modern Carmelite writer, a vocation such as that undertaken by Eleanor in the 1460s would have involved 'accepting her nothingness and making no fuss about it'.[19] Obviously anyone who chose to base their life upon such foundations can have taken no interest whatsoever in the thought of lengthy court proceedings aimed at establishing social status. 'Women mystics saw their way to the imitation of Christ through renunciation'. As for suffering, that was viewed as an integral part of the process.[20]

While she was married to Thomas Boteler, Eleanor had sealed her documents using a signet ring possibly given to her by her mother, the bezel of which bore the impression of a daisy (marguerite) – the Countess of Shrewsbury's name-flower.[21] Later, as a widow, Eleanor seems to have acquired new signets. One of these was engraved with a representation of the Carmelite brown scapular.[22] This is a rectangular length of cloth with a hole in the middle through which the head and neck pass. It is worn by members of the order, hanging down over the wearer's chest and back, as part of their religious habit. The scapular is a special token of the Carmelite order, believed to have been delivered by the Blessed Virgin (Our Lady of Mount Carmel) to the Carmelite saint Simon Stock in a vision. When Pope Nicholas V established the second and third orders (Carmelite nuns and tertiaries) he extended to them the wearing of the brown scapular. Lay members of the order (tertiaries) were (and are) required to wear the scapular, even if only in symbolic form. Wearing a representation of a scapular on the bezel of her signet ring would have been one means of fulfilling this obligation for Eleanor when she became a lay member of the Carmelite order. However, it may also have been the case that, following her taking of tertiary vows, Eleanor dressed in a manner which, to modern eyes, may have made her look rather like a nun. Such dress is depicted in what may be a later image of Eleanor, which survives in the Coventry tapestry, dating from about 1500 (see below).

In the 1460s, Eleanor also owned another seal ring, which depicted the Virgin Mary holding the Christ child on her left arm. This signet appears specifically to depict the ancient icon of Our Lady of Mount Carmel, brought from the Holy Land when the Carmelite hermits fled before the tide of Islam, and now preserved at the church of San Niccolò al Carmine, Siena.[23]

Eleanor Talbot as a Carmelite tertiary? Redrawn after a Coventry Tapestry image of *circa* 1500, possibly intended to represent one of the Countess of Shrewsbury's daughters.

It was probably in March 1462/3 that Eleanor became a tertiary, associated with the Carmelite priory in Norwich. Her commitment to the Carmel was apparently negotiated on her behalf by her brother-in-law, the Duke of Norfolk, through the intermediary of his elder cousin Sir John Howard.[24] As the young Duke of Norfolk's cousin, and a key member of the Mowbray affinity, there is no doubt that John Howard was well acquainted with members of the Talbot family. Documentary evidence survives proving his connections with Eleanor's sister, Elizabeth Talbot, Duchess of Norfolk; with her surviving brother, Sir Humphrey Talbot; and with her nephew and eventual legal heir, Thomas Talbot, Viscount Lisle.[25]

Sir John Howard also appears to have had connections with Eleanor herself – in the 1460s she seems to have become a kind of neighbour as a result of her residing in East Anglia. For example, he may have been involved in Eleanor's negotiations with the then Master of Corpus Christi College in respect of her patronage of the college.[26] Also, on 23 March 1462/3, Howard paid Thomas Yonge, sergeant at law, 13s 4d 'for his two days labour at the White Friars for my lord's matter'.[27] Whichever Carmelite priory was Yonge's destination (and it might actually have been the priory in Norwich) it seems likely that the business which Howard was conducting with the Whitefriars on the Duke of Norfolk's behalf was connected with Eleanor's oblation. A few months later, in July 1463, Howard acted once again as an intermediary for the Duke of Norfolk. On this occasion he paid John Davy 16d 'to ride on my lord's errand to Kenehale [Kenninghall]'.[28] Given Eleanor's probable residence at Kenninghall at this time, the Duke of Norfolk's message on this occasion may well have been addressed to his sister-in-law, and may once again have related to the ongoing negotiations in respect of Eleanor's oblation to the Carmelites.

14

1464: THE GREY MARE

At some stage between 1461 and 1463/4, while Eleanor Talbot was abandoning her relationship with the young Yorkist king and deepening her religious faith, Edward IV had met Elizabeth Widville,[1] the dowager Lady Grey, later known to those who disliked her as 'the Grey Mare'. Elizabeth was the eldest of a large family of children. Her mother was arguably a 'foreign princess', and a descendant of the Emperor Charlemagne – Jacquette of Luxembourg, the dowager Duchess of Bedford. However, the father of Jacquette's children was not the Lancastrian prince whom she had first married, but her second – and initially secret – husband, Richard Widville, later Lord Rivers.

As in the case of Eleanor Talbot, Elizabeth Widville's precise date of birth is not on record. But she had probably been born in 1437, soon after her parent's marriage. This would have made her about five years older than the king and about a year younger than Eleanor Talbot. So, like Eleanor, Elizabeth Widville seems to have been a little older than the king.

It is possible that Jacquette had already been pregnant at the time of her second marriage. And, as we shall see, it is conceivable that Elizabeth herself later employed a similar claim of being with child in order to push Edward IV to recognise her as his wife in September 1464. Elizabeth's place of birth is also uncertain. Her parents – like the parents of Edward IV – had spent some years in France during the early years of their marriage. It is therefore possible that, like Edward IV, Elizabeth Widville was born there. Indeed, one writer has stated that Elizabeth 'had known [Edward] literally ever since he was born, as her father was attached to the Duke of York's staff in Normandy'.[2] However, the claim that Elizabeth had known Edward all his life is only a hypothesis, not an established fact.

Back in England, Elizabeth's parents arranged a marriage for their eldest daughter with Sir John Grey. This marriage seems to have taken place at some point between 1452 and 1454. The first child of the marriage, Thomas Grey (later Marquess of Dorset), was probably born in 1455. John Grey was some years older than his wife, although the age difference between the couple in this marriage was probably smaller than it had been in the case of Eleanor Talbot's first marriage to Sir Thomas Boteler. Sir John Grey had subsequently been killed, fighting on the Lancastrian side, at St Albans in 1461.

The new evidence of Edward IV's movements around the country published here (see above, chapter 8) shows that, assuming he met Elizabeth Widville in the vicinity of Northampton, the couple could have encountered each other in July 1462, in July, August and/or September 1463, and in January 1463/4. It is frequently imagined that the initial meeting between the young and widowed Lady Grey and King Edward IV took place because Elizabeth approached Edward to appeal for the restitution of her husband's property, which Edward had confiscated because Sir John Grey had been an anti-Yorkist. However, that story is inaccurate.

The truth is that the property had not been confiscated by the Crown. Instead, a conflict over it was in process between Elizabeth Widville and her mother-in-law. This is what eventually led Elizabeth to arrange to be allowed to appeal to the king. And she made her approach via Lord Hastings. But of course, when her meeting with Edward IV took place it seems that Elizabeth (like Eleanor before her) attracted the king's attention in a way which had not formed part of her original plan. It seems that, like Eleanor, she may have been asked to have sex with the young king, but refused – leading Edward IV to once again offer marriage as a means of fulfilling his desires.

As has already begun to emerge, the start of Edward's Widville marriage story is in many respects similar to that of his relationship with Eleanor Talbot. However, in the long term, the major difference between the two stories lies in the fact that the fertile Elizabeth subsequently went on to produce for the king a large family of children (see below). If this had not happened, the Widville union might also have remained a secret, in which case many later historians would presumably have denied its existence as readily as they deny the existence of the Talbot marriage.

Elizabeth's secret marriage with Edward is said to have taken place at her family manor house of Grafton Regis, on 1 May 1464. The evidence of the king's movements published here shows that the alleged date is believable. According to the much later – and politically slanted – report by Sir Thomas More, Edward IV had previously asked the Earl of Warwick to negotiate a possible marriage for him with 'the king's daughter of Spain [*sic*]'.[3] Of course, Spain did not then exist as a single state, so the king to whom More is referring was in fact Henry IV of Castile. And since Henry IV was said to be impotent he reputedly never fathered a daughter. So presumably More is actually referring to the negotiations which took place for a possible marriage between Edward's younger brother, Richard, Duke of Gloucester (later Richard III), and King Henry of Castile's sister and eventual heiress, Isabel the Catholic.[4] However, in reality those negotiations took place much later, in 1468 or 1469. As we have seen, although various marriage plans for Edward IV were genuinely being explored by the Earl of Warwick in 1463 and 1464, they did not involve any negotiations with the kingdom of Castile. It is therefore clear that Thomas More's version of what took place is – once again – far from accurate.

However, because More's 'history' has been widely, if rather naively, accepted for almost five hundred years, we need to review what he says. His account continues:

> Now it happened that in the mean season [= meantime] there came to make a suit by petition to the king, Dame Elizabeth Grey – which was after his queen, at that time a widow – born of noble blood, specially by her mother, which was Duchess of Bedford ere she married the Lord Woodville, her father. Howbeit, this Dame Elizabeth, herself being in service with Queen Margaret, wife unto King Henry the Sixth, was married unto one John Grey, a squire whom King Henry made knight upon the field that he had on Shrove Tuesday at Saint Albans against King Edward. And little while he enjoyed that knighthood, for he was at the same field slain. After which done, and the Earl of Warwick being in his embassiate about the afore remembered marriage, this poor lady made humble suit unto the king that she might be restored unto such small lands as her late husband had given her in jointure.[5]

Once again, there are mistakes here. Elizabeth's mother had not married a lord, because her second husband did not receive a peerage until after their marriage. At the time of their union he was merely a knight. As for Elizabeth's own husband, John Grey was not made a knight just before the (second) battle of St Albans, at which he was killed, but three years earlier, in 1458. Also, More's explanation of the motive for Elizabeth's interview with Edward IV is somewhat imprecise. Moreover, his account is very unclear in its chronology, for Grey died in 1461, while Warwick's marriage negotiations (though not with the Castilian royal family) were in 1463 and 1464. So in which of those years is Thomas More suggesting the first meeting took place between Edward IV and Elizabeth Widville? However, More's version of the story continues:

> When the king beheld and heard her speak – as she was both fair, of a good favour, moderate of stature, well made, and very wise – he not only pitied her, but also waxed enamored on her. And taking her afterward secretly aside, began to enter in talking more familiarly. Whose appetite when she perceived, she virtuously denied him. But that did she so wisely, and with a good manner, and words so well set, that she rather kindled his desire than quenched it.[6]

Of course, for almost five hundred years, Thomas More's account of what took place at this first meeting has simply been accepted as accurate. But since it has now clearly emerged that More's report contains a number of inaccuracies, perhaps it should also be considered that what he claims as a description of the first meeting of Edward IV and Elizabeth Widville may also be his invention (or the invention of his source). Or perhaps it might originally have been an account of Edward's first meeting with Eleanor Talbot!

Just as seems to have been the case in his relationship with Eleanor, after meeting Elizabeth for the first time, Edward apparently continued seeing her,

> and finally, after many a meeting, much wooing, and many great promises, she well espied the king's affection toward her so greatly increased that she durst somewhat the more boldly say her mind ... and in conclusion she showed him plain that as she wist herself too simple to be his wife, so thought she herself too good to be his concubine ... and thus taking cousel of his desire, [the King] determined in all possible haste to marry her.[7]

Given that Robert Fabyan died on 25 February 1511/12, somewhat more contemporary details of how the marriage was enacted between Edward IV and Elizabeth Widville are reported in his Chronicle. However, Fabyan had forgotten where exactly Elizabeth's first husband had been killed. He reports that

> in moste secrete maner, vpon the firste daye of May,[8] kynge Edwarde spousyd Elizabeth, late the wyfe of sir John Graye, knyght, whiche before tyme was slayne at Toweton or Yorke felde, whiche spowsayles were solempnyzed erely in y^e mornynge at a towne named Graston [= Grafton], nere vnto Stonyngstratforde; at whiche mariage was no

[moo] persones present but the spowse, the spowsesse, the duches of Bedforde her moder, y preest, two gentylwomen, and a yong man to helpe the preest synge. After which spowsayles endyd, he went to bedde, and so taried there vpon. iii. or. iiii. houres, and after departed & rode agayne to Stonyngstratforde, and came i^n maner as though he had ben on huntinge, and there went to bedde agayne. And within a daye or. ii. after, he sent to Graston [Grafton], to the lorde Ryuers, fader vnto his wyfe, shewynge to hym y^t he wolde come & lodge with hym a certeyne season, where he was receyued with all honoure, and so taryed there by the space of. iiii. dayes. In whiche season, she nyghtly to his bedde was brought, in so secrete maner, that almooste none but her moder was of counsayll. And so this maryage was a season kept secret after, tyll nedely it muste be discoueryd & disclosed, by meane of other whiche were offeryd vnto the kynge, as the quene of Scottes and other.[9]

The priest who solemnised the marriage ceremony at Grafton Regis is said to have been the Dominican Master Thomas Eborall.[10] Having gone through a secret marriage ceremony with Elizabeth, Edward was, of course, able to get what he wanted from her, and as the accounts tell us, he did so. However, that did not make the relationship an official marriage or a matter of public knowledge. Just as he had presumably done with Eleanor Talbot, Edward saw – and slept with – Elizabeth without making the connection a matter of public awareness. This state of affairs continued for four months.

Since Edward had previously contracted a secret marriage with Eleanor Talbot, and since Eleanor was still living in 1464, Edward's Widville 'marriage' was, of course, bigamous. Subsequently, the degree to which the king appeared to be besotted with Elizabeth Widville was popularly ascribed to witchcraft on the part of the bride and her mother. Indeed, Jacquette was prosecuted for sorcery by the Earl of Warwick in 1469–70. 'The sorcery suit ... apparently presumed that necromancy had been necessary to secure such a marriage!'[11]

From his own point of view, having acquired the right to have sex with the woman he desired, Edward IV probably felt that he had achieved at least one of his goals. Therefore, just like the alleged earlier Talbot marriage, the Widville marriage was not made public at the time when it was contracted. It was only four months later, in September 1464, that the king publicly proclaimed his connection with Elizabeth Widville. The context in which he did so was a meeting of his council at Reading, at which his cousin the Earl of Warwick was attempting to promote the proposed royal marriage with Bona of Savoy (see above).

It is popularly assumed that it was Warwick's pressure on the king which made him announce his marriage to Elizabeth Widville. On other occasions, however, Edward IV appears to have had no problem with simply saying 'no' to proposals made by Warwick with which he did not agree. There must therefore have been some other reason why, on this particular occasion, he chose to announce that he was already secretly married. The most likely explanation for this seems to be that Elizabeth Widville had told Edward that she was with child. This is a hypothesis, but it appears to fit in with the chronology and other facts.

Of course, it could simply have been that Elizabeth – who was a clever and calculating woman – had worked out that this was the best way in which to push the king into acknowledging their partnership. In that case she may simply have been telling a lie, which could later have been covered up by feigning a miscarriage. However, it could well have been the case that she was genuinely pregnant in September 1468 but subsequently miscarried. Certainly her first living child by Edward IV was not born until February 1465/6. But a detailed study of the conceptions and births of her royal children (see below) shows that it would be more consistent with the overall chronology of her pregnancies if the first of these had commenced in the early summer of 1464. Moreover, her coronation as queen consort was delayed until 26 May 1465. A possible explanation for that delay could well have been that Elizabeth genuinely was pregnant in the autumn and winter of 1464, but then suffered a miscarriage.

It is virtually certain that, at the time of her marriage to the king, Elizabeth knew nothing of his earlier contract with Eleanor. She had not been at the Yorkist court in 1461. If she had known of the earlier marriage, she would undoubtedly have been reluctant to accept the secret wedding ceremony which the king had offered her. For, given her intelligence, she must have known that only by a public marriage with Edward could she stand a chance of contesting the earlier (pre-)contract if her own marriage was ever disputed before the Church courts. If Elizabeth Widville had married the king in public, and if Eleanor had failed to raise an immediate objection to the new marriage contract, the king's earlier spouse would thereby have destroyed her own case in the eyes of canon law. Under canon law, when a bigamous second 'marriage' was publicly celebrated, the legal first wife was required to make a public objection to the second union when the priest asked to know of any impediment.

For Edward, on the other hand, a *secret* marriage with Elizabeth Widville offered the best means of denying Eleanor the opportunity of making trouble, since if she was unaware of what was happening she would have no chance to raise an objection. The fact that the

Widville marriage was celebrated in secret effectively denied Eleanor any opportunity of asserting her claim.

When the alleged Widville marriage was revealed to him, Warwick naturally opposed it and was angered by it. 'Much heart burning was ever after between the earl [of Warwick] and the queen's blood so long as he lived.'[12] Later, Warwick pursued an accusation that Elizabeth's mother, Jacquette, had employed witchcraft for various purposes, possibly including the seduction of the young king into his dubious marriage with her daughter. In June 1483 that accusation was repeated by the Three Estates of the Realm. The petition which they sent to Richard, Duke of Gloucester, asking him to accept the crown, stated that

> the said pretensed marriage betwixt the above-named King Edward and Elizabeth Grey was made of grete presumption, without the knowyng or assent of the lordes of this lond, and alsoe by sorcerie and wichecrafte committed by the said Elizabeth and her moder, Jaquett, Duchess of Bedford (as the common opinion of the people and the publique voice and fame is through all this land; and hereafter — if, and as, the case shall require — shall bee proved suffyciently, in tyme and place convenient).[13]

Thus, whether or not Elizabeth and Jacquette really had attempted to employ the black arts to pursue their objectives, the surviving evidence clearly shows that there were contemporary rumours to that effect.

Although she was an unpopular choice with most of the English aristocracy, Elizabeth Widville was subsequently crowned queen consort of England, with some splendour, at Westminster Abbey. This was not necessarily the essential location for an English coronation, even in the case of sovereigns. For example, Henry III was initially crowned at Gloucester Abbey (though he later celebrated a second coronation at Westminster Abbey). As for queens consort, Margaret of France, the wife of Henry II's eldest son, Henry the Young King, had her coronation celebrated at Winchester Cathedral. Later, Berengaria of Navarre, the consort of King Richard I, was not even crowned in England, but in Cyprus. Indeed, a few English consorts were never crowned at all. Margaret of France, the second wife of Edward I, was never crowned.[14] As for the alleged wives of Henry VIII, after Anne Boleyn, not one of them was crowned. Nevertheless, for Elizabeth Widville a Westminster coronation was a triumphant outcome.

For reasons which, as we have seen, may have been associated with a first royal pregnancy which resulted in a miscarriage, it was not until eight months after her acknowledgement as queen, on 26 May 1465, that Elizabeth Widville was crowned. The ceremony, which was announced by Edward IV in a letter to the 'Maire of oure Citie of London' dated 14 April 1465,[15] began with a procession. In the course of this procession, Elizabeth was greeted on London Bridge by actors impersonating St Elizabeth and St Paul. This was to honour both her Christian name and the hereditary title of her mother's family (St Pol).

Elizabeth Widville then entered Westminster Abbey by the north door, which was the entrance closest to the Palace of Westminster. She was escorted by the bishops of Durham and Salisbury. Normally the Bishop of Bath and Wells would have been one of the escorts, but the see of Bath and Wells was vacant at the time.[16] It is not clear whether the king himself attended this coronation. His presence is not mentioned in any surviving sources. However, it may be that, like Henry VII at the coronation of Elizabeth of York, Edward witnessed the ceremony at Westminster Abbey out of everyone's sight, concealed in a space enclosed by tapestry.

In the Abbey Church, Elizabeth first knelt, and was anointed with holy oil. Then, she took her seat upon a throne. There she was given a ring, her crown, and two sceptres – a gold sceptre in her right hand, and an ivory rod surmounted by a dove in her left. The gold sceptre was the sceptre of St Edward; the second sceptre was 'a rode septre of ivory w[ith] a dove of gilte' (see above) which had been borne to the abbey in the pre-coronation procession by the Duke of Suffolk.[17] Despite the misleading image of the crowned Elizabeth Widville which is shown below, queens consort of England do not receive an orb. That item of the regalia is reserved for the sovereign regnant.

The anointing and coronation were followed by the celebration of Mass, at the end of which the abbey choir sang *Te Deum laudamus*.[18] After the church ceremony Elizabeth Widville donned a royal robe. Then the queen and her guests made their way to Westminster Hall for the coronation banquet. Three courses were served, comprising respectively seventeen, nineteen and fifteen dishes.[19] The ceremonies ended with a tournament on the following day. In this period, post-coronation tournaments usually lasted for three days. But in the case of Elizabeth Widville, her tournament appears to have lasted only for one day.

Following the public acknowledgement of Edward IV's marriage to Elizabeth Widville, 'the children of Lord Rivers [were] hugely exalted and set in great honour, as his eldest son made Lord Scales, and the others to sundry great promotions. Then shortly after was Lord Rivers made high treasurer of England, and the queen's eldest son was made Marquis of Dorset. And thus kindled the spark of envy which, by continuance, grew

Elizabeth Widville crowned as Queen –
but erroneously depicted holding an orb.
Redrawn after a fifteenth-century MS
illustration held by the London Skinners
Company.

to so great a blaze and flame of fire that it flamed not only through all England but also into Flanders and France.'[20]

As for the personal conduct of Edward IV's officially recognised queen, that has received various judgements. Perhaps trained by her aristocratic mother, a rather grandiose royal style seems to have come naturally to Elizabeth, and many who saw her were impressed by her. Nevertheless, she alienated much of the traditional aristocracy by her nepotism. Her political involvement, while often unclear and even disputed, seems also to have attracted adverse comment. Her interventions in the case of Sir Thomas Cook and in the executions of the Earl of Desmond and the Duke of Clarence are cases in point. The first of these will be considered briefly now (ahead of its chronological context) as one example of Elizabeth's conduct. The other cases will be reviewed later.

The case involving Sir Thomas Cook, a former mayor of London, was a typical example of the Widville behaviour. He found himself sent to the Tower of London, while his property was confiscated by Elizabeth Widville's father and his servants:

And fynally, after many persecucious and losses, was compelled as for a fyne sette vpon hym for offence of mysprysion, to paye vnto the kynge. viii. M.*li.* And after he had thus agreed, and was [set] at large for the kynges jnterest, he was thanne in newe trowble agayne the quene; the whiche demaundyd of hym as her right, for euery M.*li.* payde vnto the kynge by waye of fyne, an hondreth marke.[21]

There is also a surviving account of how one canny petitioner protested to the king about the Widville arrogance. The man in question presented himself to his sovereign 'clad in a short coat, [a] pair of boots upon his legs as long as they might be [and] in his hand a long pike. When the king beheld his apparel he asked him what was the cause of his long boots and long staff. "Upon my faith, sir," said he, "I have passed through many counties of your realm, and in places that I have passed the rivers have been so high that I could scarcely escape through them [unless I searched] the depth with this long staff." The king knew that he meant by it the great rule which Lord Rivers and his blood bore at that time within the realm.'[22]

However, despite its dubious public reception, Edward IV's Widville union was certainly potentially fruitful in terms of the succession. It was eventually to produce a large number of children, including the so-called 'princes in the Tower', and also Elizabeth of York, future mother of the house of 'Tudor'. The dramatic recent discovery by Glen Moran of a living all-female line of descent from Elizabeth Widville's younger sister, Margaret – which could potentially reveal the mtDNA of Elizabeth, and of all her children, including the famous 'princes in the Tower' – will be revealed later (see Appendix).

The following table shows the dates of birth of all Elizabeth's children by Edward IV, together with the probable approximate date and place of each conception. It also reveals the time lapses between these family events. A gap of some months between pregnancies was and is quite normal. But the time gaps which occurred in the case of Elizabeth Widville appear to indicate that from 1464 until 1473, Edward was in regular sexual contact with her.

The probable conception dates and places (based on their subsequent birth dates) of the children of Edward IV and Elizabeth Widville		
1 X(?)	conceived Grafton Regis 1 May 1464?	miscarried Oct. 1464?
gap 7 months?		
2 Elizabeth of York	conceived Greenwich 11 May 1465	born 11 Feb. 1465/6
gap 9 months		
3 Mary	conceived Westminster 11 Nov 1466	born 11 Aug. 1467
gap 10 months		

4 Cecily of York	conceived Westminster late June 1468	born 20 March 1468/9
gap 11 months		
5 Edward	conceived Westminster 4 Feb. 1469/70	born 4 Nov. 1470
gap 8 months		
6 Margaret	conceived Westminster* 10 July 1471	born 10 April 1472
gap 7 months		
7 Richard of Shrewsbury	conceived Westminster 17 Nov. 1472	born 17 Aug. 1473
gap 18 months		
8 Anne of York, Lady Howard	2 Nov. 1475	
gap 7 months		
9 George Plantagenet	conceived Greenwich± June 1476	born March 1476/7
gap 20 months		
10 Catherine	conceived Eltham(?) 14 Nov. 1478	born 14 Aug. 1479
gap 5 months		
11 Bridget of York	conceived Greenwich(?) 10 Feb. 1479/80	born 10 Nov. 1480
* or possibly a few days later at Windsor Castle		
± or possibly Westminster		

Following Edward IV's public acknowledgement of his secret marriage contract with Elizabeth Widville, one factor with which he was confronted was the fact that, in spite of Elizabeth's ignorance, he and Eleanor Talbot were not the only people who were aware of the earlier secret marriage which he had contracted with her. At least one other person had been present at that earlier exchange of vows. One certain witness had been Canon Robert Stillington.

In 1461 the canon had been the Keeper of the Privy Seal. He also held a number of Church appointments. He was the dean of St Martin's, the archdeacon of Colchester, the archdeacon of Taunton, prebend of York, prebend of St David's, prebend of St Stephen's Chapel in Westminster, and the rector of Ashbury.[23] At the time of the Talbot marriage Stillington held no high appointment in the Church. He was not then a bishop. Significantly, however, following the secret marriage the king had favoured him to the extent of awarding him an annual salary of £365. This award was granted towards the end of 1461.[24] Possibly it was a reward for the role he had played in respect of the royal relationship with Eleanor Talbot, and perhaps also a kind of bribe, to encourage Stillington to remain discreet regarding what had taken place in his presence.

Moreover, once his second secret marriage with Elizabeth Widville had become public knowledge, Edward IV acted in an even more significant way. He then pushed very hard for Stillington's promotion to a bishopric. Following the September 1464 marriage acknowledgement, the next English bishopric to fall vacant was the see of Bath and Wells. This occurred on 14 January 1464/5, as a result of the death of Bishop Thomas Bekyngton. Five days after Bishop Bekynton's demise, the royal licence for the election of his successor was issued.[25]

It is clear that Edward IV had been awaiting such an episcopal vacancy. It is also clear that, as soon as the vacancy became known, Edward's intention was for the post to be granted to Canon Robert Stillington. The moment he heard the news of Bishop Bekynton's death, Edward granted custody of the see's temporalities to Canon Stillington. This grant was made on 20 January 1464/5.[26]

But there was one major problem which confronted the king. Unbeknown to him, Pope Paul II had already reserved for himself the nomination of the next bishop of Bath and Wells. The Pope wished to honour with this episcopal see a learned English divine named John Free, who was resident in Rome.[27] When the Pope found himself confronted with the king's counter-proposal, a diplomatic crisis was born.

Meanwhile, back in England, although the bishopric of Bath and Wells remained officially vacant, as a result of the royal grant which he had received Robert Stillington had already begun to make appointments within the diocese. In other words he was already behaving as though he had officially received the bishopric from the hands of the Pope.[28] In the longer term the dispute was resolved by another death – that of the Pope's chosen candidate. When this became known, Pope Paul II publicly acknowledged King Edward's protégé. Thus it was that on 30 October 1465 Robert Stillington was finally appointed to the vacant see.[29] No doubt Edward IV hoped that he had now secured the former canon's loyal silence.

15

1465–1469: ITINERARY

1465/6
JANUARY
Westminster[1]

FEBRUARY
Westminster[2]

MARCH
Westminster[3]
REGNAL YEAR 6
Westminster and Hertford Castle[4]

1466 (age 24; regnal year 6)
MARCH
Hertford Castle[5]

APRIL
Hertford Castle and Westminster[6]

MAY
Westminster, Sheen and Windsor
Castle[7]

JUNE
Windsor Castle and Westminster[8]

JULY
Westminster[9]
Windsor Castle[10]

AUGUST
Windsor Castle, Farnham Castle,
Southampton and Salisbury[11]

SEPTEMBER
Windsor Castle[12]

OCTOBER
Greenwich and Westminster[13]

NOVEMBER
Westminster[14]
Greenwich[15]

DECEMBER
Greenwich, Westminster and
Woodstock[16]

1466/7
JANUARY
Greenwich, Windsor Castle and
Westminster[17]

FEBRUARY
Windsor Castle[18]
Westminster[19]

MARCH
Westminster[20]
REGNAL YEAR 7
Windsor Castle[21]
Westminster and Greenwich[22]
Sheen[23]

1467 (age 25; regnal year 7)
MARCH
Westminster and Windsor Castle[24]

APRIL
Windsor Castle, Westminster and
Greenwich[25]

MAY
Westminster[26]
Windsor Castle[27]

JUNE
Westminster[28]
Smithfield (tournament)[29]
Windsor Castle[30]
Westminster[31]

JULY
Westminster, Windsor Castle,
Mortlake and Chelsea[32]

AUGUST
Windsor Castle and Chelsea[33]
Windsor Castle[34]
Westminster[35]
Windsor Castle[36]
Mortlake[37]
Windsor Castle[38]

SEPTEMBER
Windsor Castle[39]
The manor of Beckley (Oxon.)[40]
The manor of Boarstall (Bucks.)[41]
The manor of Woodstock,
Cornbury (Oxon.) and Windsor
Castle[42]
Dogmersfield (Hants.)[43]
Windsor Castle and Croydon[44]

OCTOBER
Windsor Castle and Kingston
upon Thames[45]
Westminster[46]
Brentford (Middx.), Chelsea and
Windsor Castle[47]

The Royal Manor House
at Chelsea.

NOVEMBER
Windsor Castle, Reading Abbey
and Chelsea[48]
Sheen[49]

DECEMBER
Sheen and Windsor Castle[50]

1467/8
JANUARY
Coventry[51]
Fotheringhay Castle[52]

MARCH
REGNAL YEAR 8
Stamford, the Tower of London,
Westminster and Greenwich[53]

1468 (age 26; regnal year 8)
MARCH
The manor of Greenwich[54]
Derby[55]

MAY
Warwick Castle[56]
Westminster (Parliament)[57]
The manor of Greenwich[58]

JUNE
Westminster[59]
London (dismissal of George
Neville as Chancellor)[60]
Stratford Abbey[61]
London: the Wardrobe, St Paul's
Cathedral and London Bridge, and
the night spent at Stratford Abbey
(marriage of Margaret of York)[62]
Stratford Abbey[63]
Westminster[64]

JULY
Westminster[65]

AUGUST
Westminster and Fotheringhay
Castle[66]
Leicester Castle[67]
Fotheringhay Castle[68]
Westminster[69]

SEPTEMBER
Westminster[70]

OCTOBER
Westminster[71]

NOVEMBER
Westminster[72]

DECEMBER
Westminster[73]
Greenwich[74]

1468/9
JANUARY
Greenwich, Westminster and
Salisbury[75]

FEBRUARY
Westminster and Greenwich[76]
Westminster[77]

MARCH
Westminster[78]
REGNAL YEAR 9
Westminster[79]

16

1466?: THE MYSTERIOUS
CATHERINE

As we saw earlier, according to Buck, at some stage Edward IV had a
well-known mistress called Catherine de Clarington. She is described by
Buck as one of 'the most famous'. Indeed, she figures first in his list.[1] But
the order of Buck's list is clearly irrelevant in terms of chronology, since
the last partner of Edward IV who appears upon it is Eleanor Talbot –
who, in reality, was Edward IV's *first* known partner. As for Catherine
de Clarington, sadly this 'famous' mistress is mentioned by no other
surviving source.

The name Clarington exists today in the New World, both as a surname
and as a place name (in Canada). However, those appear to be modern
inventions. There seems to be no record of the surname Clarington in
medieval England, and it is therefore generally assumed that it is merely a
variant spelling of 'Clarendon'. This was the name of a park in Wiltshire
which had belonged to royalty since Anglo-Saxon times, and which had
been developed into a royal hunting lodge, and ultimately a palace, by
Henry II and Henry III.

> The site of the royal palace at Clarendon ... has been the subject of
> a recent detailed archaeological investigation, which helps to create
> a lively impression of [Queen Eleanor of Provence's] accommodation
> there in the early 1250s, shortly after a major programme of
> enlargement and refurbishment. Many of the details come from the
> chancery rolls. By 1252 Eleanor had a compact suite of apartments
> at Clarendon, comprising a hall, a chapel, three chambers and
> a wardrobe. They were situated on two floors. The rooms were
> spacious, two of them extending to a length of 40 feet, and the

amenities of her chambers had been greatly improved by the adjacent construction of a two-storey building providing access to 'a fair privy chamber, well vaulted on both floors'. The focal point of the queen's hall was an imposing new fireplace with double marble columns on each side and an overmantel carved with representations of the twelve months of the year. The windows of her rooms were glazed, perhaps mainly in plain glass or the delicate silver-grey *grisaille* patterns, but also with some figured glass, which would be coloured. The windows of her hall overlooked a garden. The chapel, on the upper floor, had a marble altar, flanked by two windows, which could be opened and closed, and above the altar was a crucifix, with the figures of Mary and John. Religious imagery was not confined to the chapel; in the window of one of the queen's chambers there was a representation of the Virgin and Child with the kneeling figure of an earthly queen, presumably Queen Eleanor herself, with an *Ave Maria* scroll. ... The walls of the chapel were initially painted with scenes from the life of St. Katharine, but later redecorated 'with symbols and stories as arranged'. One distinctively up-to-date feature of these rooms were the tiled floors, and the remaining portion of one of these, lifted in the post-war excavations at Clarendon, can be seen on the far wall in the medieval ceramics room of the British Museum. The pavement dates from 1250–2 and was laid in one of Eleanor's ground-floor chambers. Divided into panels of patterned and figured tiles, glowing in muted shades of gold, grey, and warm pink, its power to evoke is incomparable. It was in 1453 at Clarendon Palace that King Henry VI first started to show signs of insanity. Usage of the Palace declined and by 1500, the building was no longer being maintained.[2]

The name Clarendon is reported to be an Old English word meaning clover-covered hill.

Obviously, given the complete lack of solid evidence, any account given of Catherine de Clarington can only be hypothetical. The basic assumption is that Edward may have had a relationship with a girl whose family lived in the vicinity of the royal hunting lodge and palace of Clarendon in Wiltshire. Since no family with the surname Clarington / Clarendon is on record at this time, it would presumably have been a family of no special social consequence, merely living and presumably serving in some capacity in the royal hunting park in Wiltshire. It therefore seems that, if she really existed, the king would probably have met the girl in question, and engaged in his affair with her, while he himself was in the vicinity of Clarendon.

Ruins of King Johns Palace at Clarendon Aug.3.1723.

The ruins of the Palace of Clarendon in the eighteenth century.

The first occasion on which Edward IV is actually documented as having been in that area was in August 1466, roughly mid-way between the birth of his first living child by Elizabeth Widville, and her conception of their second living child. On that occasion he was in Salisbury on 25 August. In fact he may well have been in the region for longer (see above, chapter 14). Later Edward stayed again at Salisbury on 16 and 18 January 1468/9, when Elizabeth Widville was carrying their third living child. Once again, he may well have spent longer in the area. His final recorded stay at Salisbury was on 24–25 April 1470 (chapter 18), when Elizabeth Widville was in the early stages of the pregnancy which was to result in the birth of the Prince of Wales. If Catherine did indeed belong to a family living in the vicinity of Clarendon Palace, it therefore seems likely that her relationship with Edward IV would have commenced on one of these three occasions.

Records exist in the Close Rolls, dating from 1470 and 1471, containing Edward IV's instructions to the sheriff of Wiltshire for the selection of verderers for the forest of 'Claryngdon'.[3] This confirms that at that period the spelling of the place name did approximate that of the 'surname' assigned to Catherine de Clarington. But with the exception of one Walter Barowe, the names and surnames of Edward IV's Clarendon verderers and their families are not recorded in these particular documents.

However, prior to his first recorded visit to Clarendon, Edward had made grants there as follows:

July 1 [1461] Westminster. [Grant for life] to Thomas Combe of
the custody of the king's lands within his park of Claryngdon, co.
Wilts, otherwise called *le laundership*, with fees as [in the last year
of Edward III. and the first of Richard II.][4]

Oct. 26 [1462] Westminster. Grant for life to William Sandes and
Thomas Combe, esquires, of the custody of the king's launds within
his park of Claryngdon, co. Wilts, *alias* 'le laundership' of that
park, receiving fees as in the last year of Edward III. and the first of
Richard II. at the hands of the sheriff.[5]

Following his first recorded visit to Clarendon, Edward IV also made the
following grant:

Feb. 18 [1467] Westminster. Grant for life to Thomas Perkyns and
Thomas Combe, esquires, in lieu of a like grant to William Sandes,
esquire, and the said Thomas Combe by letters patent dated 26
October, 2 Edward IV. surrendered, of the office of launder of the
king's park of Clarindon, co. Wilts, receiving 3d. daily for wages
and 13s. 4d. yearly at Christmas for their robe and 10s. yearly at
Easter for their summer vesture from the issues of the county of
Wilts, as were allowed for John Cousyn, late launder of the park,
in the account of Ralph Cheyne, late sheriff of Wilts, in the year 61
Edward III. and for Walter Worth in the account of John Moigne, late
sheriff, in the year 18 Richard II. with all other accustomed profits.[6]

A later document, dating from the penultimate year of the king's reign
(1482), confirms the fact that

on 18 February, 6 Edward IV [1467], by letters patent[7] the king
appointed Thomas Perkyns, since deceased, and Thomas Combe
esquire or the longest liver of each to the office of launderer
(*landarii*) of the park at Claringdon,[8]

and commands the sheriff of Wiltshire to now make annual Christmas
and Easter payments to the survivor, Thomas Combe, who at that time
was apparently married to Margaret, *née* Echingham, the former wife
both of Sir William Blount (who had died in 1471 of wounds received at
the battle of Barnet) and of Sir John Elrington.[9]

In fact it appears that Thomas Combe, esquire, died shortly after
receiving this award. Eleven months later, similar arrangements were

made for payments to John Shorter, yeoman of the Crown, who is reported as having succeeded Thomas Combe as 'launderer (*landarius*) of the park of Claringdon' on 15 November 1482.[10]

It is now possible to speculate as to whether the real surname of Catherine de Clarington might possibly have been Perkyns or Combe. Given their royal appointments in respect of the Clarendon estate, either Thomas Perkyns or Thomas Combe might possibly have also come to be known as 'of Clarendon'. Moreover, Thomas Combe, esquire, does appear to have been a man of minor importance, as the following royal orders reveal:

> April 27 [1461] Durham. Commission to Thomas Combe, esquire, and the sheriff of Surrey and Sussex [Nicholas Gainsford / Gaynesford][11] to take into the king's hands all the possessions late of Henry, duke of Somerset, Henry, late earl of Northumberland, James, late earl of Wilts, Thomas Roos of Ros, knight, John Nevill of Nevill, knight, and John Clyfford within those counties and to certify thereto in Chancery on the morrow of Midsummer.[12]

Combe is also named in a release and quitclaim dated 24 July 1480.[13]

So could either Thomas Perkyns or Thomas Combe, esquire, have been Catherine's father? The appointment of these two men had been made about six months after August 1466, when Edward might perhaps have begun his relationship with Catherine de Clarington. Perhaps the appointment of Thomas Perkyns and Thomas Combe as 'launderer' had therefore been a reward on the part of the king to members of the family of his latest girlfriend, awarded some months after the relationship commenced.

In effect, however, given the surviving evidence (or rather the total lack thereof), both this hypothesis and the suggested possible surnames of Catherine de Clarington remain mere speculation. If Catherine genuinely existed, her family name could equally well have been Barowe, or Shorter, or some other surname held by a royal appointee at Clarendon, of which no record has survived. Indeed, one further possible surname will be suggested later (see below, chapter 19). Obviously, one alternative possibility is that – like 'Elizabeth Lucy' – Catherine did not really exist at all.

If she did exist, one possible sequel of the relationship between Edward IV and Catherine could be that the alleged daughter of the king who was later known as Isabel Mylbery may have been the fruit of this liaison. Once again this proposed connection is purely hypothetical. However, the surname Mylbery could well be a toponym, derived from one of the various Melburys of Dorset. This would imply that the holder of the name – who may have been the eventual husband of Catherine de Clarington – might, like Catherine herself, have come from the West Country. Instances of the surname Melbury certainly are recorded in Dorset, Devon and Wiltshire,[14] and we have already seen that in the second half of the fifteenth century use of the letters 'y' and 'e' was sometimes interchangeable.

The child Isabel Mylbery was probably born at about the right period (late 1460s) to have been the possible fruit of Edward IV's relationship with a Catherine de Clarington from Wiltshire, assuming, as was proposed above, that the king had met her in the late 1460s, and assuming – as was later believed during the 'Tudor' period – that Edward IV really was the father of Isabel Mylbery. But unfortunately the alleged name of Isabel's mother is nowhere on record. The only factual information available to us is that Isabel herself was apparently acknowledged in the early sixteenth century as a bastard child of Edward IV, and was granted a coat of arms which apparently reflected her kingly paternity (see plates). Significantly, it appears that Isabel was never acknowledged as his daughter by Edward IV during his lifetime. More will be said about the case of Isabel, and other alleged bastards of Edward IV, later (see below, chapter 28).

Meanwhile, however, it has to be said that, in actual fact, the existence of Catherine de Clarington, like the existence of Elizabeth Lucy, remains totally unconfirmed. Intriguingly, we have now encountered a total lack of evidence in respect of two of the women whom later sources name as alleged mistresses of Edward IV. Thus, at this point in the story, the only remaining certainties are Edward's three authentic and documented relationships. These are the relationships with Eleanor Talbot, with her cousin Henry, Duke of Somerset, and with Elizabeth Widville. What is more, two of these relationships apparently took the form of marriages.

17

1468: DISPOSING OF THE RIVAL

As we have seen, in February 1465/6 Elizabeth Widville had borne Edward IV a daughter, known to history as Elizabeth of York. In August 1467 she had given birth to a second daughter, Mary. Earlier, in the late autumn of 1464 or the winter of 1464/5, she may also have miscarried a baby of unknown gender. So far, therefore, in terms of her royal relationship the fecund Elizabeth Widville, who had successfully given birth to two sons by her first husband, was proving something of a failure. She had produced only two living female offspring for the king. Both from her point of view and from that of Edward IV himself this may have been the cause of some anxiety. From the king's secret viewpoint the circumstances may well have been rendered even more worrying by the fact that his earlier relationship, with Eleanor Talbot, had also produced no heirs. Did this mean that King Edward was incapable of begetting male offspring? Under these circumstances is it possible that the disappointed young king may have made comments which hinted at the possibility that the validity of his Widville alliance might be regarded as doubtful? If so, that would have worried and stressed Elizabeth.

It has been suggested (see above) that, at the time of her secret marriage with Edward IV, in May 1464, Elizabeth Widville had probably been unaware of his antecedent marriage with Eleanor Talbot. Yet, despite her initial ignorance, it is clear that sooner or later rumours of her husband's earlier secret marriage contract must have reached Elizabeth Widville's ears. Domenico Mancini, whose own source for English information comprised his Widville connections, reported, in the months following Edward IV's death, that in about

1475–76, when she found herself confronted by the opposition of Edward IV's brother, George, Duke of Clarence, Elizabeth recalled 'the calumnies with which she was reproached, namely that according to established usage she was not the legitimate wife of the king'.[1] Although Mancini gives no specific date for this statement, he makes it clear that it occurred between the restoration of Edward IV to the English throne (in 1471) and the execution of the Duke of Clarence (in 1477/8). The mid-point between those two dates would have been about 1475. However, since Elizabeth Widville was then reported to be *remembering* these allegations, they cannot have comprised new information which only reached her ears for the first time in the mid-1470s. Instead, they must have been current for some years. In fact, given the date of her secret marriage with the king, questions about the validity of her royal marriage must have been current – in whispered form – since the second half of the 1460s.

Moreover, her arrangement in 1468 for the execution of the Earl of Desmond (see below) – who is reported to have cast aspersions on her union with the king as early as in September 1464 – strongly suggests that question marks concerning the validity of her own royal marriage must first have come to the attention of Elizabeth as early as the autumn or winter of 1464, when the king first made his Widville union public. Indeed, if she had brought about the public recognition of her own royal marriage by claiming to be pregnant by the king, as was suggested earlier, that may indicate that some kind of awareness of her potential problem had begun to reach her ears even prior to September 1464.

It is interesting to consider what her reaction may have been when she discovered the shocking fact that her own secret marriage with the young king had been precursed by an earlier secret marriage. Obviously, this information would have placed Elizabeth herself, and the royal children whom she had begun to conceive, in a potentially perilous position, as Mancini's report of her reaction clearly emphasises. In this context it is important to stress that Elizabeth Widville was evidently a ruthless woman, as her carefully plotted revenge against the Earl of Desmond and her other subsequent actions clearly demonstrate.

It was on 15 February 1467/8 that Thomas Fitzgerald, 7th Earl of Desmond, the former deputy governor of Ireland, and a friend and ally of Edward IV, was beheaded at Drogheda. The execution was carried out under the authority of Edward IV's new governor of Ireland, the Earl of Worcester. In political terms, putting Desmond to death proved to be a big mistake. It caused consternation in Ireland, and it sent the earl's family into immediate armed rebellion. Significantly, it is also reported by a contemporary source to have surprised and upset Edward IV himself. William Worcester's Annals state:

> [1467/8] About the Feast of the Purification of the Blessed Mary [2 February], in Ireland, the Earl of Worcester had the Earl of Desmond beheaded, at which the king was initially displeased.[2]

This means that the king himself was in no way responsible for the action taken. Someone else, close to the throne, and with access to the royal seal and the ability to contact the lieutenant of Ireland, must have been the person behind the execution.

According to a later written source,

> it chanced that the said king and the queen his wife, upon some occasion, fell at words, insomuch that his grace braste out and said: 'Well I perceive now that true it is that my cousin, the Earl of Desmond, told me at such a time when we two communed secretly together;' which saying his Majesty, then in his melancholy, declared unto her; whereupon her Grace being not a little moved, and conceiving upon those words a grudge in her heart against the said Earl, found such a mean as letters were devised under the king's privy seal, and directed to the Lord Justice or governor of the realm of Ireland, commanding him in all haste to send for the said Earl, dissembling some earnest matter of consultation with him touching the state of the same realm, and at his coming to object to such matter, and to lay such things to his charge, as should cause him to lose his head.[3]

The earliest *surviving* source for this account dates from 1541 or 1542. But although no previous historians have picked up the fact, it was simply quoting in English an earlier source that was said to have been written in the Irish Gaelic language (but which has not survived).[4]

Normally, of course, earls of Desmond resided on their estates in Ireland. But in 1464 a disagreement between Thomas, Earl of Desmond, and the Bishop of Meath happened to bring Thomas to England to consult with his friend and sovereign, King Edward IV.[5] By chance, the earl's visit to England occurred at precisely the time when the king's marriage to Elizabeth Widville was publicly recognised. Reportedly, the king, who trusted Desmond, and who was well aware of the fact that his newly revealed secret marriage was the subject of wide discussion and debate, asked Thomas Fitzgerald for his opinion of it. The Earl of

Desmond is purported to have replied that the marriage was unsuitable and that recognising it had been a mistake on the part of Edward IV.

As we have seen, when she learned of what he had said, Elizabeth Widville became the permanent enemy of Thomas, Earl of Desmond. From that point onwards she looked for a way of taking vengeance on him for what he had said about her. Although the earliest surviving written account of Elizabeth's involvement in Desmond's subsequent death dates from more than half a century after the event, significantly its source is the Earl of Desmond's own family. It is therefore likely that at least an oral version of the story had been current amongst Thomas' numerous children from the moment when the execution of their father had occurred.

Moreover, there is also one extant fifteenth-century written source which strongly implies that Elizabeth had been the key person responsible for the Earl of Desmond's execution. This comprises a letter written about fifteen years after the event by King Richard III. The letter was addressed to Thomas Barrett, Bishop of Annaghdown ('Enachden'). It contains the king's instructions for the bishop who was then acting as Richard's messenger to Thomas Fitzgerald's son and heir, James Fitzgerald, the 8th Earl of Desmond:

> The said bisshop shall thank him ... as remembryng the manyfold notable service and kyndnesse by therle's fadre unto the famous prince the duc of York the king's fader ... Also he shalle shewe that albe it the fadre of the said erle, the king than being of yong age, was extorciously slayne and murdred by colour of the lawes within Ireland by certain persons than havyng the governaunce and rule there, ayenst alle manhode, reason, and good conscience; yet, notwithstanding that the semblable chaunce was and hapned sithen within this royaume of Eingland, as wele of his brother the duc of Clarence as other his nigh kynnesmen and gret frendes, the kinge's grace alweys contynueth and hathe inward compassion of the dethe of his said fadre, and is content that his said cousyn now erle by alle ordinate meanes and due course of the lawes, when it shalle lust him at any tyme hereafter to sue or attempt for the punishment therof.[6]

In this letter, Richard III makes it clear that he believed that two executions – of the Earl of Desmond, and of his own brother, George, Duke of Clarence – had both been brought about in the same way.

In 1483 it was clearly believed that the person behind the subsequent execution of the Duke of Clarence was Elizabeth Widville. As Domenico

Mancini then recorded, Elizabeth had 'concluded that her offspring by the king would never come to the throne, unless the duke of Clarence were removed; and of this she easily persuaded the king'.[7] Therefore, what Richard III wrote clearly indicates that he must have believed that Elizabeth Widville was also the person responsible for the execution of the Earl of Desmond. Some historians have rather naïvely argued against that interpretation on the grounds that Elizabeth is nowhere actually mentioned by name in Richard III's document. However, the only other possible interpretation of his written statement would be that Richard believed that the Earl of Worcester had been behind both executions. Yet that is clearly out of the question, because Worcester had been executed by the restored Lancastrian regime in 1470, seven years *before* the execution of the Duke of Clarence!

George, Duke of Clarence, never put forward a direct claim to the throne in his own name. However, in 1470 he had backed his father-in-law's attempt to finally remove the Widville family from power in the realm by dethroning Edward IV and reinstating Henry VI as king of England. Ultimately he abandoned that scheme and returned to supporting his brother. Thus, in spite of what he had done, Edward IV forgave George on that occasion. But by 1476 George was putting forward another claim. This time his case was not that Edward should be dethroned once again, but rather that he himself should be acknowledged as the legitimate heir to the throne. In other words he was obviously contending that Edward IV's children by Elizabeth Widville had no valid right to inherit the English crown. Thus, in spite of the fact that the surviving documentary evidence against him accuses George of various other things, it seems clear that the main fault for which he was condemned to death – and on this occasion, executed – was his opposition to Edward IV's Widville heirs. This can only mean that he must have been questioning the validity of the Widville marriage. It is therefore logical to assume – as George's younger brother, the future King Richard III, clearly did – that behind the king's firm hand against George on this occasion lay the steely will of Elizabeth Widville.

In the cases of both the Earl of Desmond and the Duke of Clarence, people at the time clearly believed that Elizabeth Widville was responsible for the removal of such enemies who threatened the security of her marriage to the king and the future of her royal children. It is therefore by no means illogical to explore the possibility that Lady Eleanor Talbot's sudden and unexpected death in June 1468 may also have been brought about by her rival. By that time Elizabeth Widville had almost certainly discovered that her royal 'husband' had contracted an earlier secret marriage with an aristocratic lady of English royal descent. She may also have found out that, dangerously for her, the lady in question was still living, and was under the protection of her sister and brother-in-law, the Duchess and Duke of Norfolk.

The significant fact is that Eleanor died quite young. As we have seen, she was of almost the same age as Elizabeth Widville herself. Yet the table below shows that, compared to the natural life expectancy for other members of her immediate family, Eleanor died at an unusually young age.

Length of Life of Members of the Talbot Family (The average age at death of members of this family who died naturally was 61–62)				
Name	born	died	age	natural / unnatural death
John Talbot, Earl of Shrewsbury	1387	1453	66	unnatural (in battle)
Margaret Beauchamp, Countess of Shrewsbury	1404	1467	63	natural
John Talbot, Lord Lisle	1426	1453	27	unnatural (in battle)
Sir Louis Talbot	1428	1459	30	unnatural? (injured in conflict?)
Sir Humphrey Talbot	1433	1492	59	natural
Eleanor Talbot	1436	1468	32	unnatural?
Elizabeth Talbot, Duchess of Norfolk	1442/3	1506	63	natural

Moreover, significantly, all her close relatives were out of the country when Eleanor died. By royal command, they had been dispatched to the Low Countries as part of Margaret of York's entourage on the occasion of her wedding with Charles the Bold. In a way, therefore, Eleanor's death must have taken her family by surprise. One significant result of their absence abroad was the fact that the legal requirements which arose from Eleanor's demise could not be set in motion until two weeks after her death, when her sister, the Duchess of Norfolk, finally returned to England.

Although the Duchess of Norfolk would hardly have been in a position to refuse Edward IV's command to accompany Margaret of York to Flanders, she certainly stayed on after the wedding and appears to have enjoyed all the marriage festivities to the full. Given her closeness to her sister, it is unlikely that she would have done that if she had been aware of the fact that Eleanor was on her deathbed. At all events, Elizabeth Talbot remained out of England for several weeks. Having sailed from Margate with the king's sister on Thursday 23 June, she only re-embarked to return to England on Wednesday 13 July.[8] Thus, on 30 June, while her sister lay dying at home in England, Elizabeth Talbot was still in the Low Countries.

Following the public announcement of Edward's Widville marriage, Eleanor appears to have permanently resided at her sister's dower house, East Hall, at Kenninghall in Norfolk. She apparently lived there quietly and privately, maintaining, as we have seen, her patronage of Corpus Christi College, Cambridge, and developing her religious association with the Norwich Carmelites. It has frequently been suggested that she eventually became a nun. Although that is a misunderstanding, it is certainly true that Eleanor progressively retired into a quasi-religious life as a laywoman firmly associated with the Carmelite order. If Edward IV was aware of this it is highly probable that he welcomed the move, which, for him, meant that Eleanor must have completely abandoned any claim to be recognised as his wife. Apparently she had decided that marriage with Edward was not what she wanted out of life. Instead she preferred to deeply develop her contemplative relationship with God.

Eleanor not only appears to have lived at East Hall; she also seems to have died there. In the sixteenth century, John Leland recalled a local tradition which recorded that

> there apperith at Keninghaule not far from the Duke of Northfolkes new place a grete mote, withyn the cumpace whereof there was sumtyme a fair place, and there the saying is that there lay a Quene or sum grete lady, and there dyed.[9]

Both Eleanor and Stillington (who, as we have seen, was promoted to a bishopric soon after Edward IV's public announcement of his Widville matrimony) remained completely silent in respect of Eleanor's marriage contract with the king. Nevertheless, Eleanor's death in June 1468 made the situation potentially more secure for the king – and even more so for Elizabeth Widville and her children. Given this fact, together with Eleanor's early death and the strange circumstances which surrounded it – with all her closest relatives far removed from the scene, so that she died alone – it appears distinctly plausible that she may have died of unnatural causes. And if such was the case, the most likely person to have been responsible for her demise would have been the rival who was now in a very powerful position, and who also brought about the unnatural deaths of other significant enemies, such as the Earl of Desmond and the Duke of Clarence – namely Elizabeth Widville. After all, she was the person who had the most to gain from Eleanor Talbot's death.

Following her return to her homeland, the Duchess of Norfolk had the remains of her sister interred in the choir of the Carmelite Priory Church in Norwich. Probably this was what Eleanor herself had requested in her will (the text of which does not survive). The priory church stood just across the River Wensum from Norwich Cathedral. Little remains of it today. However, in the seventeenth century Eleanor's tomb could still be seen in the priory ruins. Bones which may be Eleanor's were excavated from the priory site in 1958. They are currently preserved at Norwich Castle Museum.

PART 4
THE SECOND REIGN

18

1469–1471: ITINERARY

1469 (age 27; regnal year 9)
MARCH
Westminster[1]

APRIL
Westminster[2]

MAY
Westminster, and Windsor Castle[3]

JUNE
Windsor Castle[4]
departure predicted from
London, on pilgrimage to
Walsingham[5]
Windsor Castle[6]
The manor of The More[7]
St Alban's Abbey and Royston[8]
Bury St Edmund's Abbey[9]
Norwich[10]
Drayton and Walsingham[11]
[Castle Rising, Norfolk]
Bishop's Lynn[12]
Wisbeach, Dovesdale[13]
Crowland (Lincs.)[14]
Fotheringhay Castle[15]

JULY
Fotheringhay
riding north; (no date given)
Newark, Nottingham
Castle[16]
Stamford, Grantham and
Nottingham[17]
Olney (Bucks.)
(surrendered to Archbishop
Neville)[18]
Warwick Castle – prisoner until
October[19]

AUGUST
Coventry, Warwick Castle, and
Middleham Castle[20]

SEPTEMBER
Middleham Castle[21]
Pontefract Castle[22]

OCTOBER
Edward IV was released and went
to York[23]
The city of London[24]
Westminster[25]

NOVEMBER
Westminster[26]

DECEMBER
Westminster[27]
London[28]

1469/70
JANUARY
London[29]
Westminster[30]

FEBRUARY
London[31]
Westminster[32]

MARCH
Westminster[33]
REGNAL YEAR 10
Westminster[34]
Waltham Abbey, Essex[35]
Huntingdon[36]
Stamford[37]
Grantham and Newark[38]
Doncaster[39]
Rotherham[40]
York[41]

1470 (age 28; regnal year 10)
MARCH
York, Doncaster, Warsop (Notts.),
and the town of Leicester[42]

APRIL
Coventry, Burford (near
Oxford), Exeter, Salisbury, and
Southampton[43]

MAY
Southampton, Winchester, and
Salisbury[44]

Southampton[45]

JUNE
Battle (Hastings), Canterbury,
the City of London, and
Westminster[46]

JULY
Westminster, Lambeth, and
Windsor Castle[47]
Leicester[48]

AUGUST
Leicester Castle, Ripon and York[49]

SEPTEMBER
York[50]
Doncaster; then Edward IV
embarked at Bishop's Lynn,
Norfolk[51]
on the North Sea

OCTOBER
Texel (steward of North Holland
sent from The Hague to meet
him), Almaar, the shrine at
Egmond, Haarlem, Noordwjk,
Leiden, and The Hague[52]

NOVEMBER
The Hague[53]

DECEMBER
via Aardenburg to the Castle of
Oostcamp at Brugge[54]

1470/71
JANUARY
Aire-sur-la-Lys (met Charles the
Bold); St Pol-sur-Ternoise (met
Charles the Bold) and Brugge[55]

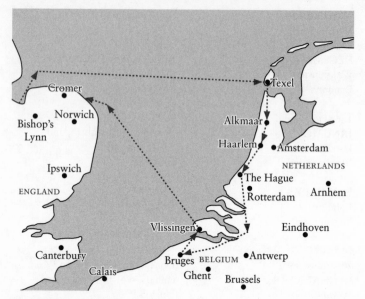

Edward IV's movements from September 1470 to March 1470/1

FEBRUARY
Brugge[56]
Vlissingen (Zeeland – known
in English as 'Flushing', and
recorded in *The Arrivall* text as
'Flisshinge'.)[57]

MARCH
Vlissingen (embarked, awaiting
good wind)[58]
REGNAL YEAR 11
Vlissingen (embarked, awaiting
good wind)
North Sea[59]
Cromer, Norfolk[60]
sailing north (up the east coast of
England)
Ravenspur / Humberhead[61]

Beverley (refused entry to
Kingston upon Hull)[62]
York[63]
Tadcaster[64]
Wakefield[65]
Doncaster & Nottingham[66]

1471 (age 29; regnal year 11)
MARCH
Nottingham[67]
crossed the river Trent (south of
Nottingham)[68]
Leicester[69]
Coventry[70]

APRIL
Warwick[71]
[Daventry]

Northampton[72]
[St Albans]
London, St Pauls Cathedral,
Westminster, Baynard's Castle[73]
left London[74]
[Watling Street going north /
Barnet]
Barnet[75]
The City of London[76]
Bath[77]
outside Bristol[78]
Abingdon[79]

MAY
Cheltenham[80]
Tewkesbury (battle)[81]
departed from Tewkesbury,
northwards (towards Worcester)[82]
Coventry[83]
London[84]
[Death of Henry VI][85]
left London for Kent[86]
Canterbury[87]

JUNE
Westminster[88]
The manor of Fulham[89]
Westminster[90]
Fulham[91]
Westminster[92]

JULY
Westminster[93]
Windsor Castle[94]

Westminster[95]
Windsor Castle[96]
Fulham[97]
Windsor Castle[98]

AUGUST
Windsor Castle, and the manor of
Henley-on-Thames[99]
Windsor Castle[100]

SEPTEMBER
The town of Tame
(?Thame?)[101]
The manor of Woodstock[102]
Northampton, the town of
Fotheringhay, and
Peterborough[103]
Canterbury (pilgrimage)[104]
Hatfield and Hertford[105]
Windsor Castle[106]
Westminster[107]

OCTOBER
Westminster[108]
Hertford Castle[109]

NOVEMBER
Hertford Castle[110]
Westminster[111]
Guildford, Farnham Castle, and
Westminster[112]

DECEMBER
Westminster[113]

19

1470?: THE LIGHT WAYTE

Understanding Edward IV's personal relationships in this period of his life, which corresponds with his brief loss of the English crown and his ensuing restoration, is in some ways more difficult to grasp than during his first reign, because there is an almost total lack of evidence in terms of any individuals with whom he may have been involved. Eleanor Talbot and her cousin Henry, Duke of Somerset, were now both out of his life – and dead. Material which shows the reality of his ongoing relationship with Elizabeth Widville does, of course, exist, and that will be examined in due course. The ongoing and fairly regular birth of the couple's children is one significant point, and the will which Edward drafted in 1475 (see below, chapter 23) also corroborates that the Widville connection was meaningful for the king.

But as for his relationship with other women, verification is hard to find. As we shall see, there is absolutely no solid contemporary documentation in respect of his alleged relationships with a member of the Wayte family of Hampshire, nor with the wife of William Shore. Nevertheless, it is absolutely clear from evidence dating from a later period that a relationship with a Wayte girl really had existed, and this liaison will be explored shortly.

There is also one significant piece of contemporary evidence, dating from the 1470s, which shows that the king had fathered a bastard son and had recognised the boy in question. However, the boy is not named, and the assumptions which have been made by previous historians in respect of his identity are not tenable based upon the available evidence.

This means that it is difficult to determine how to interpret the evidence which does exist. Certainly, previous assumptions in this respect need to be questioned, as we shall see. Thus, on the matter of the acknowledged bastard son, and the alleged relationship with William Shore's wife, the present study will offer new hypotheses. Of course, the suggestions which will be put forward here cannot be completely proved, but, as will be seen, unlike earlier theories, they are firmly based upon such evidence as genuinely exists.

In respect of the Wayte relationship, ironically one key piece of evidence definitely dates from the 'Tudor' period. There is absolutely no doubt that, in the sixteenth century, King Henry VIII gave the title of Lord Lisle to a man whom he recognised as his own illegitimate uncle. Earlier, his father, King Henry VII, had apparently recognised the man in question as his illegitimate brother-in-law, and had allowed him to assume the surname 'Plantagenet'. The evidence in respect of these 'Tudor' recognitions will be examined in detail later, in chapter 28. However, it is also clear that the man in question had previously been known by the name of Arthur Wayte.[1] In other words, during the lifetime of Edward IV and Richard III, it seems that he had used a common surname, rather than the name attributed to the medieval English royal family.[2] Thus the assumption which has previously been stated as a fact, namely that 'Arthur spent his childhood at the court of his father Edward IV',[3] and that his royal father had accorded him formal recognition, totally lacks any supporting evidence.

As we have seen, the seventeenth-century writer George Buck provides the earliest surviving record of Arthur's original surname, though he gives the spelling as *Wyat* – a small and insignificant error at a period when name spelling was often variable. In short, it seems clear that Buck knew some details of the person to whom he was referring as a bastard son of Edward IV. As for Arthur's connection with the Wayte family, definite confirmation of that does exist. However, it is not contemporary with the reign of Edward IV, but dates from the 'Tudor' period. Nevertheless, it does seem certain that at some stage in his career King Edward must have had a sexual relationship with a female member of the Wayte family.

Although George Buck described the father (whose name he does not mention) of Edward IV's Wayte mistress as a 'mean gentleman', the Wayte family was in fact well established in Hampshire. Their name first appears in the county records at about the beginning of the fourteenth century, when members of the family already held lands and possessions in the county. By the fifteenth century, Waytes held (or had held) a number of Hampshire manors, namely Lee Marks and Segenworth (both in the parish of Titchfield and adjacent to Titchfield Abbey), Limbourne (in the parish of Navant), Denmead (in the parish of Hambleden),

Bere (in the parish of Soberton), Westcote (in the parish of Binsted), West Stratton and Barton Stacey (in the parish of Micheldever), and Wayte's Court at Brighstone on the Isle of Wight. The Isle of Wight may have been the family's original home in Hampshire, and the manor they held there was possibly the origin of their surname, although a different derivation is normally cited.[4] It is not certain whether the Waytes were established first at the manor of Segenworth or at the manor of Wayte's Court. Both manors, however, were early and long-standing possessions of the family. On four occasions in the fourteenth and fifteenth centuries, members of the Wayte family held the office of escheator for the county of Hampshire, and in spite of Buck's somewhat sneering analysis regarding their social status, they also bore a coat of arms (see plates).[5]

On the basis of the earlier versions of Edward IV's story as told by Thomas More (see above) and other sixteenth-century writers, Buck, writing in the seventeenth century, not unnaturally assumed that the Wayte girl who reputedly attracted the king's amorous attention and bore him a son was one and the same person as the alleged mistress / first wife of the king, whose name was said, by Thomas More and other 'Tudor' writers, to have been 'Elizabeth Lucy'. Unfortunately, however, Buck produced not a single shred of new evidence to substantiate his surmise in this respect. Therefore, in effect, it was nothing more than an assumption on his part. It is also worth noting that not all writers arrived at the same conclusion as George Buck. For example, Harl. MS 1541 identifies the mother of Arthur Wayte not as 'Elizabeth Lucy', but as Mistress Shore![6]

Actually, there is also no justification for the assumption that the mother of Arthur, Viscount Lisle, was William Shore's wife. Based upon the evidence of the surname used by Arthur in his early years, his mother must have been a female member of the Wayte family. But although Buck later assumed that the girl in question must have borne the first name of Elizabeth, in actual fact no Elizabeth Wayte can be traced in the second half of the fifteenth century as a plausible candidate for a relationship with Edward IV. It therefore seems that George Buck must simply have been thoroughly misled by the 'Tudor' mythology relating to 'Elizabeth Lucy'. Since no authentic record survives of the first name of Edward IV's Wayte mistress, Buck's premise that her first name was 'Elizabeth' will henceforth be ignored. In the present study the girl will simply be referred to as Miss Wayte. As for Buck's conjecture that at some stage in her life the girl acquired the married surname of 'Lucy', one possible interpretation of that will be explored in a little more detail later, in chapter 28.

Buck never mentions – and presumably did not know – the first name of the father of Miss Wayte. However, his contention regarding the maiden surname of Edward IV's mistress who gave birth to Arthur Wayte / Plantagenet was confirmed and supplemented, about a hundred years later, by Anstis, who also claimed to know the Christian name of the girl's father. Antis recorded that Lord Lisle was Edward IV's natural son 'by Eliz. the Daughter of Thomas Wayte of Hampshire, the widow of Lucy'.[7]

Although we have already discounted the names of 'Elizabeth' and 'Lucy', Anstis' assertion that Edward IV's Wayte mistress was the daughter of Thomas Wayte may possibly be true. His claim was based upon the so-called Philipot Pedigree of the Wayte family recorded by John Philipot, Dragon Rouge, in 1629.[8] Unfortunately, the chronology of the Philipot pedigree sometimes appears to be inconsistent, and the alleged line of descent of 'Elizabeth Lucy' from three consecutive Thomas Waytes seems impossible. On the basis of other surviving evidence, the third of the listed Thomas Waytes was, in reality, not the son but the nephew of the second.[9] Thus the evidence presented by the Philipot pedigree is not entirely to be trusted.

Nevertheless, the surviving sixteenth-century Lisle correspondence confirms that Arthur Wayte / Plantagenet recognised, had contact with, and was acknowledged by a number of relatives called Wayte, from one of whom, his second cousin John Wayte, 'the Fool' or 'the Innocent' (who was mentally retarded), he first leased and subsequently purchased the manors of Lee Marks and Segenworth, in the hundred of Titchfield, in Hampshire, in return for taking care of John for the rest of his life.[10] Further details of Lord Lisle's relevant correspondence, together with other evidence that he was a relative both of the Wayte family of Hampshire and of the royal house of York is presented below (see chapter 28).

As for the Thomas Wayte who appears to have been the father of Edward IV's mistress, his female-line ancestors are traceable even further back than the male-line ancestors from whom he inherited his surname. His grandmother, Margaret Popham, came from a family which had been granted the manor of Popham in the twelfth century by the Empress Mathilda. Members of this family had been about the court in the earlier part of the fifteenth century, in the service of the dukes of York. In fact the Pophams were certainly regarded as firm Yorkists long before Edward IV's accession, and had suffered persecution from the Duke of Suffolk for their Yorkist allegiance.

Margaret Popham's cousin Sir John Popham had been chancellor of the duchy of Normandy and treasurer of the king's household in the reign of Henry VI. He also served Edward IV's father in France, where he had been a member of the Duke of York's council. The Duke of Suffolk evidently regarded him as a partisan of the Duke of York, for when Sir John was elected speaker of the Commons in 1449 he was regarded by the government as unacceptable, and pressure was brought to bear to make him stand down on the grounds of age and infirmity. Resident for many years in or just outside London, Sir John Popham was a benefactor of the Church of the Holy Sepulchre without Newgate, and of the London Carthusian monastery (Charterhouse), at both of which traces of his building activities are still to be seen. Sir John was buried at the Charterhouse.[11]

Margaret Popham was born on 1 May 1400 and was dead by 1447.[12] Thomas Wayte I (also, confusingly, referred to in some contemporary documents as William Wayte or Edward Wayte) was the second of Margaret's three husbands. Her first marriage, to John de Coudray, was arranged while Margaret was still young, and the marriage had been celebrated by 1415. But John (de) Coudray was dead by 1422 at the latest. Even so, it appears likely that John Wayte II, the younger son of Thomas Wayte I and Margaret Popham, could not have been born prior to 1420. John Wayte II himself subsequently fathered several children, of whom Thomas III – identified as the father of Edward IV's Wayte mistress – was probably the eldest.

On the basis of this chronology, it would appear that Thomas Wayte III may have been born in about 1440. In 1465, at the age of about 25, Thomas married (as her second husband) Elizabeth, daughter of John Skillyng, who held the manor of Shoddesden, also in Hampshire. In addition, the Skillyngs held land at Collingbourne in Wiltshire, which Elizabeth Skillyng inherited, and which both of her

TENTATIVE WAYTE FAMILY TREE

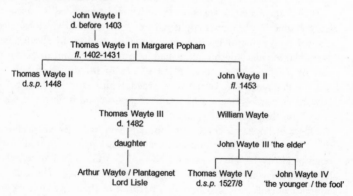

husbands held by virtue of their marriages to her. Her first husband had been John Wynnard, who is recorded as having been alive as late as 1464, though he must have died very soon after that record was made. The Wynnard marriage appears to have been childless.[13] The marriage of Elizabeth Skillyng to Thomas Wayte was also without offspring. However, evidence exists that Thomas had at some point in his life fathered an illegitimate daughter, Alice, who is named in his widow's will of 1487.[14]

There is no evidence in Elizabeth Wayte (Skillyng)'s will, or elsewhere, of the birth, the life or the death of a Miss Wayte who bore the first name Elizabeth. Thomas Wayte died in 1482 and was buried at St Michael's Church, Stoke Charity, Hampshire. It is not known why this particular church should have been chosen, but the Wayte family held lands in two adjoining parishes: Barton Stacey and Micheldever. Also, the family of Thomas' grandmother Margaret Popham had connections with this region, and her family's ancestral manor is only a few miles from Stoke Charity. Thomas' wife, Elizabeth Skillyng, survived him,[15] and may perhaps have been responsible for Thomas' rather fine monument, which seems to have been intended to serve also as an Easter Sepulchre during the observations of Holy Week. It is, however, also possible that Thomas himself had the tomb prepared during his lifetime, perhaps in the 1470s, when a number of other improvements and modernisations were carried out in the church, including the insertion of a new window in the south wall of the nave, just above the site of Thomas' tomb.

The tomb is a raised monument of the 'table' type, topped by a purbeck marble slab four feet seven inches long and two feet one inch wide, positioned under an arch in a recess of the south wall of the nave. The purbeck marble slab has brass insets. These include, at the base of the figure, the inscription:

Hic iacet Thomas Wayte Armiger qui obiit Xo die Aprilis Anno Domini MCCCCLxxxij° cuius anime propitietur Deus. Amen.
(Here lies Thomas Wayte Esquire who died on the tenth day of April in the year of Our Lord 1482 on whose soul may God have mercy. Amen.)

There is a figure of Thomas, depicted as a good-looking man with his hair long in the style of Edward IV's reign. His age is hinted at discreetly by the lines on his face, the slightly hollow cheeks and the deep-set eyes. He is dressed in fine armour. The figure is similar to that on another brass, installed only a year later in the same church,[16] although the other person – Thomas de Hampton – is depicted as taller and his brass image appears to represent a slightly younger man. Of course, the brasses are not portraits in the modern sense. Memorial brasses are seldom, if ever, actual portraits, since they were normally only produced when the person commemorated was already dead and buried.

On the Wayte tomb, in a scroll (the medieval brass equivalent of a speech bubble), Thomas again asks for God's mercy: *Iesus fili Dei miserere mei.* Above Thomas' head, reflecting both his own hope of the resurrection, and the tomb's probable secondary purpose as the church's Easter Sepulchre, is inset a scene of Christ rising from the tomb. At the four corners of the slab were brass shields, only one of which now survives intact. It shows the arms of Wayte impaling Skillyng. Windows in the church contain stained glass bearing the same arms of Wayte impaling Skillyng, although in the glass the Wayte arms have been somewhat sketchily restored in comparatively recent times. Elsewhere in the stained glass there are numerous representations of Edward IV's emblem, the sunburst, sometimes with straight rays, sometimes with curly rays.[17] These may have been intended to convey discreetly the Wayte family's connection with the king.

In fact quite a lot of medieval glass survives in this little church, albeit in a somewhat fragmentary condition. This glass all dates from about 1475, at which time someone paid to have the church windows enlarged and replaced with tracery of a more up-to-date design. In addition to the Yorkist sunburst, another royal emblem also figures in the pattern of the new fifteenth-century glazing, for the east window, which depicts the Annunciation, has a number of decorative roundels, each one containing a crowned lion's head.

Despite the claim put forward by Anstis, it cannot be regarded as absolutely proved that Arthur's mother was the daughter of Thomas Wayte. Nevertheless, as we saw earlier, it is certain that at some stage in her life the surname of Arthur's mother must have been Wayte, because that was the surname which her bastard son also bore in his youth. But since there is no certainty that Miss Wayte's Christian name was Elizabeth, might it even be possible that her first name was Catherine, and that, because of the vicinity of the Wayte Hampshire lands to the royal estate at Clarendon she has gone down in history as 'Catherine de Clarington'?

At all events, the Thomas Wayte whom Anstis claims was the father of the king's mistress has only one child of whom records survive. The person in question was his illegitimate daughter, Alice Wayte. Curiously, Thomas also had a wife who bore the name Elizabeth Wayte – though her maiden name had been Skillyng. Alice Wayte was alive and unmarried in 1487, when her name was mentioned in her stepmother's will.[18] She is therefore a possible candidate for the role of Edward IV's Wayte mistress, and her illegitimacy might account for some of the aspersions which George Buck later cast upon her family background. Another possible candidate might be her stepmother, Elizabeth Wayte (*née* Skillyng). A third possibility is that the mother of Arthur was a daughter of Thomas Wayte who died soon after giving birth to the baby – so that no record of her or her first name survives. The fourth possibility, of course, is that Anstis got it wrong – that Edward's mistress was not the daughter of Thomas Wayte, but belonged to some other branch of the Wayte family.

Scofield and others have assumed that Arthur Wayte's mother, whom (following Buck's precedent) they identify with 'Elizabeth Lucy', was also the mother of Edward IV's illegitimate daughter, Elizabeth, who later became the wife of Sir Thomas Lumley. That couple appears to have living descendants. Scofield also suggests that this illegitimate daughter was born in about 1463/4.[19] If this were true it would mean that Edward IV must have met Miss Wayte in 1462. But in actuality there is absolutely no proof that Edward IV's daughter, Elizabeth Lumley and Arthur Wayte / Plantagenet had the same mother. Very little is known for certain about Edward's illegitimate daughter, but she is said by Leland to have married Thomas Lumley, and as can been seen from the Lumley pedigree, such a match, while not otherwise documented until a much later period, would have been possible chronologically, if the girl had been born in about 1463/4.[20] It is therefore possible – though by no means proved – that she might have been one of the bastards whom Edward IV was later alleged to have claimed that he had fathered in the autumn of 1464.

The problem is that, as we have seen, there is no genuine evidence that Edward IV claimed in the autumn of 1464 to have fathered bastards. Moreover, there is no evidence that he himself ever claimed – either in 1464 or later – to be the father of Arthur Wayte / Plantagenet. The fact that Arthur apparently bore the surname 'Wayte' as a child may well imply that he was initially brought up under the care of his mother's relatives at that period. Very significantly, for reasons which will be explored later, it was Henry VII and his family who brought Arthur – by then already an adult – into a degree of prominence as a royal bastard and established him with the surname 'Plantagenet' and the title Viscount Lisle (see below, chapter 28).

The itineraries of Edward IV which are published here show that the first possible occasion for a meeting between the king and a daughter of the Wayte family of Hampshire would probably have been in August 1461, when the young king was in the county of Hampshire. The next possible date at which the king was in the correct geographical area was August 1466. However, he also spent some time in and around Southampton in April 1470, and arguably that is the most likely time for the begetting of Arthur Wayte.

If the Wayte sexual relationship did take place in April 1470 that would mean that Arthur must actually have been born in January 1470/1 – at a time when his father had lost the English crown and was living in exile in the Low Countries. It would also imply that the relationship between Arthur's parents had been a very brief affair, at a time when the king found himself separated from his consort, Elizabeth Widville, and was on the move, trying to deal with troubles and threats. That would certainly explain logically why so little survives on record of Miss Wayte and her relationship with Edward IV. It would also account for the fact that Arthur only became formally recognised as a royal bastard – and allowed to adopt the surname Plantagenet – years later, when Edward IV was dead and Henry VII had founded a new ruling dynasty. Obviously, it would also mean that Miss Wayte cannot possibly have been the mother of Edward's alleged earlier bastard, the future Lady Lumley. But, as we have seen, no surviving contemporary source exists which names Miss Wayte as Lady Lumley's mother.

When Thomas Wayte, esquire, died, in 1482, his manors were inherited by a brother. As we have seen, only one living child is recorded as having been in existence at the time of his death. This was his bastard daughter, Alice, who was still unmarried in 1487, when her stepmother died. If Alice had been begotten when her father was in his mid-teens (c. 1455) she would have been old enough to have slept with Edward IV in April 1470. Alternatively, if the mother of Arthur had been a sister – or half-sister – of Alice, the individual in question must either have died or have married at some time after the birth of Arthur, but before the death of Thomas Wayte in 1482. As the surviving wills of the Talbot family show,[21] married daughters were often omitted from mention in the wills of their blood relatives, because as a result of their marriage they had, in effect, become part of their husband's family.

1. Edward IV's mother, Cecily Neville, Duchess of York. Redrawn by Geoffrey Wheeler after the Neville Book of Hours.

2. Edward IV's father, Richard, Duke of York. Redrawn by the author after BL MS Royal 15 E VI, fol. 3.

3. Edward IV's eldest sister, Anne of York, Duchess of Exeter. Nineteenth-century engraving of her funerary monument at St George's Chapel, Windsor.

4. Edward IV's paternal aunt, Isabel of York, Countess of Essex, from her funerary brass at Little Easton Church, Essex.

5. Edward IV's middle sister, Elizabeth of York, Duchess of Suffolk, from her alabaster tomb effigy at Wingfield Church, Suffolk.

6. Edward IV's youngest surviving sister, Margaret of York, Duchess of Burgundy: copy of her 1468 marriage portrait.

7. Jean II, King of France, great grandfather of both Charles VII and his queen. Copy of a contemporary portrait.

8. Charles VII, 'the Victorious', King of France, father of the first proposed brides of Edward, Earl of March. Nineteenth-century engraving after a fifteenth-century portrait.

9. Marie of Anjou, cousin and consort of Charles VII, and mother of the first proposed brides of Edward, Earl of March. Nineteenth–century engraving after a fifteenth-century portrait.

Right: 10. Jeanne of France, daughter of Charles VII, and later Duchess de Bourbon. Redrawn from her Book of Hours. Jeanne was the elder of the young Edward's potential French royal brides – the one favoured by his father, the Duke of York.

Below: 11. Madeleine of France, sister of Jeanne and later Princess of Viana. Redrawn from a contemporary portrait. Madeleine was the younger potential French royal bride – the one favoured for that role by her father, King Charles VII.

12. Edward IV as a young king, after the Rous Roll.

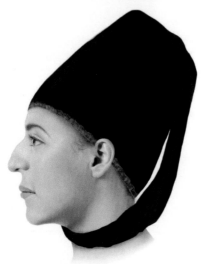

13. Eleanor Talbot? A facial reconstruction based on the CF2 skull found at the Norwich Carmel, commissioned by the author from Caroline Erolin, Medical and Forensic Artist, Centre for Anatomy and Human Identification, University of Dundee, in 2015.

14. Eleanor's sister, Elizabeth Talbot, Duchess of Norfolk. From her dedicatory window at Long Melford Church, Suffolk.

15. Eleanor's father, John Talbot, 1st Earl of Shrewsbury. Redrawn from his wife's Book of Hours, FitzWilliam MS 41-1950.f.2v.

16. Eleanor's mother, Margaret Beauchamp, 1st Countess of Shrewsbury. Redrawn from her Book of Hours, FitzWilliam MS 41-1950.f.2v.

17. Eleanor Beauchamp, Duchess of Somerset, the aunt of Eleanor Talbot, and the mother of Henry Beaufort, Duke of Somerset. From an effigy from the tomb of her father, at St Mary's Church, Warwick.

Right: 18. Possible image of Edward IV's male partner of 1463, the handsome but rather irascible Henry Beaufort, Duke of Somerset. Redrawn from a figure depicted in the Coventry Tapestry.

Below left: 19. Funerary brass of Thomas Wayte, grandfather of Arthur Wayte / Plantagenet, Viscount Lisle, from St Michael's Church, Stoke Charity, Hampshire. Brass rubbing by Dave Perry.

Below right: 20. The arms of Thomas Wayte.

21. Mary of Gueldres, Queen of Scotland. Redrawn from a contemporary image. She was proposed as the potential bride of Edward IV in 1462.

22. Bona of Savoy. Redrawn from a contemporary portrait. She was proposed as Edward's potential royal bride in 1464.

23. King Edward IV in about 1470, from the chancel arch of Barnard Castle Church.

24. Elizabeth Widville, Lady Grey. Copy of a contemporary portrait.

Left: 25. Elizabeth Lambert, Mistress Shore. From her brass memorial at Hinxworth Church, Herts.

Below left: 26. William Shore, (annulled) first husband of Elizabeth Lambert. From his alabaster funerary monument.

Below right: 27. 'Jane Shore', a fantasy image of this imaginary character, engraved by F. Bartolozzi R. A., and published in 1807.

Right: 28. Edward IV. Redrawn from an image produced in the 1470s.

Below: 29. Anne Mowbray, Duchess of York and Norfolk, daughter-in-law of Edward IV and niece of Eleanor Talbot. Facial Reconstruction by Amy Thornton, Centre for Anatomy and Human Identification, University of Dundee.

30. Possibly the last woman visited by Edward IV, in September 1482: Our Lady of Walsingham.

31. Edward V.

Above: 32. Images of Arthur Wayte / Plantagenet, left: redrawn from the 1534 Black Book of the Garter and right: an engraving based on the 1534 painting, which was published by J. Anstis in 1724. The original image appears to show a younger man than the later engraving.

Right: 33. The arms of Arthur Wayte / Plantagenet, Viscount Lisle. Courtesy of the Society of Antiquaries.

Below: 34. Arms of Isabel Mylbery, illegitimate daughter of Edward IV.

35. 'Richard of England', a possible illegitimate son of Edward IV. Redrawn from the contermporary portrait at Arras.

36. Elizabeth of York, the eldest daughter of Edward IV and Elizabeth Widville. A nineteenth-century engraving based on a contemporary portrait.

20

1470–1471: WINTER IN EXILE

As was mentioned briefly in connection with Miss Wayte's story, in 1469, 1470 and 1471 Edward IV was, at times, forcibly separated from Elizabeth Widville. In 1469 he was for a time a virtual prisoner in the hands of the leading anti-Widville campaigners, his cousin the Earl of Warwick and his brother the Duke of Clarence. Subsequently those two were forced to flee to the European mainland, whereupon Warwick adopted the role of a Lancastrian supporter and brought about the brief restoration of King Henry VI. As a result, Edward IV and his loyal brother the Duke of Gloucester then found themselves forced into exile in the Low Countries.

Ironically, however, not only did Edward's forced separation from Elizabeth Widville make no significant break to the then regular pattern of conceptions by the latter of royal children, but it also coincided with her most significant pregnancy – the one which finally resulted in the delivery not of yet another royal daughter but of a son. It seems, therefore, that his period of serious trouble may have been the very period which started producing sons for Edward IV. In November 1470, while the king himself was in exile in the Low Countries and Elizabeth Widville was in sanctuary at Westminster Abbey, the latter gave birth to the son whom she named Edward after his father, and who was subsequently proclaimed Prince of Wales. As for Miss Wayte, it may have been about two months after the birth of Edward, Prince of Wales, that she gave birth to little Arthur Wayte, an initially insignificant and unrecognised royal bastard who would have been born while his father was still out of the country. What is more, that may not be the end of the story of royal sons at that period.

Edward IV and his brother Richard, Duke of Gloucester, had fled from England on 29 September 1470. The dethroned king

> fled straight to Holland. At this time the Easterlings were enemies of both the English and the French and had several warships at sea. The English were very frightened of them and not without cause, for they were good fighters. ... The Easterlings espied the ships in which the king was fleeing from a great distance and seven or eight ships began to give chase. But he was too far ahead of them and reached Holland or rather a little further up the coat because he landed close to a small town called Alkmaar in Frisia [just north of Amsterdam]. He anchored his ship because the tide was out, and they could not enter the harbour, but they came as close to the town as they could. The Easterlings did the same, anchoring close to him with the intention of boarding him at the next tide. ... [But] by chance my lord of Gruthuse, the duke of Burgundy's governor in Holland, was then at the place where King Edward wanted to disembark. He was immediately told about this, for they had landed some men, and about the danger they were in from the Easterlings. Straight away he sent word to the Easterlings forbidding them to attack Edward, and went aboard the ship the king was in to welcome him. Edward then landed together with fifteen hundred men, including the duke of Gloucester, his brother, who later became King Richard.[1]

By 11 October the two brothers were in The Hague.[2]

The small group of loyal supporters who had accompanied them probably included the Portuguese Jew Duarte Brandão. Duarte had first come to England in 1468. There, he had converted to Christianity. The English king, whose name he subsequently shared, acted as his godfather. In England Brandão's name was anglicised as Edward Brampton (or Brandon). As we shall see, the possible presence of Brampton amongst the small party of Yorkist supporters in Flanders in the winter of 1470 may have been significant.

Edward IV and his brother Gloucester spent the winter of 1470 as guests of Louis de Gruuthuse, the governor (*stadtholder*) of The Hague. Gruuthuse, whose family came from Brugge, was already known to Edward, because he had helped to arrange the wedding of the king's sister Margaret to Charles the Bold. Moreover, he was related by marriage to the Scottish and French royal families.

Since the Duke of Gloucester was still unmarried, while his elder brother had been forcibly separated from Elizabeth Widville, either of them might have found local erotic companionship by taking on one of the women in the Gruuthuse household as his mistress during the winter of 1470–71. As a result an illegitimate English royal son may have been born in the Low Countries in about September 1471 – after his father's return to England.

A little evidence for this hypothesis survives, both in the royal household accounts of the 1470s and in some versions of the story of the young man who subsequently emerged as a Yorkist claimant to the English throne in the 1490s. The claimant in question called himself 'Richard of England', and put himself forward as the surviving younger son of Edward IV and Elizabeth Widville – Richard of Shrewsbury, Duke of York. However, his opponent, Henry VII, claimed that he was a young Fleming whose real name was Pierre Osbek / Werbecque. He is generally referred to by English historians as 'Perkin Warbeck'.

Bernard André, a French priest who became one of Henry VII's historians and who was appointed tutor to his son Arthur, Prince of Wales, later set out his version of the story of 'Perkin Warbeck' as follows:

> They feigned that a certain Pierre of Tournai, brought up by a certain Jew named Edward and subsequently sponsored as a godfather by King Edward and reared in this nation, was the younger son of King Edward IV and pretended that he had grown up in various nations.[3]

It is significant that André reports that 'Richard of England' had been brought up by 'a certain Jew named Edward', for Edward is not, of course, a Jewish first name, and the only fifteenth-century Jew who is known to have borne that Christian name is the Portuguese Jew Edward Brampton. And although André's text leaves it a little unclear to whom he is referring as Edward IV's godson, Edward Brampton certainly held that role.

It appears, therefore, that 'Richard of England / Perkin Warbeck' was believed by at least one significant figure in the entourage of Henry VII to have been born in the Low Countries, but brought up in England. Apparently it was also André's understanding that Edward Brampton played some significant role in the boy's upbringing in this country. So could it have been Brampton who, in about 1472, had been sent to the Low Countries to bring a royal bastard, engendered during the winter exile of 1470–71, to the homeland of the boy's father for recognition of some kind? It is also an interesting fact that Brampton fled from England in 1485, when the Yorkist cause was defeated. He then returned initially to the Low Countries (though he later went back to Portugal). Moreover,

'Richard of England / Perkin Warbeck' seems possibly to have been with him. If the boy had been brought up in England, as André tells us, then perhaps it was Edward Brampton who took him out of this country when Richard III was killed at Bosworth, as a kind of rescue.

It remains unclear precisely how, or when, or where, Brampton became acquainted with 'Richard of England / Perkin Warbeck'. Indeed, one surviving seventeenth-century account makes the incredible suggestion that Brampton himself was 'Richard's father.[4] However, Brampton may have been personally responsible for the boy's transportation from England to the Low Countries in the autumn of 1485. If so, Brampton must obviously have been aware of the boy's true identity. He would also have assumed some kind of responsibility for him from August 1483 – which fits with the surviving evidence regarding the subsequent Yorkist pretender.

Since Edward IV and Richard Duke of Gloucester had been in exile in the Low Countries from October 1470 until the end of February 1470/1, either one of them could potentially have taken a local mistress there, and made her pregnant. It is also possible that the girl in question may have been related somehow to the Osbek / Werbecque family of Tournai. As a result, a son may have been born, in The Hague, or in Brugge, in about August or September 1471. Curiously, the surviving alleged confession of 'Richard of England / Perkin Warbeck' actually suggests that he was initially taken to have been a son of one of Edward IV's brothers. People in Ireland are said to have identified him either as the legitimate son of the Duke of Clarence, or as a bastard son of Richard III.

> The citizens of Cork ... insisted on doing him honour as a member of the Royal House of York. At first they made him out to be the son of Clarence [Edward, Earl of Warwick / 'King Edward VI'], who had been in Ireland before; but he refused to acknowledge it and took oath to the contrary before John le Wellen, Mayor of Cork. Then they said he was a bastard of King Richard III; but this, too, he denied.[5]

The fact that 'Richard of England' reportedly denied being the legitimate son of the Duke of Clarence or a bastard son of Richard III, but did not deny that he was a son of Edward IV, may be significant. Evidence from the accounts of King Edward IV undoubtedly prove that, in the 1470s, the royal household included an acknowledged bastard son of the reigning sovereign. Nothing whatever is known about the child in question, but in 1472 clothes were ordered for 'the Lord Bastard'. The bill was paid in

1477. First there is a list in the accounts of clothes ordered for 'my Lord the Prince' – the son born by Elizabeth Widville in 1470. This is followed by a second list, as follows:

Item, for my Lord the Bastard
 Item, for making of a coat of black velvet 5s.
 Item, for making of a gown of black   2s.
 Item, for making of a gown of russet   2s.[6]

Scofield – followed by a number of other writers – assumed that this had to be a reference to Arthur Wayte. However, there is absolutely no surviving evidence that Edward IV ever formally recognised Arthur Wayte during his own reign. It was only later, in the reigns of Henry VII and Henry VIII, that Arthur appears to have been accorded formal recognition as a bastard son of Edward IV.

Curiously, André's account of the same slightly later period seems to have acknowledged that Edward IV gave some kind of recognition to 'Richard of England / Perkin Warbeck', who had been brought to him by Edward Brampton. Could it be, then, that 'the Lord Bastard' for whom the king was providing clothing in the 1470s, and who was being brought up in the royal household, was none other than the subsequent claimant to the throne of England – a bastard son of King Edward IV, who had been fathered in the Low Countries during the winter exile of 1470–71?

One further intriguing piece of evidence in respect of 'Richard of England / Perkin Warbeck' is his linguistic background. Strangely, Henry VII and his supporters never cited linguistic evidence against the alleged 'Perkin Warbeck' in an attempt to prove his birth and upbringing in the Low Countries. Yet, obviously, if he was born and brought up there, either French or Dutch (Flemish) would have been his native language – whether it was the former or the latter would have depended upon the native language of his unknown mother, and upon precisely where in the Low Countries he had been brought up as a child. But in either case, it should have been easy to demonstrate to the public that the claimant to the throne was not a native speaker of English.

The fact that this evidence was never cited strongly suggests that 'Richard of England / Perkin Warbeck' had been brought up in England (even though he may have been born in the Low Countries), and that he was therefore, in effect, a native speaker of English. In other words, the linguistic evidence appears to back André's account that the boy in question had been brought up here. Moreover, the fact that 'Richard of England' appears to have had some knowledge of the royal household of

Edward IV would certainly be consistent with the possibility that he was none other than King Edward's 'Lord Bastard'.

Of course, another possible explanation would be that the pretender was none other than the person he claimed to be, namely the second son of Edward IV and Elizabeth Widville – Richard of Shrewsbury, Duke of York. It is difficult to resolve this issue now, and it would also have been difficult when he made his claim to the throne. After all, in 1490 there would only have been a difference of a maximum of two years between the age of 'the Lord Bastard' (nineteen, if conceived during the winter exile) and the age of Richard of Shrewsbury (seventeen). Since 'Richard of England / Perkin Warbeck' was an unusually tall young man, it must have been difficult to determine, just from his appearance, which age was correct. Another relevant piece of information is, of course, the notable physical resemblance between the 1490s pretender and the late King Edward IV, which clearly implied that the former was closely related to Edward, and may well have been one of the latter's sons.

However, irrespective of whether or not he is to be identified with the later 'Richard of England / Perkin Warbeck', the evidence of the royal household accounts shows very clearly that, in the 1470s, Edward IV genuinely had recognised, and was bringing up, a bastard son of his. If the child in question was not 'Richard of England', there appears to be no surviving subsequent evidence of the existence of 'the Lord Bastard', so that what became of him would then remain a mystery.

21

1471–1476: ITINERARY

1471/2
JANUARY
Westminster, Brentford (Middx)
['Bramefford'],[1] Windsor Castle,
and Westminster[2]

FEBRUARY
Westminster[3]

MARCH
REGNAL YEAR 12
Westminster and Windsor Castle[4]

1472 (age 30; regnal year 12)
MARCH
Windsor Castle[5]
Chelsea[6]

MAY
Windsor Castle, Westminster, and
Guildford[7]

JUNE
Windsor Castle, Greenwich,
Westminster, and the manor of
Kennington[8]

Westminster, and the manor of
Kennington[9]

JULY
Westminster, Canterbury and
Kennington[10]

AUGUST
Kennington, Windsor Castle, and
Westminster[11]
Westminster, and Windsor Castle[12]

SEPTEMBER
Westminster, and Windsor Castle[13]

OCTOBER
Westminster[14]
Windsor Castle and Hertford
Castle[15]
Westminster[16]

NOVEMBER
Westminster[17]

DECEMBER
Westminster[18]

The manor of Guildford[19]
Southampton[20]
The manor of Sheen[21]

1472/3
JANUARY
Sheen, and Windsor Castle[22]
Westminster[23]
Sheen[24]
Westminster, London and
Chelmsford[25]

FEBRUARY
Westminster[26]

MARCH
Westminster[27]
REGNAL YEAR 13
Westminster[28]

1473 (age 31; regnal year)
MARCH
Westminster[29]

APRIL
Westminster[30]
Edward IV left London, and was
riding towards Northampton[31]
St Alban's Abbey, and
Northampton[32]

MAY
Leicester Castle, Nottingham,
Lichfield, and Ludlow[33]
Coventry, Killingworth Castle,
and Leicester Castle[34]
? Fotheringhay Castle[35]

JULY
Leicester Castle, Nottingham Castle,
Stamford, and Fotheringhay Castle[36]

AUGUST
Liddington (Wilts.), Shrewsbury,
and Lichfield[37]

SEPTEMBER
Lichfield, Burton-upon-Trent
Abbey, and Nottingham
Castle[38]

OCTOBER
Westminster (Parliament
reopened)[39]

NOVEMBER
Westminster[40]

DECEMBER
Westminster[41]

1473/4
JANUARY
Sheen[42]
Westminster and Berkhamsted[43]

FEBRUARY
Westminster, Chelsea, and
Windsor Castle[44]

MARCH
REGNAL YEAR 14
Berkhamsted Castle, Leicester
Castle, and Nottingham
Castle[45]

1474 (age 32; regnal year 14)
MARCH
Derby, and Burton-upon-Trent
Abbey[46]

APRIL
Nottingham Castle[47]

MAY
Coventry[48]
Daventry[49]
Westminster[50]

JUNE
Westminster[51]

JULY
Westminster[52]

AUGUST
Westminster, and Windsor
Castle[53]
Woburn[54]
The City of London, the manor of
Guildford, and Farnham[55]

SEPTEMBER
The manor of Woodstock,
Kenilworth Castle, and Nottingham
Castle[56]

OCTOBER
Kenilworth Castle, the city of
Worcester [*Wigorniensis*], Gloucester,
Bristol, and the town and abbey of
Cirencester[57]
Norwich[58]

NOVEMBER
Kenilworth Castle, and Bedford[59]
London[60]
Westminster[61]

DECEMBER
Bury St Edmund's Abbey, and the
manor of Westhorpe[62]
Westminster[63]
Coventry[64]

1474/5
JANUARY
Nottingham Castle, Lincoln, and
Westminster[65]

FEBRUARY
Westminster[66]

MARCH
Westminster[67]
REGNAL YEAR 15
Westminster[68]
Gravesend[69]
Sandwich[70]
Canterbury, and Westminster[71]

1475 (age 33; regnal year 15)
MARCH
Westminster[72]

APRIL
Westminster, and Greenwich[73]

MAY
Greenwich[74]
Westminster, and Canterbury[75]

JUNE
Westminster, Canterbury, and
Sandwich[76]

JULY
Sandwich, and Dover Castle[77]
Calais[78]
The Castle of Guisnes, and Fawconbergh[79]

AUGUST
St Quentin
Lihons-en-Santerre (nr. Peronne)
camp outside Amiens[80]
Picquigny (met Louis XI)[81]

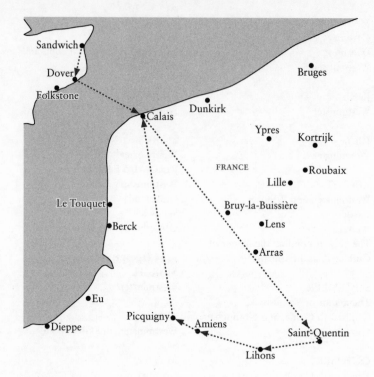

SEPTEMBER
Calais[82]
Westminster[83]

OCTOBER
Westminster, and Windsor Castle[84]

NOVEMBER
Westminster, the manor of
Guildford, Farnham, the manor of
Farringdon, and Winchester [*the
city of Winton*][85]

DECEMBER
The cities of Winchester and
Salisbury; Westminster[86]

1475/6
JANUARY
Greenwich, and London[87]
Westminster[88]

FEBRUARY
Westminster[89]
Windsor Castle[90]

MARCH
REGNAL YEAR 16
Buckden[91]
Windsor Castle[92]

22

1470?: THE CONFUSING THIRD ELIZABETH

For strange reasons, a fifteenth-century lady whose real name was Elizabeth Lambert has gone down in history under the partly invented name of 'Jane Shore'. She did indeed bear the married surname of Shore legally for approximately eight years of her life, from about 1468 until 1476. Subsequently, it seems that she continued to be known as 'Mistress Shore' until her second marriage, at the end of 1483 or early in 1484, even though legally that name had become incorrect because her marriage had been annulled. It is certain, however, that she was never known as 'Jane' during her lifetime. That first name was invented for her almost a century after her death by the Jacobean playwrights Beaumont and Fletcher. It was merely their theatrical solution to the practical problem caused for them by the fact that her name was only preserved as 'Mistress Shore' (no recorded first name) – at a time when they needed her to appear on stage as a character in their 1609 play *Knight of the Burning Pestle*.

In one respect Elizabeth Lambert (Shore) is unique. Of the four alleged mistresses of King Edward IV, she is the only individual whose existence appears to be reasonably well documented. Unlike 'Elizabeth Lucy', she was definitely a real person, and unlike 'Mistress Wayte' and Catherine de Clarington, we have solid evidence in respect of her family, and even a little evidence regarding her whereabouts. If her alleged relationship with the king ever truly existed, it must have dated during his second reign, and it would presumably have begun some time after his restoration to the throne in 1471. Nevertheless, the story of her alleged relationship with Edward IV as it has been passed down to the present day is just as completely lacking in contemporary evidence – and just as full of later mythology – as are the stories of the king's other so-called mistresses.

According to popular accounts it is normally claimed that Edward IV was a notoriously unfaithful man, who simply cast off each one of his girlfriends as soon as he had had enough of her and had found someone else. To those who believe in this piece of Edward IV mythology, it must seem very strange and unusual that Elizabeth Lambert reportedly remained very close to him for some years, from the 1470s until he died, in April 1483. In fact, however, as has already been observed, not a shred of real evidence exists that Edward IV ever had (and then cast off) a continuous succession of girlfriends. Nor, as we shall see shortly, is there any genuine contemporary evidence of his alleged relationship with Elizabeth Lambert.

In reality, Edward appears to have maintained his genuine, known and documented relationships. Thus he remained considerate in his treatment of Eleanor Talbot – and her former father-in-law, Lord Sudeley – until Eleanor's death in 1468. Edward also remained close to Henry, Duke of Somerset, until the latter deserted him and once again sided with his enemies; and he remained committed to Elizabeth Widville, despite the problems which she and her unpopular family caused him, fathering children by her on a regular basis throughout their lives together. When compared to the clear documentary evidence of Edward IV's relationship with the only two women who can be proved to have been his partners, his allegedly well-maintained relationship with Elizabeth Lambert would actually not have been in any way unusual, if the later accounts of it were true. But although there is genuine contemporary evidence of Elizabeth Lambert's existence, of her bloodline and of her marriages, there is actually not one shred of genuine contemporary evidence of her alleged relationship with the king.

Elizabeth was the only daughter of John Lambert, a London mercer, and his wife, Amy Marshall. She had three brothers, one of whom eventually became the parish priest of St Leonard's Church, Foster Lane, near Aldgate.

On the basis of her known chronology (see below), the girl was probably born in about 1453. It has often been claimed that she was born in about

The Lambert Family

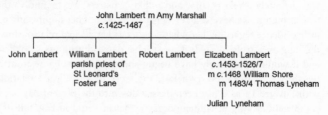

The Lambert Family.

The Church of St Leonard, Foster Lane, redrawn from an Elizabethan map of London.

1445, but no evidence has been presented to substantiate that statement. During her later life Elizabeth maintained a close relationship with her parents for as long as they lived. Her father was an alderman, so he must have owned goods worth at least £1,000. He was a lively, assertive, and even difficult man, as is shown by surviving records of his litigations. However, he was on the right side politically, because his wealth was used to help to finance the cause of Edward IV. Nevertheless, on one occasion he seems to have crossed swords with the goldsmith Edmund Shaa. It is alleged that, some years later, when he was Lord Mayor of London (and Edward IV was dead), Shaa took revenge on his old adversary's daughter by making her do public penance as a harlot. However, the real motivation for that move may have been Elizabeth's relationships with men who, by that time, had become politically dubious (see below).

Elizabeth Lambert married William Shore in about 1468, when she was about fifteen years old. Her husband was then in his early thirties – an age difference which was by no means unusual at the period. As has already been noted, similar age differences existed between Eleanor Talbot and her first husband. William Shore had been born in Derby in about 1436. In 1451–52 he was apprenticed to John Rankyn, citizen and mercer of London, and his apprenticeship may have included a period in Ghent.[1] He had a sister who married John Agard of Foston in the early 1470s. John Agard had been married before and had a son, Ralph, by his first wife.[2] This step-nephew was later associated with William Shore. Shore was by this time both a mercer of London and a merchant adventurer, and was developing business connections in East Anglia.[3] During the 1470s Lord Howard apparently became his patron. There is one certain reference, and one probable reference, to William in the Howard accounts for 1481.[4]

Sadly, William Shore's marriage with Elizabeth Lambert did not prove to be a happy one. According to her later petition to the Pope, she lived with Shore for three years, but never became his sexual partner. This was frustrating for a girl who apparently wanted to have children. She initially petitioned the Bishop of London for an annulment of her marriage on grounds of non-consummation. Her case was later referred to the Pope. The sovereign pontiff handled the matter through the intermediary of three bishops. No doubt a commission of suitably experienced local women was then appointed to carry out in London, on behalf of the Church, the physical examination of the husband which was required in such cases. The test would have sought to establish William Shore's ability (or lack thereof) to achieve an erection when stimulated by females. Such testing was required by the Church to clearly prove whether or not the husband possessed the physical ability to consummate his marriage.[5] Evidently Shore must have failed this somewhat embarrassing test, because in due course his marriage with Elizabeth was annulled. For William, one outcome of this was that, having been formally declared impotent, he then found himself banned from any subsequent attempt to remarry. But perhaps he was one of those men who preferred partners of his own sex.

The Pope formally declared the marriage of 'Elizabeth Lambert, alias Schore' null and void on 1 March 1476, on the grounds that it had never been consummated. Although Elizabeth had cohabited with William Shore

> for the lawful time ... he is so frigid and impotent that she, being desirous of being a mother and having offspring, requested the official of London over and over again to cite the said William before him to answer her ... seeing that the said official refused to do so, she appealed to the apostolic see.[6]

Of course, the Church courts moved slowly and ponderously. It is therefore probable that the outcome which Elizabeth desired had taken some time to achieve. She may have launched her petition several years before, in the early 1470s. It has been claimed by later historians that this had possibly been at about the same time as she began her liaison with the king, but of course that is merely an assumption on their part. The fact remains that, given that her marriage to William Shore was officially set aside as null and void (meaning that, as a marriage, it had never really existed), it is somewhat ironic that Elizabeth should generally be known to history by *William's* surname rather than the one she was born with.

Curiously, unlike the name of Elizabeth Lambert, the name of William Shore is recorded in connection with Edward IV in contemporary documents preserved with the patent rolls, the close rolls and elsewhere. In the king's fourteenth regnal year (1474/5), William made a significant loan to the monarch in connection with the latter's planned expedition to France.[7] On 4 December 1476 Edward IV bestowed his protection on William Shore and his servants in respect of all Shore's lands and property, both in England and elsewhere.[8]

Shore also figures in records which associate him with the king's distant cousin Lord Howard. Described there as a merchant (*mercator*), Shore first figures in the Colchester court rolls towards the end of 1476, when he appeared at the town's Moot Hall to prosecute John Williamson in respect of a debt of 26s 8d.[9] Conducting the case for Shore was the Colchester lawyer Richard Hervy, who may have been a relative of John Hervy, Colchester's town clerk in the 1480s, and who is known to have acted as a lawyer for Lord Howard.[10] Although this is the earliest surviving record of Shore's name in the Colchester court records, the fact that he alleged that a debt was owed to him by a Colchester man implies that this was not Shore's first connection with that town. The following spring (on Thursday 19 March 1476/7) William appears again in the court rolls. Described this time as 'citizen and mercer of London', he is associated with Ralph Agard, gentleman, in the prosecution of Roger More of Colchester for another debt.[11]

On 11 May 1477 the Colchester attorney John Algood senior and his wife Alianora issued a quitclaim to Lord Howard, Sir William Pyrton,

The old Moot Hall, Colchester.

William Shore, citizen and mercer of London, Ralph Agard, gentleman, John Daubeney and Richard Hervy, and granted 'to the use of William Shore ... all those lands and tenements [... &c] called Algoods, formerly Bulbekkes in West Donyland', just south of Colchester.[12] Pyrton was a well-known member of Lord Howard's circle. Agard was Shore's step-nephew, and John Daubeney was one of Shore's apprentices.[13] Hervy, as we have seen, was a Colchester lawyer. It seems that Shore was acquiring a *pied-à-terre* in the vicinity of the town. There were later difficulties over this transfer, however, and Shore took the case to Chancery.[14] The Lord Chancellor referred the case to the Abbot of Colchester and to John Sulyard, a noted East Anglian lawyer and the Colchester *legisperitus* at this time. The final outcome is unknown, but no land in Essex is mentioned in Shore's will of 21 November 1494.

There are various other mentions of William Shore in the Colchester records, including:

Roger More of Colchester, miller: licence to agree with William Shore citizen and mercer of London and Roger Agard, gentleman.[15]

William Shore, citizen and mercer of London, otherwise merchant, *versus* John Page of Mersey, husbandman and merchant, in the custody of the serjeant for debt of £10. Shore appeared in person and stated that on 7 March 1476 in the South Ward an obligatory bond was agreed, due for payment on 4 February. The bond was not paid. Shore claimed 100s. damages and produced the bond, which the defendant could not deny.[16]

William Shore, citizen and merchant of London, *versus* Robert Hill, John Sticheford and Roger West, for trespass against the protection of the Lord King.[17] The three defendants failed to appear and were fined.[18]

John Deth: licence to agree with William Shore, merchant (breach of contract).[19]

In April 1481, Dalamar, Lord Howard's steward, recorded a payment of £3 13s 4d to 'Master Shore' for a tun of wine.[20] William Shore is known to have had other commercial dealings with Lord Howard which involved wine. On 19 September 1481 Shore and others chartered two of Howard's ships, the *Barbara* and the *Paker*, for a wine run to Bordeaux. The two vessels sailed from Harwich, and brought back a total of sixty-four tuns of wine.[21]

In 1482 William Parker, one of Howard's shipmasters, brought ten tuns of Gascony wine belonging to Shore into Ipswich. In this year Shore accounted for 33 per cent of Ipswich's wine imports. At the same time he was exporting other goods, including English woollen cloth, through the port of Ipswich.[22] Shore's influence in East Anglia survived the Yorkist collapse and the death of John Howard. In November 1485 he was appointed a searcher of ships in the ports of Ipswich and Yarmouth, and 'on 13 January 1490 he delivered to the bailiffs of Colchester a copy of a proclamation under Henry VII's signet requiring them to proclaim at the next market that all creditors of the king's purveyors from the first day of his reign to 1 October last' should present their documents for payment.[23] In all probability this referred to outstanding debts incurred during the king's visit to Colchester in 1487.

The precise date of William Shore's death is not known, but he was buried by his sister's family in their parish church at Scropton, where his tomb, with its incised alabaster effigy of him, survives (see plate 26).[24]

How and when – and even whether – Shore's wife, Elizabeth Lambert, met Edward IV is completely unknown. Such an encounter could well have come about through her first husband, who, as we have seen, undoubtedly had links with both Edward IV himself and with his distant cousin Sir John, Lord Howard (later Duke of Norfolk).[25] However, the evidence which asserts that she then became Edward IV's mistress (like the evidence which claims the existence of 'Elizabeth Lucy') is exclusively due to the later writing of Thomas More. Indeed, this point has been noted by earlier writers, including Rosemary Horrox, who produced the entry on Elizabeth Lambert (Shore) for the *Oxford Dictionary of National Biography*. Curiously, however, while recognising that no contemporary evidence exists to prove that Elizabeth had been Edward IV's mistress, Rosemary Horrox appears not to question the basic veracity of that later allegation (which she correctly attributes to Thomas More).

Nevertheless, the truth is that no documentary evidence survives from the reign of Edward IV himself – or from the reigns of his two immediate successors, Edward V and Richard III – which refers to Elizabeth as the king's mistress. According to More's later account (which is based on no known evidence), Elizabeth Lambert's alleged relationship with the king, who was eleven years her senior, reportedly lasted until Edward's death in 1483. Nevertheless, the children she supposedly desired to produce continued to elude her until the time of her second marriage. Of course, More's account is far from contemporary, and there is no genuine evidence to substantiate anything of what More claims in respect of Elizabeth's alleged role as a royal mistress.

The only existing contemporary evidence we have in respect of Elizabeth Lambert comprises the record of the dissolution of her marriage,[26] together with the later references to her imprisonment in the summer of 1483 and her subsequent remarriage. As we have seen, in respect of her imprisonment in 1483, it has been claimed that, after the death of Edward IV, Elizabeth found herself subject to the vengeance of her father's old adversary Edmund Shaa. Unluckily for her, Shaa was then Lord Mayor of London, and he imprisoned her at Ludgate and made her do public penance for her immorality. However, there is no surviving evidence that the immorality in question related to the late king. As we shall see, the contemporary accounts state very clearly that it referred to Elizabeth's alleged relationships with Lord Hastings and the Marquess of Dorset (see below).

First there is mention of her imprisonment in a surviving letter written on 21 June 1483 by Simon Stalloworth:

> Mastres Chore is in prisone: what schall happyne hyr I knowe nott.[27]

Fuller details are provided by the Great Chronicle of London, which records that

> shortly afftyr [Richard III's coronation, which took place on 6 July] was a woman namyd – Shoore that before days, after the common ffame, the lord Chambyrlayn [Lord Hastings] held, contrary his honour, called to a Reconnyng ffor part of his goodys & othyr thyngys, In soo much that alle hyr movablys were attached by the Shyrevys of London, and she lastly as a common harlot put to opyn penaunce, ffor the lyfe that she ledd w^t the said lord hastyngys & othir grete astatys.[28]

One other aristocrat with whom Elizabeth Lambert was involved was Edward IV's stepson (and Lord Hastings' son-in-law), Thomas Grey, Marquess of Dorset. On 23 October 1483, in Leicester, Richard III issued a proclamation denouncing the Marquess of Dorset for holding 'the unshameful and mischievous woman called Shore's wife in adultery'.[29] However, it is very notable that, while the Great Chronicle refers specifically to Elizabeth's immoral relationship with Lord Hastings and other noblemen, and Richard III's proclamation refers to her relationship with the Marquess of Dorset, neither of these sources asserts at any point that she had been the mistress of King Edward IV.

After doing public penance, Elizabeth was released on the order of the new king, Richard III, who gave her into her father's custody, pending an enquiry into whether or not she was lawfully able to marry Richard's solicitor, Thomas Lynom, who was in love with her. The king's letter reads as follows:

By the king

Righte Reverend fadre in god etc. Signifying unto you that it is shewed unto us that our servant and Sollicitor Thomas Lynom merveillously blynded and abused with the late [= former] wife of William Shore nowe being in Ludgate by our commandement hathe made contract of matrimony with hir, as it is said, and entendethe to our fulle grete mervaile to procede totheffect of the same. We for many causes wold be sory that hee soo shuld be disposed. Pray you therefore to sende for him. And in that ye goodly may exhorte and sture hyme to the contrary. And if ye finde him utterly set forto marye hur and noon otherwise wolbe advertised, than if it may stande with the lawe of the churche we be content, the tyme of marriage deferred to ourcommyng next to London, that upon sufficient suertie founde for hure good abering ye doo sende for hure keper and discharge hym of our saidcommaundement by warrant of thise, committing hure to the Rule and guyding of hur fader or any other by your discrecion in the meane season yeven etc.

To the Righte Reverend fadre in god etc The Bisshop of Lincolne, our Chancellor.[30]

In due course it was found that, according to the law of the Church, Elizabeth was indeed free to marry. The wedding duly took place – and was perhaps attended by Richard III – either late in 1483 or early in 1484 (modern calendar), when the king was back in London.[31]

Despite the fact that Richard III seems to have treated her kindly, as his surviving letter regarding her indicates, Thomas More asserted later that Richard had accused Elizabeth Lambert of witchcraft against him. More's account claims that Richard accused her of association, in respect of her alleged dabbling in black magic, with her namesake, Elizabeth Widville. If she had indeed been Edward IV's mistress, the logical assumption appears to be that Elizabeth Widville would have regarded her as a rival and potential enemy, not as an ally. But again – as is the case with Elizabeth Lambert and Edward IV – not a shred of genuine evidence survives to show what (if any) real relationship existed between the two Elizabeths.

23

1475: THE ROYAL WILL

The known children of Edward IV and Elizabeth Widville				
Name	Age	Born	Died	Married
Elizabeth of York	37	11 Feb. 1465/6	11 Feb. 1502/3	Henry VII
Mary	14	11 Aug. 1467	23 May 1482	
Cecily of York	38	20 Mar. 1468/9	24 Aug. 1507	1. Ralph Scrope; 2. John Welles; 3. Thomas Kyme or Keme.
Edward	12?	4 Nov. 1470	22 Jul. 1483?	(betrothed 1480 to Anne of Brittany)
Margaret	8 mths	10 April 1472	11 Dec. 1472	
Richard of Shrewsbury	??	17 Aug. 1473	?	1. Anne Mowbray
20 JUNE 1475 EDWARD IV MADE HIS WILL AT SANDWICH				
Anne	36	2 Nov. 1475	23 Nov. 1511	Thomas Howard, 3rd Duke of Norfolk.
George Plantagenet	2	Mar. 1476/7	Mar. 1478/9	

| Catherine of York | 48 | 14 Aug. 1479 | 15 Nov. 1527 | William Courtenay |
| Bridget of York | 37 | 10 Nov. 1480 | 1517 | nun |

On 20 June 1475 Edward IV drafted his will, a copy of which still survives (see below for the full text). The king did this at Sandwich, just before he set off on his expedition to France. Presumably the main reason why the will was drafted (or possibly redrafted and updated) at that point in time was because the king wished to take account of the fact that if things went wrong in France he could conceivably be killed.

In respect of the living members of his family, Edward mentions in the will his own mother; his cousin the Cardinal Archbishop of Canterbury; the mother of his children, Elizabeth Widville; and all their living children, namely Edward, Prince of Wales, Richard, Duke of York, Elizabeth, Mary and Cecily. For obvious reasons, mention of their daughter, Margaret, who had died young two and a half years previously, is omitted from the will. There is also no mention of any of the king's sisters (all of whom were married, and had therefore become the legal responsibility of their spouses). Nor is there any mention of either of his surviving brothers, both of whom had already been provided for by the king in other ways.

The will is very explicit in respect of Elizabeth Widville. She is referred to as 'oure derrest wiff the Quene', 'oure said derrest and moost entierly beloved wiff Elizabeth the Quene' and 'oure said derrest Wiff in whoom we moost singulerly put oure trust'. Moreover, the king names her as the first of his listed executors. It is obvious, therefore, that in 1475 the relationship of the couple was still meaningful, and that Elizabeth had influence on Edward, who appears both to have trusted her, and to have recognised her as a capable woman who had a good brain and was well-versed in the handling of the royal business. Edward's relationship with Elizabeth, as it emerges from the wording of the will, raises serious questions as to whether he could ever have been sexually involved with other women in any serious or long-term manner following his acknowledgement of his commitment to Elizabeth Widville. It is possible, of course (given her clear influence upon the king), that it was Elizabeth Widville herself who had made sure that his will referred to her in clear and unequivocal terms. After all, Edward IV was writing it at about the time when, as we know from another source, she was deeply concerned about the question marks which surrounded her royal marriage (see above, chapter 17).

From the wording of the will it appears that the king definitely expected his younger son, the little Duke of York, to live. This implies that the boy in question was a strong and healthy child, even though he was still just under two years of age at the time when the will was made. Typically, therefore, the king generally states without reservation what should happen 'after oure said son the Duk of York comme to the said age of xvj. Yeres'. For example,

> *after that oure son Richard Duk of York come to the age of xvj. yeres* thay make estate unto him of the Castell Lordshippes Manoirs lands and tenements of Fodrynghay Staunford and Grantham with thair appertenances and of all other Manoirs lands and tenements in the Shires of North't' Rutland and Lincoln which were in the possession of my said Lord and Fader. [Present author's emphasis.]

Only on one occasion does Edward IV specify what should happen to the relevant parts of his inheritance if the Duke of York were not to survive. However, on that occasion he merely says,

> If it fortune the same oure son the Duk of York to deceasse, as God forbede, without heires masle of his body commyng and afore the said age of xvj. yeres, then we wol the revenues of all the premises expressed in this article be applied by oure Executours to the paiement of our said debtes and restitutions making.

Curiously, however, there seems to be a definite implication in the wording of the will that Edward IV felt somewhat unsure as to whether his elder son, the Prince of Wales, would survive long enough to succeed him. Thus the king leaves certain bequests to 'oure said son the Prince *if God fortune him to comme to age of discrecion; And if he decease afore such age, as God defende, then by such as God disposeth to bee oure heire*'. (Present author's emphasis.) This suggests that, even in 1475, when he was still only four and a half years old, the Prince of Wales may have been known to be sick or weakly. Indeed, the king sounds distinctly pessimistic at one point, when he states that

> we wol and in the straitest wise charge oure son Edward the Prince *or such as shall please almighty God to ordeigne to bee oure heires and to succede us in the Corone of England* that he suffer every personne that have proved his debte or dueties according to the said Acte to bee contented and paied therof according to the tenour

and fourme of the same Acte without let or interruption. [Present author's emphasis.]

One other possible interpretation of the king's choice of words here is that he knew, or suspected, that his son by Elizabeth Widville would not be permitted to succeed to the crown of England. Thus God would ordain another member of the royal family to be Edward IV's heir – as in fact proved to be the case!

Also, based, presumably, upon the fact that, as he mentions,[1] Elizabeth Widville was some four months pregnant in June 1475, Edward IV speculates in his will upon the possibility of the birth of another son at some time in the future. He does not, however, mention any illegitimate royal children in the will. This might be interpreted as meaning that no illegitimate royal children existed – or that, if they existed, they had not been recognised by their father. However, contemporary evidence from another source shows clearly that, three years earlier, the king had been providing clothes for 'the Lord Bastard'. This clearly means that in 1472 an illegitimate royal son not only existed, but had been accorded formal recognition.

Of course, there are various ways of attempting to explain why 'the Lord Bastard' is not mentioned in his father's will. One possibility is that, like his half-sister Margaret, the boy had died before the summer of 1475. Another possibility is that 'the Lord Bastard' was excluded from the royal will because of his illegitimate status. If that were the case, it might also have been the case that there were other royal bastards living in 1475, who were not mentioned anywhere in their father's will. However, as was seen earlier (in chapter 19), it was not apparently considered improper in the second half of the fifteenth century to name illegitimate children in wills, and to make some provision for them.

THE TEXT OF THE ROYAL WILL:[2]

In the name of the moost holy and blessed Trinitie, the Fader, the Sonne and the holy Goost, by and undre whoom alle Kings and Princes reigne. We Edward, by the grace of God, King of England and of Fraunce and Lord of Irland, remembring inwardly that we, as other creatures in this world, bee transitorie and have noon abidunt therin certain, considering also that we be nowe upon oure journey and in taking oure passage, by Godds sufferance and assistence, toward oure Reame of Fraunce, for the recouveryng of oure undoubted right and title unto the same, Willing therfore to dispose us in alle things to the pleaser of God, for the helth and relief of oure soule, as ferforthly as we by his grace and assistance can call to oure mynde, the xx day of Juyn, the yere of oure Lord God M.cccc.lxxv, and the yere of oure Reigne the xvth, beeing in helth of body and hole of mynde, thanked bee his Grace, at oure Towne of Sandwich make this oure last Wille and testament in the manere and fourme herafter enswing.

Furst we bequeth [our soul] to allmighty God and to his glorious Moder oure Lady Saint Marie, Saint George, Saint Edward and all the holy Companie of heven, and oure body to bee buried in the Church of the Collage of Saint George within oure Castell of Wyndesore by us begonne of newe to bee buylded, in the place of the same Church by us limited and appointed and declared to the Reverende Fader in God oure right trusty and welbeloved the Bisshop of Sarum, where we will oure body be buried lowe in the grownde, and upon the same a stone to bee laied and wrought with the figure of Dethe with scochyne of oure Armer and writings convenient aboute the bordures of the same remembring the day and yere of oure decease, and that in the same place or nere to it an Autre bee made metely for the rome as herafter we shall devise and declare.

Item we wol that overe the same Sepulture ther bee made a vawte of convenient height as the place wil suffre it, and that upon the said vawte ther bee a Chapell or a Closet with an Autre convenient and a Tumbe to bee made and set there, and upon the same tumbe an Image for oure figure, which figure we wil bee of silver and gilte or at the lest coopre and gilt, and aboute the same tumbe scripture made convenient remembring the day and yere of oure deceasse.

Item we wol that nere to our said Sepulture ther bee ordeigned places for xiij personnes to sit and knele in, to say and kepe such observance divine service and praiers as we herafter shall expresse and declare.

Item we wil that all oure debtes that can bee proved due bee contented and paid afore all things excepte the costs of oure buryeing; and where as it is ordeigned by auctorite of oure Parliament last holden at oure Palois of Westm^r that all debtes due by us to eny personne wherof assignation or assignement was made for contentation therof by letters patents tailles debentures or billes or otherwise before the furst day of Decembre in the xth yere of oure Reign, that he to whoom eny such assignation or assignement was made shuld appiere before the Barons of oure Eschequier in his personne or by his attourney or servant afore certain daies limited there to shewe and prove the sommes of money specified in such assignation to bee due unto him upon a trewe grownde or cause at the making or rearing therof shuld after that doon have assignement made unto him for paiement of the same duelie to bee had unto him his executours or assignes in xx yeres, and that all assignations made by lettres patents taille or bille not soo shewed before the saide daies limited shuld bee voide and we therof acquited and discharged, as more at large and more clerely is expressed in the said Act We wol and in the straitest wise charge oure son Edward the Prince or such as shall please almighty God to ordeigne to bee oure heires and to succede us in the Corone of England that he suffer every personne that have proved his debte or dueties according to the said Acte to bee contented and paied therof according to the tenour and fourme of the same Acte without let or interruption, and that in the next Parliament to bee holden after our decease the said acte bee auctorised and confermed by auctoritie of the same Parliament for the more seurtie of paiement of the same debte.

Item where in the said Parliament last holden at oure said Palois by auctoritie of the same the moost Reverende Fader in God oure entierly beloved cousin Thomas the Cardinall Archbisshop of Cantrebury, William Bisshop of Ely, Ric' Bisshopp of Sarum, Robert Bisshop of Bathe, Thomas Bisshop of Lincoln, Henry Erl of Essex, Antonie Erl Ryvers, William Lord Hastyngs, John Lord Dynham, Maister John Russell Clerk Keper of oure Prive Seall, Maister William Dudley Deane of oure Chapell, Thomas Borugh, William Parre, Thomas Mountgomery Knights, Maister John Gunthoys Clerk, Richard Fowler and William Husee have astate in fee of and in the honours Castelles Lordships and Manors of Tuttebury Kenelworth Leycestre Bolyngbroke Longebenyngton Pountfrete Tykhull Knaresburgh Pykeryng and Dunstanburgh with thair membres and appertenances and of all other lands and tenements and other the premisses in the said Shires of Warr' Leyc' Staff' Derby Not' Lincoln' York and Northumbr' as wil serve and suffise to the full paiement of asmuch of oure said debte after the said rate of xx yeres as shal remaigne unpaied the tyme of such interrupcion had, and that thay in noo wise make astate unto oure said Son or unto oure said heires or eny other unto the tyme the same oure debte bee fully contented and paied and restitucions and satisfaccions made according to this oure Wille.

Item we wol that all oure other debtes bee contented and paied by oure said executours with the residue of the said revenues in as hasty wise as it may bee borne, respecte had to the other charges that we have and shall by this oure Wille and testament ordeigne to bee doon with the same.

Item in cas it can bee proved before oure said executours that eny debte or dueties be owing to eny personne upon a true grownde and that he to whoom such debte is owing have not proved it for his duetie according to thacte above rehersed concernyng the paiement of oure debtes for litelnesse of the debte or for povertie or for lakke of knowlege of the same Acte or other cause reasonable and that duely proved before oure executours, that then we wil that he have paiement therof after the rate of xx yeres paiement and as it may bee borne of the said revenues appointed by this oure Wille to the paiement of oure said debte.

Item we wol that if it can bee shewed unto oure said executours that eny personne to whom eny such debte is due by us and hath made his prove therof according to the saide Acte or have not proved it for eny of the causes above shewed and may nat for povertie abide the length of paiement of xx yeres and that duely proved before oure executours, then we wil that every such personne have paiement of his debte as hastely as it may bee borne of the said revenues appointed to the paiement of oure debtes afore declared, consideracion had to the other charges to bee borne therof as afore is declared.

Item we wil that if eny personne complaigne to oure said executours of eny wronge doon unto him by us or oure commaundement or moyen, we wil that every suche complaincte bee tendrely and effectuelly herd and the matiere complaigned duely and indifferently examined, and in cas that by such examination it can bee founden that the complaincte be made upon a grownded in conscience that then he bee recompensed by the discretion of oure said Executours of the said revenues appointed to the paiement of oure said debtes and as it may bee borne of the same, respecte had to the other charges, and in this we wil that every personne complaignyng in this partie be considered after his degree and have, and he that is moost pourest and ferrest from helpe bee furst herd and satisfied.

Item we wil that oure doughtre Elizabeth have x^{ml} marc' towards her mariage, and that oure doughtre Marie have also to her marriage x^{ml} marc', soo that they bee gouverned and rieuled in thair marriages by oure derrest wiff the Quene and by oure said son the Prince if God fortune him to comme to age of discrecion; And if he decease afore such age, as God defende, then by such as God disposeth to bee oure heire and by such Lords and other as then shal bee of their

Counsaill; and if either of oure said doughtres doo marie thaim silf without such advys and assent soo as they bee therby disparaged, as God forbede, that then she soo marieing her silf have noo paiement of her said x^{ml} marc' but that it bee emploied by oure Executours towards the hasty paiement of oure debtes and restitucions as is expressed in this oure last Will.

Item where we trust in God oure said Wiff bee now with childe, if God fortune it to bee a doughtre then we wil that she have also x^{ml} marc' towards her mariage, Soo alwayes that she bee rieuled and guyded in her mariage as afore is declared in tharticle touching the mariages of oure said doughtres Elizabeth and Marie, and elles to bee emploied by oure said Executours to the hasty paiement of oure said debtes.

Item to the mariage of oure doughtre Cecille for whoom we have appointed and concluded with the King of Scotts to bee maried to his Son and heire, for the which mariage we have bounden us to paie unto him xviij^{ml} marc' in certain fourme expressed in writing thereupon made over and above m^l.m^l marc' paied to the same King of Scotts in hande, we wol that the said xviij^{ml} marc' bee paied by oure said son Edward and oure heires according to the said appointement and bonde, considering that the said mariage was by thadvis of the Lords of oure blode and other of oure Counsaill for the grete wele of all this oure Reame and of oure heires in tyme to comme concluded, and for that cause we have bounden us and oure heires to the paiement therof, and therfore eftsones we wil and straitly charge oure said Son and such as shall please God to bee oure heires in the said Corone to see that the said xviij^{ml} marc' bee contented and paied as afore is said, soo as the revenues of such Lordshippes and Manoirs as we shal by this oure Wille ordeigne and appointe to the paiement of the mariage of our other doughters bee in noo wise applied to the paiement of the said xviij^{ml} marc' or eny part therof.

Item that if the mariage betwix the same oure doughter and the said King of Scotts Son bee not accomplisshed, then if the same oure doughtre Cecille bee maried to eny other by the counsaill and advys of oure said Wiff and other afore named we wol that the said xviij^{ml} marc' or asmuch therof as shal remaigne unpaied bee paied by oure said son the Prince and his heires to such an other as she shal bee maried unto.

Item if it fortune eny of oure said doughtres other then oure said doughtre Cecille to deceasse, as God forbede, afore she bee maried or afore the money appointed to her mariage paied for it, then we wol that the hool somme of that appointed to her mariage soo dieing not paied bee disposed by oure Executours for the hasty contentacion and paiement of oure said debtes and restitution making if nede bee, and aftre oure debtes paied and restitution made therof the residue to bee emploied by the discretion of oure Executours for the helthe of oure sowle.

Item to thentent that the said sommes of money appointed by this oure Wille towards the mariages ofoure said Doughtres other then to the mariage of oure said doughtre Cecille bee wel and truly paied in the fourme afore declared, we wol that all the revenues issues proffits and commodities commyng and growing of oure Countie Palatine of Lancastre and of alle oure Castelles Lordshippes Manoirs lands tenements rents and services in the Countie Palatine and Shire of Lancastre parcell of oure said Duchie of Lancastre with thair membres and appertenances, and of the honours Castell Lordship Manoirs lands and tenements in Suth Wales and the Marches therof parcell of oure said Duchie with thair members and appertenances, bee received yerely by oure said Executours, and the money commyng and growing therof over the ordinarie charges and expenses of the same bee emploied and paied by oure said Executours to the mariages of oure said doughtres by thadvis of oure said Wiff and Son or such as shal please God to ordeigne to bee oure heire in the fourme afore declared.

Item where by fyne reared afore the Justices of oure Comen Place oure said cousin the Cardinall and other have estate in certain Castell Lordships Manoirs lands and tenements which were in the possession of my Lord and Fader, in the which fyne the names of the same Castell Lordshippes Manoirs lands and tenements bee expressed at large, we wol that the same oure feoffees after the deceasse of my Lady and Moder and after that oure son Richard Duk of York come to the age of xvj. yeres thay make estate unto him of the Castell Lordshippes Manoirs lands and tenements of Fodrynghay Staunford and Grantham with thair appertenances and of all other Manoirs lands and tenements in the Shires of North't' Rutland and Lincoln which were in the possession of my said Lord and Fader or in the possession of eny other to his use, to bee had to the same oure son the Duk of York and to the heires masle of his body commyng and for defaulte of such heires the remaindre therof to oure right heires; and if my said Lady and Moder deceasse, as God forbede, afore the same oure son the Duk of York come to the said age of xvj. yeres and afore all oure debtes and restitutions paied and made, then we wol the revenues of all the premisses specified in this article bee applied to the paiement of oure said debts till he come to the said age.

Item we wol that after oure said son the Duk of York comme to the said age of xvj. yeres that oure said cousin the Cardinall and his Coofeoffees beeing enfeoffed amongs other of and in the above named honour Castell Lordship and Manoir of Bolyngbroke with the members and appertenances and of and in all Manoirs lands and tenements in the shires of Lincoln Norh't' and Rutland parcell of oure said Duchie of Lancastre with thair appertenances doo make astate unto him of the same honour Castell Lordship and Manoir of Bolyngbroke with the membres and appertenances and of and in all the said Manoirs lands and tenements in the said shires of Lincoln Norh't' and Rutland, the Lordship and Manoir of Longbenyngton with thappertenances in the same shire of Lincoln oonly except, to bee had unto him and to the heires masle of his body commyng, and for defaulte of such heires the remaindre therof to oure right heires; and in this we wol that if it fortune the same oure son the Duk of York to deceasse, as God forbede, without heires masle of his body commyng and afore the said age of xvj. yeres, then we wol the revenues of all the premises expressed in this article be applied by oure Executours to the paiement of our said debtes and restitutions making.

Item where we have ordeigned and appointed that oure said Cousin and other shall have astate by a like fine of and in certain Lordshipps Manoirs lands and tenements parcell of oure said Duchie of Lancastre in the shires of Somers' Dors' Wiltes' Berk' Oxon' Glouc' and Buk' Sussex Surr' Kent Essex Suff. and Norff. parcell of oure said Duchie, in the which fyne the Lordshipps Manoirs lands and tenements bee expressed at large, we wol the same oure feoffees after the deceasse of oure said derrest Wiff stande feoffees of and in the same to this entent, that thay shall suffre oure said derrest Wiff to take and perceive during her liff all the revenues issues and profiits commyng and growing of all such part of the same as she hath estate in for terme of her liff, and after her deceasse to suffre oure Executours to take and perceive the oon half of the hool revenues issues and profits of all the said honours Castell Lordshipps Manoirs and other the premisses expressed in this article towards the paiement of oure said debtes and restitutions making if eny shal nede, and the other half of the same revenues issues and proffits to bee applied and paied for and aboute the contentation of oure said Wyves detts if eny shal fortune to bee by the hands of her Executours or such other as shal have the charge of paiement therof, and that doon to make astate therof to oure said Son yet not borne after he commeth to his age of xvj yeres and to the heires masle of his body commyng, and for default of such issue, or if God fortune noo such sonne to bee borne, the remaindre of all Lordshippes Manoirs lands and tenements rents reversions and services in the said shire of Norff. to oure said son the Duk of York, and to the heires masle of his body commyng, and for defaulte of such heires the remaindre therof to oure right heires; and as to all the residue specified in this article, we wol for defaulte of heires masle of the body of oure said son yet nat borne begoten, or if God fortune noo such son to bee borne, the remainder therof be to oure right heires.

Item we wol that the Church of the said Collage begonne by us of newe to bee buylded bee thorughly finisshed in all things as we have appointed it by the oversight and assent of the said Bisshop of Sarum during his liff and after his deceasse by the oversight of the Dean of the said Collage for the tyme beeing, soo alway that our Executours and Supervisour of this our last Wille and testament bee prive to all charges and expenses that shal bee expended about it.

Item we wol that oure said Executours and Supervisour here oons in the yere thaccompts and rekenyng aswell of the said Bisshop as of the said Dean and all other that shal have the charge and governance of the said buyldings, soo as the charges therof may bee provided for from tyme to tyme as the cas shal require.

Item where we have graunted unto oure said cousin the Cardinall and other to oure use and behove all Castelles Lordshippes Manoirs lands and tenements that were late John Erl of Shroosbury and John late Erl of Wiltes' or either of hem and commen unto oure hands after thair deceasse and by reason of the nonnage of thair heires, and also all such Manoirs lands and tenements as late were Thomas Tresham Knight and commen to oure hands by vertue of an Acte of forfaiture made in our said last Parliament, withouten eny thing yelding unto us for the same, we wol that the revenues issues and proffits of all the same Castelles Lordshippes Manoirs lands and tenements, the rents issues and proffits of the Lordshippes Manoirs lands and tenements graunted by us to oure welbeloved Conseillour William Lord Hastyngs for the sustentation and fyndyng of the newe Erl of Shroesbury son and heire of the said late Erl of Shroesbury oonly except, bee emploied by the oversight aforesaid about the buildings of the said Church as ferre as it wil strecche over the ordinarie charges therof; and if the said Erles or either of thaim deceasse or that thay or either of thaim have lyveree of thair londes

beeing within age and afore the said Church and oure other werks
there thoroughly buylded and finisshed, then we wol that asmuch of
the revenues issues and proffits of the premisses parcell of oure said
Duchie of Lancastre put in feoffement by auctoritie of Parliament
aforesaid as the revenues of the said Erles lands or either of thaim
soo dieing or having liveree of his lands extendeth unto in yerely
value, bee emploied by oure Executours aboute the same buylding
aud werks by the oversight abovesaid.

Item we wol that ther bee two prests perpetuelly founden within
the said Collage to synge and pray for us and oure said Wiff oure
faders and other of our auncestres in such fourme and manere as
herafter we shal doo to bee ordeigned and devised, which two
prests we wol bee chosen and named by the Dean and Chanons of
the same Collage for the tyme beeing and thair successours by the
oversight and assent of the said Bisshop of Sarum during his liff,
in the which election we wol that the said Dean and Chanons bee
sworne upon the holy Evangelists that they shall name noon of the
said two prests for favour or affection or at the desire or request
of enypersonne what soo ever he bee, but that thay shall chose
such as bee notarily knowen good and of vertuous conversacion
and nat promoted to eny manere benefice Chaunters prebende
nor free Chapell, in the which eleccion we wol that such Clerks
of the Universities of Oxonford and Cambrigge as bee Doctours
of Divinitie or Bachelers of Divinitie at the lest, beeing of good
conversation as afore is said, bee preferred afore all other, which
prests and either of hem soo chosen we wol thay bee sworne upon
the holy Evangelists upon thair admission before the said Deane
and Chanons truely to observe and kepe all observances and divine
service as we shall ordeigne to bee doon and at such tyme and place
as shal also bee limited and appointed.

Item we wol that ther bee founden perpetuelly within the said
Collage xiij poure men whoo we wol that thay daily pray and say
such service and praiers as we shall ordeigne to bee said by thaim
and at such tyme and place also as we shall ordeigne and devise, for
observation of the which we wol that thay bee straitlie sworne upon
the holy Evangelists at thair furst admission in the presence of the
said Deane and Chanons.

Item we wol that the said xiij poiire men bee chosen and named
by the said Dean and Chanons for the tyme being by the oversight
of the said Bisshop during his liff, in the which election we wol that
the said Dean and Chanons bee sworne in the fourme as afore is

declared in thellection of the said prests with this addicion, that thay shall noon chose but such as bee moost poure and nedy and next dwelling to the said Collage and unmaried, and in this election we wol that oure servants and such other as were servants to my said Lord and Fader have preferrement afore all other albeeit that thay bee not next dwelling or abiding to the said Collage.

Item we wol that either of the said two prests have yerely for thair salarie xx marc' in redy money at iiij termes of the yere by even porcions by the hands of the said Deane and Chanons and their successours, and that every of the said xiij poure men have two pens by the day to bee paied wekely thorugh out the yere, that is to say every Satirday immediatly after even songe of the day said in the said Collage by the hands of the said Dean and Chanons for the tyme beeing or oon of thaim to bee deputed in that behalve.

Item for seurtie of paiement aswell of the salarie of the same two prests as of the almesse of the same xiij. poure men we wol that oure said cousin the Cardinal and his Coofeoffees of and in the Lordship and Manoir of Wicomb called Basset Bury with the Fee ferme of the towne of Much Wicomb, and of and in the Manoir of Dadyngton in the shire of Oxenford, doo make estate therof to the said Dean and Chanons of Wyndesore and to thair successours for evermore undre such fourme as shall bee thought to oure Executours raoost seurtie and convenient for the paiement of the said salarie and almesse truely to bee had and made to thaim according to this oure Wille.

Item we wol that the said two prests bee discharged of keeping divine service in the Chauncell of the said Collage or in any other place within the said Church other then aboute oure sepulture and tumbe as afore is said, of lesse then it bee upon the principall Fests in the yere, or that the Quere goo a procession, which daies we woll thay goo a procession with the Quere weryng surplees and copes as the Vicairs there doo.

Item we wol that the said two prests and xiij poure men bee contynuelly abiding and resident within the said Collage and that thay daily kepe and say thair observances and divine services aboute oure sepulture and tumbe in the fourme as shal more at large bee declared in oure Ordenance therof; and if eny of the said two prests bee promoted to eny manere of benefice, bee it with cure or without cure, that immediatly after his promocion he bee avoided and removed from this his service, and a newe to bee chosen, as afore is declared, and put in his place.

Item if eny of the said poure men bee promoted to eny manere of lyvelode rents offices fees or annuities by enheritaunce or by eny other moyen to the value of v. marc' by the yere, that he immediately after he bee discharged of his service and have noo lenger paiement of our said almes, and an other to bee chosen, as afore is said, and put in his place.

Item if eny of the said prests or poure men absente thaim from the said Collage for eny cause more then xxviij. daies in all by the yere, or elles he bee necligent or remisse in keping the said observance divine service or praiers that shall be in his charge to doo and say, of lesse then it bee by occasion of sekenesse or feblenesse notorili knowen to the Dean and Chanons for the tyme beeing there present, that he soo absentyng him or bee necligent or remisse in keping or dooing the said observances divine service or praiers, after certain monissions yeven unto him soo dooing, bee discharged of his service and an other for that cause chosen, as afore is declared, and put in his place.

Item we wol that the hows and Hospitall of Saint Antonies with all the possessions rents proffits commodities and advayles thereunto belonging bee in the moost seure wise appropred and annexed to the said Collage to bee had to the said Dean and Chanons and thair successours for evermore, thay with the same to fynde and bere in the same place in London and elleswhere all manere observances divine service almes and all other charges in as large manere and fourme as it hath bee ordeigned by the foanders and benefactours of the same place to bee had and doon, and specially as it hath been used and accustumed to bee doon at eny tyme within xl. yeres last passed, and with the residue of the revenues commyng therof we wol that the said Dean and Chanons and thair successours for evermore doo fynde ten Vicaires with Calaber ameses vj. Clers and iiij Children over their nombre that thay nowe have, under such manere and fourme as we shall doo to bee ordeigned and stablisshed.

Item we wol that oure said feoffees contynue thair astate and possession of and in all the said honours Castelles Lordshippes manoirs lands tenements and all other the premisses ordeigned to the paiement of oure said debtes, restitution of wrongs if eny bee, the marriages of oure said doughtres, and buylding of the said Church and other the charges above expressed, unto the tyme this oure Wille and testament in the manere and fourme afore expressed and declared in that behalve bee thoroughly and perfitely executed and perfourmed, without eny astate making therof or eny part therof to oure said son Edward or to such as shall please God to ordeigne to bee oure heire or eny other oure Sonnes or other personne what soo ever.

Item we wol that cc^{li} bee disposed yerely for evermore in almes, wherof I^{li} to bee disposed by the discretion of the said Bisshop of Sarum during his liif and after his deceasse by the said Dean of the said Collage and his successours by the oversight of the Bisshop of Sarum for the tyme beeing to the mariages of poure mayd[ens] as nat having fader or moder nor other frende able to preferre thaim; other I^{li} to bee departed by the same oversight to the moost miserable and pourest people next dwelling to the said Collage, wherin we wil that oure olde servants have preferrement afore all other albee it thay bee nat next dwelling to our said Collage; the third I^{li} to bee departed by the said oversight amongs prisoners condempned for debte or other cause where the duetie or damages excede not iiij^{li}, or elles to such as remaigne in prison for lakke of paiement of thair fees; and the fourth I^{li} to bee applied yerely by the said oversight about high weyes next lieing to the said Collage moost necessarie to bee repaired; and to thentent that this oure ahnes may seurly bee had for evermore, we wol that our feoffees of and in the Manoir of Westcote in the said shire of Buk', the Manoir of Purton Haseley Kyrtelyngton, Dadyngton and Ascote in the shire of Oxon', the Manoirs of Asparton and Stretton with thappurtenences in the shire of Glouc', and the Manoir of Longbenygnton in the shire of Lincoln with thair appurtenances doo make estate therof to said Dean and Chanons and thair successours for evermore under such seure fourme in that behalve as shall seme to oure Executours moost seurtie and convenient.

Item if oure said son Edward and his heires suffre the personnes above named and all other havyng astate in the premisses to oure behove and oure Executours to perfourme and execute this oure Wille and testament in all thing yn manere and fourme afore expressed and declared without let or interruption of him or thaim, then we woll that the said personnes after oure said Wille soo in all thing perfitely executed and perfourmed doo make astate unto oure said son Edward and the heires of his body commyng, and for [default] of such heires the remaindre therof to oure right heires, aswell of and in all the honours Castelles Lordshippes Manoirs lands and tenements specified in the said Act concernyng the Feoffement for the perfourming of oure Wille, the said honour Castell Lordship and Manoir of Bolyngbroke with the membres and appertenances and the Lordship and Manoir of Longbenyngton with thapperteriances in the shire of Lincoln with all other lands and tenements in the same shire parcel of oure said Duchie of Lancastre oonly except as of the said Countie Palatine of Lancastre, and all Castells Lordshippes Manoirs lands and tenements with thappertenances in the said Countie Palatine and shire of Lancastre with all thair membres and appertenanees, to thentent that all the same honours Castell Lordshippes Manoirs lands and tenements with thair membres and appertenances except afore excepted may perpetuelly remaigne hooly to oure said son Edward and his heires aforesaid, nat oonly for thenlarging of the possessions of oure Corone of England toward the bering of the charges therof, but also for the more seure and restfull governance to bee had in the same oure Reame, desiring therfore and also traicly charging oure said son Edward and his heires that he nor thay, for eny thing that may falle, depart from thoos possessions to eny personne what soo ever he bee, as he and thay wil answere afore God at the day of Dome and as thay love the wele of thaim silf and of the said Reame.

Item if this oure Wille and testament bee perfitely executed and doon in all things as afore is said without let or interruption of oure said son Edward and his heires, then after the same oure Wille soo executed and perfourmed we wol that oure feoffees doo make astate aswell of and in the Manoirs of the More Busshy and Eggeware in the shires of Hertford and Midd' as of the Manoirs of Ditton and Dachett in the shire of Buk' with thair appertenances to oure said son Edward and his heires for evermore in recompense of the said Castell Lordshippes and Manoirs of Fodrynghay Staunford and Grantham with thair membres and appertenances and all lands and tenements in the [shires] of Norh't' Rutland and Lincoln; and if the perfite execution of this oure last Wille and testament bee in eny wise letted or interrupted by oure said son Edward [or his] heires, then we wol that the said Manoirs of the More Busshy Eggeware Dachet and Ditton with all thair membres and appertenances bee sold by oure said Feoffees and Executours to the moost avauntage, and the money commyng therof to bee disposed by oure Executours to the paiement of oure debtes and restitutions making and other charitable dedes and werks of pitie thought unto thair discretion moost meritorie to the relief of oure sowle.

Item for soo much as diverses of the Lords aswell of oure blode as other and also Knights Squiers and diverses other oure true loving subgietts anxl servants [have faithfully] and lovingly assisted us and put thaim in the extreme jeopardie of thair lyves losses of thair

lands and goods in assisting us aswell aboute the reco[verie] of oure
Corone and Reame of England as other diverses seasons and tymes
of jeopardie, in consideracion wherof we have made to diverses of
thaim grauntes som of lands and tenements and offices, and som of
offices fees and annuities, we wol and require and straitly charge
oure said son Edward and other oure heires that every Lord Knight
Squire and other having eny thinge of our graunte what soo ever
it bee, that he and his heires have and enjoye every graunte soo by
us [graunted] for eny of the said considerations or eny other cause
according to the tenoures fourraes and effects of every of the same
without eny manere let or interruption of oure said Son or eny other
of oure heires.

Item as to all oure goods, that is to say beddyng' arrases tapestries
verdours stuff of oure houshold ornaments of oure Chapell with
boks apperteignyng to the same, plate and jouelx excepte, excepte
also such part of the same ornaments and boks as we shall herafter
dispose to goo to oure said Collage of Wyndesore, we wol that
oure said wiff the Quene have the disposicion therof without let or
interruption of the other oure Executours, to thentent that she may
take of the same such as she shall thinke to bee moost necessarie and
convenient for her, and have the use and occupation therof during
her liff, and after her deceasse oure said son the Prince hooly to have
and enjoye that part, and the residue of all the said goods except
afore excepted to bee departed by her discrecion betwix our said
sonnes the Prince and Duk of York, wherin we wol that oure said
son the Prince have the preferrement in such therof as shal seme to
her discrecion raoost necessarie and convenient for his astate; and
as unto all oure jouelx and plate aswell of oure Chapell as other,
we wol thay bee sold by our Executours to the moost avauntage,
and with the money commyng therof the costs and charges of oure
buryeing and couvereing of oure body to the said Collage, and a
m^l marc to bee disposed the day of oure buryeing or afore amongs
prests and poure people to syng and pray for oure soule, bee borne,
and the residue therof to bee disposed by oure said Executours
aboute the hasty paiement of oure debtes, restitution of wrongs if
eny bee, with other charitable dedes and werks of pitie thought by
thair diserecion moost acceptable to God to the relief of oure sowle;
and over this we wol that oure said wiff the Quene have and enjoye
all her owne goods catelles stuff beddying arrases tapestries verdours
stuff of houshold plate and jouelx and all other thing which she
now hath and occupieth, to dispose it freely at her will and pleaser

without let or interruption of oure Executours; and for the perfite execution of this oure last Wille and testament we ordeigne and make oure said derrest and moost entierly beloved wiff Elizabeth the Quene, the Reverende Faders in God William Bisshop of Ely, Thomas Bisshop of Lincoln, John Bisshop of Rochestre, William Lord Hastynges oure Chamberleyn, Maister John Russell Clerk Keper of oure Prive Seall, Sr Thomas Mountgomery Knight, Richard Fowler oure Chaunceller of the Duchie of Lancastre, Richard Pygot oure Sergeant, and William Husee oure Attourny, oure Executours, praieing and requiring and also straitly charging thaim and specially oure said derrest Wiff in whoom we moost singulerly put oure trust in this partie, that she and thay put thaim in thair uttermast devoirs to see this oure last wille and testament bee truely executed and perfourmed in all things in manere and fourme afore declared as oure singler trust is in her and thaim and as she and thay wil answere afore God at the day of dome; and we ordeigne and make oure said cousin Thomas the Cardinall Archbisshop of Cauntrebury overseer of the same oure wille and testament, by whoos advyse we wol this oure wille and testament bee executed and perfourmed as afore is declared, requiryng and in oure moost herty wise praieing him to bee helping and assistyng oure said Executours in that behalve according to the grete trust that we have in him; and we wol that every of the said Bisshoppes, William Lord Hastynges, and Maister John Russell, have c marc in money for thair laboures in this behalve, and that every of the said Sr Thomas Mountgomery, Richard Fowler, Richard Pygot, and William Husee have xl^{li} in money for thair laboures, and that oure said cousin the Cardinall have also c marc in money for his labour.

Yeven undreoure grete Seall at our said towne of Sandwich the day and yere
above writen. R. E.

PART 5
THE LEGACY

24

1476–1479: ITINERARY

1476 (age 34; regnal year 16)
MARCH
Westminster[1]

APRIL
Westminster, and Windsor Castle[2]
The manor of Greenwich[3]

MAY
Windsor Castle[4]
The manor of The More,
Westminster, and Greenwich[5]
Westminster[6]
The manor of Greenwich[7]

JUNE
The manor of Knolle, Greenwich,
Westminster, Ware, and
Fotheringhay Castle[8]

JULY
Coventry, Leicester Castle,
Nottingham Castle, and
Fotheringhay Castle[9]

AUGUST
Fotheringhay Castle[10]
Coventry[11]

SEPTEMBER
The manor and town of Bewdley[12]
?Conderton [Cauden or Canden]
and Winchcombe Abbey[13]
The manor of Woodstock[14]

OCTOBER
Woodstock, Windsor Castle,
Westminster, and Greenwich[15]

NOVEMBER
Westminster[16]
The manor of Greenwich[17]

DECEMBER
Greenwich, and Westminster[18]
The manor of Waltham (Essex /
Herts. border)[19]
The forest of Waltham[20]

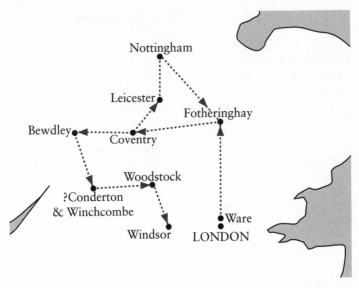

Edward IV's movements from June to October 1476

1476/7
JANUARY
Westminster, and Greenwich[21]

FEBRUARY
Greenwich, and Westminster[22]
Westminster[23]

MARCH
Westminster[24]
REGNAL YEAR 17
Westminster[25]
Sheen, and Windsor Castle[26]

1477 (age 35; regnal year 17)
MARCH
Greenwich[27]
Windsor Castle[28]

APRIL
Windsor Castle, and Westminster[29]

MAY
Windsor Castle, Westminster, and
the manor of Kennington[30]
The Great Wardrobe, and the City
of London[31]
Windsor Castle[32]

JUNE
Windsor Castle, and the manor of
Knolle[33]
Westminster, and Greenwich[34]

JULY
The manor of Kennington, and
Windsor Castle[35]
Westminster[36]

AUGUST
Windsor Castle[37]
The City of London[38]
The Tower of London[39]
Westminster, and the manor of
Shipridge[40]
Southampton[41]
The manor of Waltham (Essex /
Herts. border)[42]

SEPTEMBER
Waltham (Essex / Herts. border),
Wardlam(?), and Windsor Castle[43]
The City of London, and Windsor
Castle[44]

OCTOBER
The House of St John's Guild, and
the City of London[45]
Windsor Castle[46]
Westminster[47]

NOVEMBER
Westminster[48]

DECEMBER
Westminster[49]

1477/8
JANUARY
Westminster[50]

FEBRUARY
Westminster, and Greenwich[51]

MARCH
Greenwich[52]
REGNAL YEAR 18
Greenwich[53]

1478 (age 36; regnal year 18)
MARCH
Greenwich[54]

APRIL
Greenwich[55]
Westminster[56]

MAY
Greenwich, Westminster, the
manor of Waltham (Essex / Herts.
border), and Farley (Farley Hill,
near Luton, Beds.?)[57]

JUNE
Greenwich[58]
Westminster[59]
Greenwich, the manor of
Faltebourne (Faulkbourne, near
Braintree, Essex? – held by
Sir Thomas Montgomery),
and Westminster[60]

JULY
Greenwich, and Westminster[61]
The City of London[62]
Windsor Castle[63]
The manor of Ditton (near Windsor)[64]
The manor of Sutton, and
Windsor Castle[65]
Berkhamsted Castle, Moorend
Castle (near Carlisle), and Higham
Ferrers[66]
Windsor Castle, and Benefield[67]

AUGUST
Nottingham Castle, and Windsor
Castle[68]
Greenwich[69]
The City of London[70]
Greenwich[71]

SEPTEMBER
St Alban's Abbey, Nottingham
Castle, and Doncaster[72]

OCTOBER
Dunstable[73]
Greenwich[74]
Westminster, the manor of
Waltham (Essex / Herts. border),
and the manor of Eltham[75]

NOVEMBER
The manor of Eltham[76]
The manor of Greenwich[77]
The City of London, Westminster,
the manor of Eltham, and the
manor of Kennington[78]

DECEMBER
The manor of Eltham[79]
London[80]
Westminster, and the manor of
Eltham[81]
The manor of Eltham[82]
Windsor Castle[83]
The manor of Eltham[84]
Windsor Castle[85]

1478/9
JANUARY
London[86]
The town of Brentford [*Braynforde*],
the manor of Easthampsted
(Easthampstead Park, near
Windsor), and Croydon[87]
The manor of Eltham[88]

FEBRUARY
The manor of Eltham, the City
of London, Westminster, the
manor of Sheen, and the manor

of Easthampstead (Easthampstead
Park, near Windsor)[89]

MARCH
The manor of Sheen[90]
REGNAL YEAR 19
The manor of Sheen[91]

1479 (age 37; regnal year 19)
MARCH
The manor of Sheen[92]

APRIL
Windsor Castle[93]

MAY
Windsor Castle, the manor of The
More, and Berkhamsted Castle[94]

JUNE
The manor of The More[95]
The manor in the Great Park at
Windsor[96]
The manor of The More, and the
manor of Ditton (near Windsor)[97]
The manor of Easthampstead
(Easthampstead Park, near
Windsor)[98]

JULY
The manor of Easthampstead
(Easthampstead Park, near
Windsor), the town and priory of
Guildford, and Vachery [*Bachery*]
(near Cranleigh)[99]

AUGUST
Guildford (town and priory)[100]

SEPTEMBER
Chichester[101]

OCTOBER
Chichester[102]
The manor of Woking[103]
NOVEMBER
The manor of Woking, the manor
of Guildford, and Windsor Great
Park[104]

DECEMBER
Greenwich, the manor of Woking,
and Windsor Castle[105]

1479/80
JANUARY
Greenwich[106]

FEBRUARY
Greenwich, the City of London,
and Westminster[107]

MARCH
Greenwich[108]
REGNAL YEAR 20
Greenwich[109]

25

1475–1478: GONE BUT NOT FORGOTTEN

Although the young Eleanor Talbot had died suddenly and unexpectedly in the summer of 1468, neither she nor her relationship with the king had been forgotten, as later events show very clearly. Evidence exists proving that the subsequent political propaganda of the 'Tudor' regime did its best in a very determined way to airbrush Eleanor out of history.[1] Ironically, at the same time Eleanor and her significance in respect of the inheritance of the English crown remained well-remembered, both in England and in other lands which lay outside 'Tudor' control, well into the sixteenth century.[2] Another significant point, however, is the thought that the government of King Henry VII may not have been the first English regime which did its best to ensure that Eleanor's story was concealed. As we shall see shortly, there is possible evidence of the murder of some of Eleanor's relatives in the 1470s.

Certainly Eleanor was always remembered with love and affection by her younger sister, Elizabeth Talbot, Duchess of Norfolk. Like Eleanor herself, Elizabeth Talbot appears to have experienced some difficulty in conceiving children. In the autumn of 1471, when she was twenty-seven, and her husband was twenty-six, the couple remained childless despite the fact that they had been married for twenty years. In September 1471, they therefore embarked on a pilgrimage on foot to the shrine of Our Lady of Walsingham,[3] which was then already a popular centre for couples who were experiencing a difficulty in this respect.

Our Lady of Walsingham appears to have responded to their pilgrimage to her shrine, for by the following summer the hitherto fruitless Elizabeth 'for serteyn is gret wyth chyld'.[4] Her baby was born at Framlingham Castle, on Thursday 10 December 1472. Unfortunately it proved a daughter, not a son and heir. Nevertheless, this birth was a hopeful sign. A week later, in the chapel at Framlingham Castle, Bishop William Waynflete of Winchester christened the baby, standing as godfather to the child himself:

> The Byshop cam to Framlyngham on Wednysday at nyght, and on Thursday by 10 of the clok before noon my yong lady was krystend and namyd Anne. The Byshop crystynd it and was godfadyr bothe, and wyth-in ij owyrs and lesse aftyr the crystenyng was do, my lord of Wynchester departyd towardys Waltham.[5]

Significantly, on Friday 18 December – the day following his first baby's baptism – John Mowbray, Duke of Norfolk, set off from Framlingham on a thank-you pilgrimage to Walsingham. Although it was winter and not the best season for travelling, he went in all haste in order to show the gratitude of himself and his wife to Our Lady of Walsingham for giving them a healthy child, and for Elizabeth's safe delivery.

Just over two years later, enough time had elapsed following the birth of Anne Mowbray for Elizabeth Talbot to entertain hopes of a second conception. Since her earlier appeal to Our Lady of Walsingham seemed to have worked, she decided to have recourse to the same assistance once again. The night of Wednesday 29 March found her in Norwich, where she was staying en route for Walsingham.[6] Perhaps while she was in Norwich she also found time to visit the tomb of her sister, Eleanor, at the Whitefriars' Priory, near Norwich Cathedral, and to pray for her soul.

Elizabeth's second appeal to Our Lady of Walsingham also seems to have been speedily answered. The summer of 1475 found her with child once again. On 10 October 1475, John Paston III wrote to his elder brother to tell him that the duchess 'lythe in Norwyche, and shall do tyll she be delyvered'.[7] This was in spite of the fact that the birth of her second baby was not scheduled for several months. Perhaps the duchess was residing in the Norfolk's palace on the south side of Tombland, just to the west of the cathedral's Ethelbert Gate. For some reason it was apparently thought wiser for Elizabeth not to travel about too much during her pregnancy.[8] Probably the Duke of Norfolk wanted to take no risks over the birth of his son and heir. He may also have been aware of the growing anxiety about the validity of her royal marriage on the part of Elizabeth Widville. Assuming that he and his wife already suspected the cause of death of his sister-in-law, Eleanor Talbot, this may well have made him anxious regarding his wife's safety. His anxiety may well have been increased by awareness of the fact that Bishop Stillington was in trouble. The bishop was summoned to Rome in 1475 to answer serious charges which had been raised against him, though precise details of the nature of those charges have not been preserved.[9]

John Mowbray may have spent Christmas with Elizabeth in Norwich, but early in January he left to return to Framlingham Castle, apparently leaving his wife in Norwich. Sir John Paston II waited on the Duke at Framlingham, and it is he who has recorded for us the dramatic event which then followed:

> It is so fortunyd that wher as my lorde off Norffolke yisterdaye beyng in goode heele, thys nyght dyed a-bowte mydnyght; wherffor it is alle that lovyd hym to doo and helpe nowe that that may be to hys honoure and weel to hys sowele.[10]

It must have been in his apartment in the up-to-date, central block of Framlingham Castle, which then stood within the enclosure of the outer walls, facing the main gate, that John, the fourth and last Mowbray Duke of Norfolk, died, early in the morning of Wednesday 17 January 1475/6. Sir John Paston gives no hint as to what caused his death, but makes it clear that the event was sudden and completely unexpected, and that on the day before it happened the duke had been in good health.

Possibly the date of the death, together with other events going on at that time, and the Duke of Norfolk's family connections, are significant in respect of the cause of his early and unexpected demise. As Domenico Manicini has told us, it was at about this time that Elizabeth Widville was experiencing renewed worries about the validity of her royal marriage and the chance of her royal sons ever succeeding to the English throne. This was directly connected with the latest campaign of the Duke of Norfolk's cousin and apparent friend the Duke of Clarence,[11] who was now claiming that he, rather than the Widville children, should formally be recognised as the heir to Edward IV's crown. This was a campaign promoted on behalf of the Duke of Clarence by the publishing and circulation in London and Westminster of political poems. The existence of the poems was first recorded in March 1476/7.[12] Unfortunately, no copies of them have survived. Presumably they were later destroyed by the government in order to conceal the claims they made. Eventually Thomas Burdet, the servant of the Duke of Clarence who was responsible for the publication and distribution of the poems, was executed for his 'treasonable intent' against 'the King and ... *Edward Prince of Wales, his eldest son*'.[13]

Earlier, the thesis was put forward that, on a previous occasion, when Elizabeth Widville had faced similar problems, she may have taken action to remove those problems by ending the existence of two of the people in question. The occasion in question was the year 1468 when, in terms of individuals, the chief problems confronting Elizabeth Widville comprised Eleanor Talbot and the Earl of Desmond.

Of course, Eleanor had been the Duke of Norfolk's sister-in-law. Therefore, he would almost certainly have been aware of her relationship with Edward IV, and we have already seen that further deaths had occurred in 1468, when some of his and his wife's servants had been put to death by the government – possibly as a kind of warning both to John Mowbray and to Elizabeth Talbot to behave carefully and to keep quiet. Now, the unexpected death of the Duke of Norfolk himself had ensued. Moreover, 1475/6 proved to be not only the date of *his* unexpected demise, but also of other significant and suspicious deaths, the evidence for which will be presented shortly.

As we have seen, the Duchess of Norfolk was not at Framlingham at the time of her husband's death. Presumably she was still in Norwich, where she was supposed to remain until the birth of her second child. However, once she received the shocking news of her husband's sudden and totally unexpected death, she immediately rushed home to Framlingham Castle. She was there only ten days after her husband's demise, on 27 January, when Sir John Paston wrote again to his younger brother, discussing the fact that already Edward IV, with his eye on the Mowbray inheritance, was now seeking to marry his two-and-a-half-year-old younger son to little Anne Mowbray, the late duke's infant daughter. Possibly Elizabeth Widville was also behind the king's rapid plan in respect of this matrimonial project. After all, even if she was able to ensure that her elder royal son, Edward, ultimately succeeded to the throne of England, she still had to make provision for the future of her younger royal son, Richard. And it is absolutely certain that Elizabeth Widville would have seen marriage to an aristocratic heiress as the obvious way forward in this respect, for she had earlier formulated similar projects on behalf of her own younger brothers and sisters.

Sir John Paston was evidently concerned regarding the proposed royal marriage for Anne Mowbray, for he wrote earnestly to his brother: 'late vs alle preye God sende my lady off Norffolke a soone'.[14] Sadly, however, this was not to be. Perhaps the shock of John's death caused Elizabeth to miscarry, or perhaps the speed of her unscheduled return to Framlingham when she heard the news (at a time when she was apparently meant to be resting quietly in Norwich) did some mischief. At all events, we hear nothing more of the child she was carrying in her womb when her husband died. Whether his baby was a boy or a girl, clearly it did not live. The only heiress of the Mowbrays was thus Elizabeth's little daughter, Anne.

Significantly, her husband's death, the loss of her possible son and heir, and the proposed royal marriage of her daughter and heiress, was not the only sad family news to reach Elizabeth Talbot in 1476. In December of that year, her first cousin, Isabel, Duchess of Clarence, also died, soon after the birth of her second son, Richard. Moreover, the baby Richard followed his mother into the grave. The Duke of Clarence himself, who had been with his family when the two deaths had occurred, clearly believed that both the deaths were unnatural. His subsequent actions show that he was firmly convinced that both his wife and his new son had been murdered by the deliberate and malicious administration of poison. His belief in that respect may well have sounded all too familiar to his wife's cousin, Elizabeth Talbot, who had similarly experienced the sudden and unexpected deaths of two members of her own immediate family, namely her sister, Eleanor, and her husband, John Mowbray.

The most direct surviving evidence in respect of the murder of the Duchess of Clarence and of her younger son, Richard, is preserved in the *Baga de Secretis*, Bundle 1 (records of court cases from the reign of Edward IV):

Tuesday next after the Clause of Easter [15 April], 17 Edw. 4 [1477]. Warwickshire Indictment taken before the Justices of the Peace, whereby it is found that Ankerett Twinnewe, otherwise Twymowe, late of Warwick, widow, late servant of George, Duke of Clarence and Isabella his wife, did on [Thursday] 10th October, 16 Edw. 4 [1476] at Warwick give to the said Isabella poisoned ale, of which poison she died on Sunday next before the then following Christmas [22 December 1476].

Also against Roger Tocotes, late of Warwick, Knight, servant of the said Duke and Duchess, for that on the said 10 October, he abetted the said Ankarett to commit the said felony.

Also that John Thuresby, late of Warwick, yeoman, late servant of Richard Plantagenet, second son of George Duke of Clarence, compassing the said death of the said Richard, gave him, on [Saturday] 21st December 16 Edw. 4 [1476], certain poisoned ale, of which poison he died on [Wednesday] 1st January then next ensuing [1477].

And furthermore that the said Roger Tocotes, otherwise Tokettes, late of Warwick, Knight, on the said [Saturday] 21st December, procured and abetted the said John Thuresby to commit the said felony.[15]

More fortunate in respect of her fecundity than her first cousin, the Duchess of Norfolk, the Duchess of Clarence had become pregnant for the fourth time in 1476. Her baby son, Richard, came into the world at the end of the first week of October of that year. His place of birth is usually cited as Tewkesbury Abbey, but possibly that is an error, because the report of the case brought against Ankarette and Sir Roger Tocotes by the Duke of Clarence speaks of Isabel as having been poisoned at the family home – the castle in Warwick. It has often been claimed in modern accounts that Isabel had been attended during Richard's birth by Ankarette Twynyho (*née* Hawkeston). However, no surviving documents relating to the Twynyho case offer any evidence that Ankarette had served Isabel in the role of midwife, or that she later served as the nurse for Isabel's newborn son. The report of the court case against her merely refers to Ankarette as a servant of the duke and duchess.

Ankarette was a widow in her sixties. Born probably in about 1412, she had married William Twynyho of Keyford (Frome), Somerset. The couple produced at least two sons and one daughter. She and her family were undoubtedly in the service of the Clarences in the 1470s. According to the account of the court case (see above), on Thursday 10 October 1476 Ankarette had been in Warwick, in the service of the Duchess of Clarence. The subsequent case against her states that on 10 October 1476, Ankarette, aided and abetted by Sir Roger Tocotes, gave Isabel poisoned ale, which made the Duchess of Clarence seriously ill, and which finally brought about her death on the Sunday before Christmas.

In the immediate aftermath of Isabel's death, her deeply shocked husband was initially caught up with making arrangements for her interment. However, he then suddenly found himself also having to cope with a second shocking bereavement – the death of his newly born baby son, Richard. The later court hearing established not only that Isabel had been poisoned by Ankarette and Sir Roger Tocotes but that Richard had also been poisoned. In his case the poison had been administered by a servant called John Thursby. Since Sir Roger Tocotes also incited this second killing, he was obviously the person *in situ* at Warwick Castle who was leading the anti-Clarence campaign on the spot. However, the chief person behind the campaign was presumably the key Clarence enemy in London – and the power behind the throne – Elizabeth Widville.

Sir Roger Tocotes was a leading member of the Wiltshire gentry. His wife, Elizabeth, was the widow of Sir William Beauchamp, brother of Richard Beauchamp, Bishop of Salisbury. These two Beauchamp brothers were cousins of the Duchess of Clarence. Sir Roger had been with Clarence and Warwick in France, and was one of those who accompanied Clarence when the duke defected to Edward IV before the battle of Barnet. He was a member of Clarence's council from 1475, and Hicks considers that 'his career suggests that he was the duke [of Clarence]'s friend as well as his servant and one of his leading officials'.[16] Nevertheless, Tocotes seems to have been a man of rather adaptable loyalty – based on the best sources of influence for his own promotion. He served Edward IV as well as his brother, George. For example, in the months following George's execution Sir Roger continued to be appointed to royal commissions. It is not precisely clear what stance he adopted on Edward IV's death, but in September 1483 he became one of the leaders of Buckingham's Rebellion, as a result of which he was attainted – though subsequently pardoned. However, two years later he appears to have fought on the side of Henry 'Tudor' at the battle of Bosworth.[17] This record implies possible connections with Dr John Morton and perhaps also with members of the Widville family.

It seems that the Duke of Clarence was so stunned by the actions which had now been taken against two members of his family by those in power that his first reaction was to desperately seek some means of preserving the life of his only surviving son and heir, Edward of Clarence, the young Earl of Warwick. George was the lieutenant of Ireland, and had an excellent relationship with his deputy there, the Earl of Kildare. One eighteenth-century writer states that George travelled to Ireland in 1477,[18] and later, at his trial, Edward IV accused George of plotting to send his son to Ireland or Flanders. Since very detailed plans seem to have been in place for such a rescue of the little Earl of Warwick, it may well be the case that his father did indeed make such a journey. And since George was definitely in Warwick in April, and in London in May and June, while from June onwards he was a prisoner in the Tower of London, if he did visit Ireland in 1476/7 it must have been in February or in March – just after the murders of his wife and younger son. This would explain why he was not able to pursue any legal action against the murderers until April.

But on Saturday 12 April 1477, George sent a force of twenty-six men, led by Richard Hyde of Warwick and Roger Strugge, clothier, of

Beckington (near Frome) to the manor of Keyford, at Frome in Somerset,[19] where Ankarette was living quietly in her late husband's home. She was captured and transported to Warwick, via Bath and Cirencester, arriving in Warwick at about eight o'clock in the evening of Monday 14 April. The following morning, Tuesday 15 April, Ankarette was brought to trial at the Guildhall in Warwick, together with John Thursby. Although Sir Roger Tocotes was also accused, it seems that he had escaped capture, because he was not apparently held – or punished.

As we have seen from the records, the court in Warwick found Ankarette and John Thursby guilty, and ruled that Ankarette 'should be led from the bar to the said lord king's gaol of Warwick aforesaid, and drawn from that gaol through the centre of that town of Warwick to the gallows at Myton, and be hanged there on that gallows until she is dead'.[20] Thursby was also sentenced to death, and the sentences were duly carried out.

There is no indication that the legal proceedings were in any way untoward. However, Ankarette's grandson (taking advantage, perhaps, of the subsequent arrest of the Duke of Clarence) presented a formal petition at the parliament of 1478 for the verdict against his grandmother to be overturned, which was successful. Indeed, either he or possibly Sir Roger Tocotes may have approached the king on this subject earlier. At all events Bundle 1 of the *Baga de Secretis* contains a writ of *Certiorari* (High Court review) of the Warwick court indictment. The writ of *Certiorari* is dated 20 May 1477. Thus, in due course, it appears that the power behind the throne which may have brought about the deaths of Eleanor Talbot, of the Earl of Desmond, of servants of the Duke and Duchess of Norfolk, of the Duke of Norfolk himself, and of the Duchess of Clarence and her baby son, was also able to overturn the court decision which had attempted to justly punish the perpetrators of the last two murders.

The final death that was definitely brought about by Elizabeth Widville in her attempt to ensure the safety of her union with Edward IV, and so the rights of her children to succeed to the throne of England, was the execution of her brother-in-law George, Duke of Clarence, himself. Although George had been somewhat reluctantly caught up in his father-in-law's project of 1470–71, he himself had backed away from that at the earliest opportunity. He never subsequently attempted to oust his brother, King Edward IV, from the throne. However, he did put forward a claim that he should be recognised as the heir of Edward IV. This can only mean that he was disputing the validity of the Widville marriage, and the right of the children of that marriage to claim the crown.

George had opposed the Widville marriage from the beginning – as indeed did other members of the royal house of York. However, it was only in the 1470s that he began asserting that he, rather than young Edward, Prince of Wales, should succeed his brother on the English throne. This can only mean that he had somehow become aware that, according to the laws of the Church, the Widville marriage was invalid because of Edward's earlier marriage contract with Eleanor Talbot. And of course the date when this happened clearly coincided with the date when Domenico Mancini reports that Elizabeth Widville 'remembered ... the calumnies with which she was reproached, namely that ... she was not the legitimate wife of the king'.[21] Significantly, it also coincided with the period when Eleanor's brother-in-law, John Mowbray, Duke of Norfolk – a friend, as well as a cousin, of the Duke of Clarence – died suddenly and unexpectedly, and when Eleanor's first cousin, the Duchess of Clarence, and her younger son were murdered, so that the Duke of Clarence became panic-stricken and made plans to smuggle his surviving son and heir across the sea to Ireland in order to prevent him too from being killed.

As for Elizabeth Widville, her final conclusion was now 'that her offspring by the king would never come to the throne unless the duke of Clarence were removed'.[22] Her fear of her brother-in-law strongly suggests that by 1477 she was aware that George had discovered the hitherto secret history of Edward IV's marriage to Eleanor Talbot.

The king appears to have initially assumed that Robert Stillington was George's source for this information. As we have seen, Stillington had first been summoned to Rome to answer charges. Subsequently Edward IV arrested the bishop and investigated what he had been doing and saying. On 19 January 1477/8 Stillington had presumably still been at liberty, because on that date he had been appointed to a commission of the peace for Southampton.[23] However, by Friday 6 March he was a prisoner in the Tower of London.[24] He had probably been arrested on about 15 February.[25] In the end, the bishop appears to have convinced Edward IV that he had not given away the marriage secret. On Tuesday 14 April 1478 Stillington was again appointed to a commission of the peace for Berkshire, which implies that he had then been released.[26] Thus he appears to have remained in the Tower for two months. Apparently he was only released following his payment of a fine.[27] Subsequently, on Saturday 20 June 1478, he was granted a formal pardon, which declared 'that Robert, Bishop of Bath and Wells, has been faithful to the king and done nothing contrary to his oath of fealty, as he has shown before the king and certain lords'.[28] It seems that Edward IV had finally been convinced that the bishop had not given away his secret.

However, the Bishop of Bath and Wells may not have been the only possible source of information to the Duke of Clarence regarding the Talbot marriage contract. Another potential source close to George would have been his own servant Thomas Burdet, who had previously been in the service of the Boteler family of Sudeley, at the time when Eleanor had been married to Thomas Boteler. As we have already seen, Thomas Burdet was undoubtedly the man responsible for those pro-Clarence political poems (all now destroyed), which had been circulated in London and Westminster, and which were probably the source for the famous 'prophecy of G', which proclaimed that Edward IV would be succeeded by someone whose name began with the letter G.

It is possible that Burdet's publications also included verses which contained specific references to the invalidity of Edward IV's marriage to Elizabeth Widville, together with allegations of bastardy against the couple's children. But unfortunately for George, one of the chief results of Burdet's publications – and of the subsequent trial and execution of him and his associates – was that the king now required very little input from Elizabeth Widville to persuade him to now take firm action against his brother: 'Loe sudaynly [Edward IV] fell into a fact most horrible, commanding rashly and upon the suddane his brother George of Clarence to be apprehendyd.'[29]

The Duke of Clarence was tried, and condemned to death. Of course the case as presented before Parliament had to be carefully worded.[30] It would have been a fatal mistake for Elizabeth Widville and her royal children if the question regarding the validity of her marriage had been exposed in that context. Thus, although it certainly was stated in the trial that a wicked plot had been set in motion by the Duke of Clarence, which was aimed not only against Edward IV, but also against Elizabeth Widville, against their son the Prince of Wales, and against all their other children, the Duke of Clarence ultimately found himself condemned on other grounds. These included his earlier (and previously forgiven) involvement in the Earl of Warwick's campaign against Edward IV, and – somewhat ironically – his Lancastrian claim to the throne! George was also accused of involvement in the black arts via his servant Thomas Burdet, whose execution by the king he had contested, and of planning to ship his own young son and heir out of the country.

In the final analysis, it was probably Elizabeth Widville who ensured that George's death sentence was carried out, on Wednesday

18 February 1477/8. The execution took place just over a month after the splendid marriage of her younger royal son, Richard of Shrewsbury, to Eleanor Talbot's niece and Elizabeth Talbot's daughter, Lady Anne Mowbray. In connection with that marriage, it was probably also Elizabeth Widville who persuaded Edward IV to enact dubious legislation to ensure that if little Anne Mowbray died childless, Richard of Shrewsbury would retain her Norfolk inheritance. This legislation became effective in November 1481, when the eight-year-old Duchess of York and Norfolk passed away. The cause of Anne Mowbray's death is unknown.

26

1480–1483: ITINERARY

1480 (age 38; regnal year 20)
MARCH
Greenwich[1]

APRIL
Greenwich[2]
Westminster[3]
The Tower of London[4]

MAY
London and Westminster[5]
Greenwich[6]
Windsor Castle, and Sheen[7]
The Tower of London[8]
The City of London[9]

JUNE
Greenwich, the Tower of London, Westminster, and the forest of Waltham[10]

JULY
Greenwich[11]
The City of London[12]
'our manor called Potels within our forrest of'[13]

Waltham Abbey, and Greenwich[14]
The City of London[15]
The manor of Easthampstead (Easthampstead Park, near Windsor), and Greenwich[16]

AUGUST
Sheen, and Windsor Castle[17]
Westminster and London[18]

SEPTEMBER
The City of London and the manor of Falburn (Faulkbourne, near Braintree, Essex? – held by Sir Thomas Montgomery),[19]
The City and Tower of London[20]
Canterbury, and Dover Castle[21]

OCTOBER
The Tower of London, the manor of Eltham, Greenwich and Westminster[22]

NOVEMBER
The manor of Eltham[23]
Westminster[24]

DECEMBER
Westminster, and the City and
Tower of London[25]
The manor of Eltham[26]
Greenwich[27]

1480/81
JANUARY
Greenwich and the City of
London[28]

FEBRUARY
The City and Tower of London,
and Greenwich[29]
Greenwich[30]

MARCH
The Tower of London[31]
REGNAL YEAR 21
The Tower of London, and
Greenwich[32]

1481 (age 39; regnal year 21)
MARCH
The Tower of London[33]

APRIL
Greenwich, the Tower and City of
London[34]

MAY
Windsor Castle[35]
The Tower of London[36]
Greenwich[37]
Sandwich[38]

JUNE
The Tower of London[39]
Westminster[40]
Windsor Castle and
Westminster[41]

JULY
The Tower of London[42]
Westminster[43]
Potel's Manor, and the forest of
Waltham[44]
The manor of Waltham (Essex /
Herts. border)[45]
The Tower of London[46]
Sheen[47]
Windsor Castle[48]

AUGUST
The manor of Wardelham
(Hants.), and Windsor Castle[49]
Westminster[50]

SEPTEMBER
The manor of Woodstock[51]

OCTOBER
Greenwich, Nottingham Castle,
Fotheringhay Castle, Greenwich
and the Tower of London[52]

NOVEMBER
Greenwich and the Tower of
London[53]
Westminster and Windsor Castle[54]

DECEMBER
The town of Southampton, 'the
city of Winton' (Winchester – early
medieval name 'Wintan ceastre'),
the manor of Sheen, 'the monastery
of Winton' (Winchester Cathedral
Priory), and Windsor Castle[55]

1481/82
JANUARY
Windsor Castle[56]
Westminster[57]

FEBRUARY
The Tower of London[58]
Westminster, the Tower of
London, Windsor Castle, 'the
manor of Goldeford' (Guildford?)
and the manor of Eltham[59]

MARCH
The Tower of London and the
manor of Eltham[60]
REGNAL YEAR 22
The manor of Eltham and the
Tower and City of London[61]

1482 (age 40; regnal year 22)
MARCH
Westminster[62]

APRIL
The Tower of London[63]
The manor of Eltham[64]
The Tower and City of London,
Greenwich and Westminster[65]

MAY
Windsor Castle, the Tower of
London, and Westminster[66]
Leeds ('Lode') Castle[67]
Canterbury, and Dover
Castle[68]
Westminster[69]
The Tower of London[70]
Royston[71]
Cambridge[72]

JUNE
Fotheringhay Castle[73]
Westminster and the Tower of
London[74]

JULY
The Tower of London[75]
The manor of Knoll,
Canterbury, and Dover
Castle[76]
The Tower of London and
Westminster[77]

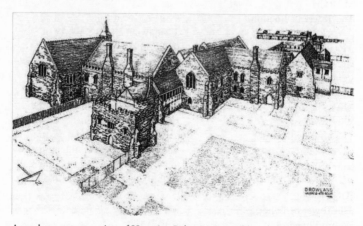

A modern reconstruction of Havering Palace as it would probably have appeared
in 1578, viewed from the north-east, copyright Elizabeth Fann (CC BY 3.0,
https://commons.wikimedia.org/w/index.php?curid=19988227).

AUGUST
Westminster, the Tower of
London, and Windsor Castle[78]
Guildford[79]
The Tower of London and the
manor of Havering [*Haueryng of
the Bower*][80]

SEPTEMBER
The Tower of London, Cheshunt
(Herts - 'Chesten'), and Lavenham
(Suffolk – 'the manor of Lanam')[81]
Walsingham pilgrimage[82]

OCTOBER
Warwick, the manor of Eltham,
the Tower of London, and
Westminster[83]

NOVEMBER
Westminster[84]
The manor of Eltham[85]
The Tower of London[86]
City of London[87]

DECEMBER
The Tower of London[88]
The manor of Eltham[89]

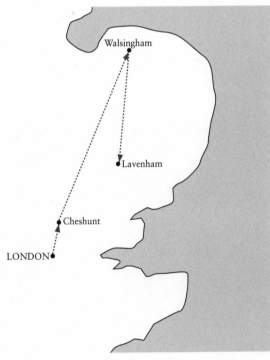

Edward IV's last pilgrimage to the shrine of Our Lady of Walsingham,
September 1482

1482/3
JANUARY
The manor of Eltham,
Westminster and the Tower of
London[90]

FEBRUARY
Westminster[91]
The manor of Eltham[92]
Chelsea[93]
The Tower of London[94]

MARCH
Westminster[95]

REGNAL YEAR 23
Westminster[96]
Windsor Castle[97]

**1483 (age would have been 41 –
but he did not live long enough to
reach his birthday; regnal year 23)**
MARCH
Westminster

APRIL
died at Westminster

27

1483: THE SUCCESSION PROBLEMS

It is clear that by 1477 the succession problems relating to the validity of Elizabeth Woodville's royal marriage, which had been worrying her for quite a while, had, to some extent, come into the open. In April 1483, after King Edward IV had fallen ill and died, that fact, coupled with her own natural worldly ambition, combined to push Elizabeth into an active but illegal plot which was aimed at achieving permanent power for herself and her family. In the context of this Widville plot, account must now be taken of the curious fact that the precise date of Edward IV's death is unclear. This important point has generally been overlooked by historians.

According to the contemporary York Records, Edward must have died either on Tuesday 1 April or on Saturday 5 April 1483, depending on whether his York Requiem Mass was celebrated on the seventh day or the third day after his decease.[1] Most probably the king had died on Saturday 5 April. It is clear that the news of his death had reached the Dean of York by the evening of Sunday 6 April. Presumably a message had been speedily dispatched to the dean by his archbishop.

As the Lord Chancellor of England, in April 1483 Archbishop Rotherham of York was himself present at the Palace of Westminster, where the king died. He is also known to have subsequently been one of the celebrants of the king's funeral Mass. Moreover, following Edward IV's demise, he clearly sided with Elizabeth Widville. Unfortunately, though, he seems not to have possessed a great deal of talent for prognostication. Had he anticipated Elizabeth Widville's plans more wisely he would probably have kept quiet. Instead, it appears that he hastily dispatched news of the king's death to his cathedral in the north of England, in order to ensure prompt prayers there for the soul of his departed sovereign.

According to Domenico Mancini's slightly later account (written in 1483, but about six months after the event) Edward IV died on Monday 7 April.[2] However, the 1486 Crowland Chronicle continuator, and most other later accounts, claim that the king died on Wednesday 9 April.[3] Indeed, a *circa* 1509 addition to the Anlaby Cartulary appears to claim that Edward IV died even later, on Tuesday 15 April. Only thus could the reign of his son, Edward V, have lasted for two months and eight days, as stated in the cartulary![4] But since the same later addition to the Anlaby Cartulary also erroneously records the reign lengths of Richard III and Henry VII, its suggested date for Edward IV's demise can be ignored.

Of course, the Anlaby Cartulary is a later account. However, the genuine conflict which emerges from the *contemporary* narrations of Edward IV's death date raises the significant issue that the king may well have expired a few days before the date on which the news was officially released by the royal council. Elizabeth Widville and her co-plotters presumably decided to conceal the royal death from the public for a short time in order to facilitate their seizure of power. Unfortunately they must have reached this decision just a little too late to prevent Archbishop Rotherham from dispatching news of the king's passing to his dean at York Minster.

The contemporary records of the London Mercers' Company prove that the official announcement was revealed by the King's Council early on the morning of 9 April. This government-authorised account asserted that the king had died during the previous night.[5] Since then, 9 April – the date on which the news was released – has been misinterpreted by the Crowland continuator and others as the actual date of the royal death.

Fortunately for Elizabeth Widville, she had already succeeded in eliminating the Duke of Clarence. His young son and heir, the Earl of Warwick, had also been legally excluded from any claim to the Yorkist inheritance by the act of attainder which had been passed against his late father. Warwick was also too young to be capable of initiating the putting forward of any claim on his own behalf at this time. Moreover, assuming that the Duke of Clarence's plan for shipping his son and heir to safety abroad had not succeeded (which actually it may have done),[6] the boy had effectively been brought under Widville control. A little boy had been sent to Edward IV, in London, from the Clarence nursery at Warwick Castle, and this little orphan, who remained in England bearing the title 'Earl of Warwick' (whether or not he really was the son of the

Duke of Clarence), had then cleverly been consigned to the guardianship of Elizabeth Widville's eldest son, the Marquess of Dorset.

As for Edward IV's younger brother, Richard, Duke of Gloucester, he was in command of the north of England. However, unlike the Duke of Clarence, Gloucester had always been a loyal servant of their brother, the king. Also, although he was not entirely happy with the Widville power in the realm, he had never openly campaigned against that family.

According to English custom, as the senior living adult prince of the blood royal, the Duke of Gloucester should have acted as regent – or 'Lord Protector' as the role was then known in England – for the young Edward V, eldest son of Edward IV and Elizabeth Widville, who had now been proclaimed king in London. Appropriately, when he heard the news of his brother's death the Duke of Gloucester summoned the nobility of the north to York and had them take oaths of loyalty to his nephew.

At the time of his father's death the boy-king himself was living at Ludlow Castle, under the guardianship of his maternal uncle, Earl Rivers. But in London, Elizabeth Widville wrote a message to her brother ordering him to bring the young king to the capital as soon as possible, so that she could have him crowned. She was anxious to speedily guarantee that her son would reign. She was also anxious to ensure that she, rather than the Duke of Gloucester, should exercise the powers of regent for the boy-king. Her Widville family backed her attempted coup in this respect, even though it was illegal and in contravention of the established English practice of that period during the reign of a king who was a minor.

However, some leading members of the nobility, who had always had some problems with the ascent of the Widvilles, were eager to prevent this latest attempted Widville coup. The leading roles in this respect were taken by the Duke of Buckingham and Lord Hastings. Both of these were cousins of the late king and shared his descent from King Edward III. Buckingham was descended from Edward III's youngest son, Thomas of Woodstock, Duke of Gloucester, while Hastings shared Edward IV's descent from Lionel of Antwerp, Duke of Clarence. Despite the fact that Buckingham had been married to one of her sisters, he was no friend of Elizabeth Widville, as we shall see shortly. As for Lord Hastings, he had been a close friend and supporter of Edward IV, but was also not on good terms with Elizabeth. Acting independently, both Hastings and Buckingham wrote to the Duke of Gloucester, warning him that Elizabeth Widville was attempting to seize power, and urging him to prevent this.

Gloucester therefore rode south. On Tuesday 29 April he met both Earl Rivers and the Duke of Buckingham at Northampton. The following morning he went on to Stony Stratford, where he met his nephew. Initially, on 29 April, Gloucester appears to have acted in a friendly way towards the boy's maternal uncle, Earl Rivers, but 'eventually Henry, Duke of Buckingham, also arrived [when] … it was late'.[7] Apparently it was only after Buckingham's arrival – and possibly, therefore, as a result of his influence – that the decision seems to have been made to arrest Rivers. The arrest was carried out on the morning of 30 April. Gloucester is said to have stated that he was only doing this 'to safeguard his own person because he knew for certain that there were men close to the king who had sworn to destroy his honour and his life'.[8]

When Gloucester and Buckingham were received in Stony Stratford by the young king, the Duke of Buckingham was furious to hear Edward V asserting strong trust in his mother. The boy-king told his paternal uncle and his cousin that

> as for the government of the kingdom, he had complete confidence in the peers of the realm and the queen … On hearing the queen's name the duke of Buckingham, who loathed her race, then answered, it was not the business of women but of men to govern kingdoms, and so if he cherished any confidence in her he had better relinquish it.[9]

The new king and his uncle, the Duke of Gloucester, were probably virtual strangers to one another. Gloucester may occasionally have met Edward V as Prince of Wales in London, but because of his own role in the north of England, and the fact that young Edward had been brought up at Ludlow, such meetings must have been very rare. For the boy-king his paternal uncle would have therefore been a very unfamiliar figure. However, it was under the leadership of the Duke of Gloucester that the royal party now made its way onwards towards London.

There, Elizabeth Widville, who had received the news of what had happened at Stony Stratford – including the arrest of her brother, Earl Rivers – on the evening of Thursday 1 May, had promptly fled with the rest of her royal children from the palace of Westminster into sanctuary at the adjacent Westminster Abbey. Obviously she realised that her attempted coup had failed. Her family also understood that their attempt to seize power had proved unsuccessful. One other result of the news was that Elizabeth's youngest brother, Edward Widville, who had been given charge of the English navy, illegally seized part of the royal treasury and fled with the bullion and his ships to Brittany to link up with Henry 'Tudor'.

As for Edward V, when he reached the capital he was initially received at the Bishop of London's palace, where the Duke of Gloucester once again had oaths of fealty taken to the young king. Gloucester's repeated practice in this respect shows very clearly that at this point he had no personal intention of anything other than the coronation of his nephew and the exercise of power on the boy-king's behalf, and in his name, until he came of age. Once again, it was the Duke of Buckingham who subsequently made a suggestion which significantly altered the situation. Buckingham's proposal was that the most appropriate residence for the boy-king in the lead-up to his coronation would be the Tower of London.

The Duke of Gloucester was now formally acknowledged as the Lord Protector of the kingdom during the minority of his nephew.[10] Ironically, Gloucester's tenure of this position is frequently described as a 'coup' by historians who apparently have no real understanding of what had taken place, or of the relevant legal precedents in fifteenth-century England. Under Gloucester's legitimate authority, preparations were now once again formally set in motion for the coronation of the young sovereign. But it was at one of the preparation meetings for the organisation of the coronation that Robert Stillington, Bishop of Bath and Wells, apparently finally decided to go public in respect of Edward IV's Talbot marriage. The result, as Simon Stallworth reported on the day in question, in a letter to Sir William Stonor, was that suddenly and unexpectedly 'there is gret besyness ageyns the Coronacione'.[11]

Of course, Stillington's motive had nothing whatever to do with the question of the marriage itself, since the two key parties – the only people who would have had the right to raise the issue of having their marriage publicly acknowledged – were both now dead. Rather, Stillington was stating that the ongoing preparations for the coronation of Edward V could not proceed, because the boy was not Edward IV's heir but merely a royal bastard. Nevertheless, it seems that the bishop made this amazing statement to a meeting of the royal council which was held at the palace of Westminster on Monday 9 June between 10 a.m. and 2 p.m. As was noted earlier (see above, chapter 7), this date was almost precisely the 22nd anniversary of the day upon which Stillington appears to have celebrated Edward IV's Talbot marriage at one of Eleanor's manors in Warwickshire! The outcome of Stillington's announcement to the royal council was precisely the consequence which Elizabeth Widville had dreaded ever since she discovered that her royal marriage was questionable.

On the basis of the evidence of the Bishop of Bath and Wells, Edward V was set aside. Account was also taken of the earlier Act of Attainder against the Duke of Clarence, and its resultant exclusion of his children from the Yorkist line of inheritance. Based upon these two factors, the three estates of the realm offered the throne to Richard, Duke of Gloucester, as the legitimate male heir. When he had been persuaded to accept their offer, Gloucester was proclaimed king as Richard III.

The decision of the three estates of the realm was ratified by a full Parliament the following year. The relevant Act of Parliament states in completely unequivocal terms that Edward IV 'was and stoode marryed and trouth plight to oone Dame Elianor Butteler, doughter of the old Earl of Shrewesbury', and that his subsequent 'pretensed marriage' to Elizabeth Widville was invalid. As we saw earlier, secondary evidence against the Widville marriage, including the allegations of witchcraft against Elizabeth Widville and her mother, is also mentioned.

The entire royal family appears to have backed the decision. In England, Cecily Neville, Duchess of York, and mother of both Edward IV and Richard III, closed ranks with her middle daughter, the Duchess of Suffolk and the latter's family, in support of the new king. The youngest daughter, Margaret of York, dowager Duchess of Burgundy, made no public statement either way in 1483, but her later behaviour – and her ultimate choice of a burial location for herself which precisely reflected that assigned to Richard III – shows which side she was on. Even Elizabeth Widville said nothing against the decision. After all, she was an intelligent woman who for a number of years had been only too well aware of the fate which would await her royal children if Edward IV's Talbot marriage ever became public knowledge.

The decision of the three estates of the realm – and later of Parliament – produced one very interesting result. Whereas previously, as we have seen, it had been highly questionable whether King Edward IV had fathered very many bastard children, all his numerous offspring by Elizabeth Widville had now officially been declared illegitimate. As a result, the late king was now suddenly perceived to have produced a very considerable number of bastards!

Interestingly, like the royal family, Eleanor Talbot's surviving relatives also backed the new king. Her sister, the Duchess of Norfolk, was well treated by the new king, and seems to have enjoyed a good relationship with him.[12] Other members of Eleanor's family also served Richard III. Indeed, William Catesby, who was Eleanor's relation by marriage, is best remembered nowadays as 'the Cat' who served Richard so faithfully that he was put to death by Henry VII after the battle of Bosworth in August 1485. Curiously, Eleanor was also related by marriage to Sir James Tyrell. In 1502 Tyrell was posthumously accused by Henry VII of having murdered the 'princes in the Tower' on behalf of Richard III. However, that accusation was probably a 'Tudor' government invention.

Naturally, the government of Richard III could not acknowledge Elizabeth Widville as ever having been a true queen. In March 1483/4, when Richard III negotiated with her to come out of sanctuary at Westminster Abbey, and to bring her daughters with her, Richard referred to her as 'dam Elizabeth Gray late calling her self Quene of England'.[13] Nevertheless, he promised to secure suitable marriages for his nieces, the illegitimate daughters whom Elizabeth had borne to the late king. Subsequently, in 1484, he arranged a marriage for his niece, Cecily (the second surviving daughter of Edward IV and Elizabeth Widville), to Ralph Scrope, a younger brother of Thomas, 6th Baron Scrope.[14] This marriage was annulled by Henry VII soon after his accession, and Henry subsequently married Cecily to his own ally, Lord Welles.

In 1485, following the death of his own queen, Anne of Warwick, Richard III negotiated a second marriage for himself, with the Infanta Joana of Portugal. As part of this marriage contract, he also arranged for quite a splendid wedding for his eldest illegitimate niece, Elizabeth of York. She was to have married a junior cadet member of the Portuguese royal family.[15] Both of these Portuguese royal marriages would certainly have taken place had it not been for the battle of Bosworth.

The unexpected defeat of King Richard III at Bosworth, and the ensuing usurpation of Henry VII changed the situation completely. Following his seizure of the English throne, Henry not only executed William Catesby, he also re-imprisoned Bishop Stillington.[16] This shows that he was very concerned about Edward IV's marriage question. Indeed, in his first parliament Henry VII organised a bizarre and unique procedure. He ordered the repeal of the Act of Parliament of 1484, and prevented the words of the original act from being quoted. Normally, when Acts of Parliament were annulled they were quoted in full. At the very least, if the act was not fully quoted, its contents were summarised in the act of repeal. However, Henry VII merely permitted the first thirteen words of the Act of 1484 to be cited. Significantly, these few words revealed nothing of the contents of the Act.

Henry VII also ordered all copies of the 1484 Act to be destroyed 'upon Peine of ymprisonment ... so that all thinges said and remembered in the said Bill and Acte maie be for ever out of remembraunce and also forgott'.[17] This makes it absolutely clear that he was determined that Eleanor Talbot and her marriage with Edward IV should be wiped out of history. He was aided in this by the subsequent invention of his government to the effect that the bastardisation of Edward V had been brought about by Richard III's claim that his elder brother had married 'Elizabeth Lucy' (see above).

The motivation behind Henry's actions comprised two significant threads of political thinking. The first was that by airbrushing Eleanor Talbot and her genuine relationship with Edward IV out of history, Richard III could be presented to the world as a usurper – a thesis which was completely unjustified but which proved highly effective from the 'Tudor' point of view. The second thread was that Henry VII, whose own claim to the throne was extremely weak, aimed to reinforce it by marrying the eldest surviving daughter of Edward IV and Elizabeth Widville, and by presenting this girl to the nation and to the world as the Yorkist heiress. Of course, he could only achieve this by reinstating the girl's mother, Elizabeth Widville, as England's dowager queen. That is what he did, and in that respect also, his action proved highly successful.

One outcome was that, for about two years, Elizabeth Widville found herself back at court, where she was now honoured not as the consort of the reigning monarch, but as the mother of the new queen consort, and thus the prospective grandmother of a new dynasty. However, in 1487, Henry VII found himself facing a threat to his throne from a Yorkist pretender whom at least one of his servants mistakenly suggested claimed to be the second of Elizabeth Widville's sons by Edward IV.[18] In actual fact, the pretender claimed to be (and possibly was) the Earl of Warwick. However, Henry VII apparently then decided that the wisest move would be to ensure that his mother-in-law never caught a glimpse of her alleged son or nephew. Obviously, if she had recognised the boy, that would have proved a major disaster. Elizabeth Widville was therefore disgraced. Deprived of her dower lands, and left with only a very small pension, she then retired to Bermondsey Abbey. One curious result is that, in one way, Elizabeth Widville can be seen as having come closer to being a nun than her rival, Eleanor Talbot!

At one point there was a brief political fantasy that Elizabeth Widville might make yet another royal marriage – this time becoming the queen consort of Scotland. However, nothing ever came of this. Thus Elizabeth simply spent the last five years of her life at Bermondsey Abbey. She died there in utter poverty in April 1492. At the time of her death she was not in a position to leave anything to her children beyond her blessings. Her final request was for her dead body to share the royal tomb of Edward IV at St George's Chapel, Windsor. Thus she hoped to retain forever the rank of queen consort. In one sense she succeeded. However, her funeral hardly seems to have been a genuine royal event. Her wooden coffin was so cheap that it rapidly decayed in the damp Windsor soil, leaving virtually nothing to be found, four hundred years later, by the late eighteenth-century antiquarians who explored the burial site. As for the accounts of Elizabeth's funeral, they clearly reveal that the entire event was a penny-pinching act on the part of her son-in-law, King Henry VII. We are even told that second-hand candles were used.[19] What is more, it seems that Elizabeth's own royal children were excluded from her burial. Instead, Elizabeth Widville found herself accompanied to Windsor by one of Edward IV's illegitimate daughters.

28

1485–1574: FATES OF THE
ROYAL BASTARDS

The book *Royal Bastards*, by P. Beauclerk-Dewar and R. Powell, offers a rather curious account of its stated subject. It provides strong, fascinating – and scientific – evidence in relation to Stuart and later royal bastards and their descendants. But it has nothing to say about any royal bastards prior to the end of the fifteenth century, despite the fact that the existence of illegitimate offspring of Henry I, Henry II and many other early English kings and their sons is well documented. Curiously, the book's account of royal bastards begins with King Edward IV. Presumably this is because, as we have seen, Edward IV is popularly perceived as the father of numerous royal bastards. But, ironically, the book's account then seems to be able to cite only one single bastard child of Edward IV, namely Arthur Wayte (whom it claims was the son of the mythical 'Elizabeth Lucy').[1]

In fact this is inaccurate in several ways. Edward IV was not the first English king to produce royal bastards. And although he did father at least one bastard son whose existence he himself recognised, the son in question was not Arthur Wayte. Instead, it may have been the person who later became known as 'Richard of England / Perkin Warbeck'. Nevertheless, it is true that Arthur Wayte was subsequently recognised as a bastard son of Edward IV – by the new reigning dynasty of King Henry VII. For political reasons, the new royal dynasty also allowed Arthur to adopt the surname 'Plantagenet'. Moreover, there is some evidence (also not contemporary in terms of their royal father's life and reign) that several other children (namely four daughters) were also recognised by 'Tudor' authorities as the illegitimate offspring of King Edward IV. Possible reasons for this will be considered shortly.

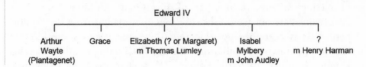

The alleged illegitimate children of Edward IV recognised by the 'Tudor' regime.

Earlier, of course, Parliament had formally recognised a numerous family of Edward IV's bastards. But, as we have seen, the individuals in question were Edward IV's sons and daughters by Elizabeth Widville! Although the relevant Act of Parliament was subsequently quashed by the government of Henry VII, for political reasons it may well have comprised part of the motivation behind subsequent 'Tudor' recognition of Edward's other alleged illegitimate children. The same motivation may also explain the 'Tudor' political allegations to the effect that Edward IV had had numerous mistresses.

During the period of the Norman kings of England there seems to have been absolutely no difficulty over acknowledging royal bastard offspring. This situation continued into the reign of Henry II. Although by no means all of his descendants fathered bastards, acknowledgement of illegitimate royal children – when they did exist – appears to have continued into the fourteenth century. However, there are no acknowledged bastards of any of the Lancastrian kings, and only one bastard child fathered by one of Henry V's younger brothers was apparently acknowledged in the first half of the fifteenth century.

As for the house of York, the father, Richard, Duke of York, appears to have produced no illegitimate offspring. Neither does his middle son, George, Duke of Clarence. But both Edward IV and Richard III did so. King Richard, it seems, showed no greater difficulty in acknowledging his genuine illegitimate children than his royal ancestors had done. He acknowledged two such children, one son and one daughter. Later accounts have sought to attribute other, unacknowledged bastard children to Richard. However, the evidence for his paternity of these subsequently alleged offspring remains highly disputable. There is no documentary evidence from Richard himself to indicate that he acknowledged the people in question – or even that he was aware of their existence. It therefore seems probable that in reality Richard only fathered those two royal bastards whom he recognised and cared for during his own reign and lifetime.

As for Edward IV, like his younger brother, Richard, he is accused of having fathered a number of illegitimate children. But these allegations date not from Edward's own lifetime but from the 'Tudor' period. It is therefore possible that they constituted some kind of 'Tudor' political manipulation. During his lifetime, rather like his younger brother, Richard, Edward IV appears to have recognised only one bastard son and perhaps one bastard daughter. The possible daughter was Lady Lumley. As for the son, his name was not recorded at the time, but he figures in Edward IV's household accounts as 'the Lord Bastard'. As we have seen, the boy in question may possibly have been the subsequent Yorkist claimant to the English throne who gave out his own name as 'Richard of England'. Of course, this person was later designated 'Peter of Tournai' (alias 'Perkin Warbeck') by the government of Henry VII. He was ultimately executed for treason, and his remains were interred in the Church of the Austin Friars in Broadgate, London.[2]

As for Arthur Wayte, there is not a shred of evidence that his existence was ever formally acknowledged by his royal father. Although for some time he was subsequently supported and employed by the

The Austin Friars, Broadgate. Redrawn from Anthonis van den Wyngaerde's 'Panorama of London', *circa* 1544. Here 'Richard of England' was buried following his execution in 1499.

'Tudor' government of England, he too ultimately found himself on the wrong side of the new ruling dynasty. There is no reason to doubt that Arthur was an illegitimate royal child. It is shown, for example, by his coat of arms, which are identical to those used after August 1485 by his half-sister, Elizabeth of York, consort of Henry VII, with one addition – a bend sinister across the royal arms, indicating bastard descent in Arthur's case. Additional proof, if it were needed, can be found in *The Lisle Letters* in the form of the following letter 'To my loving Cousyn my Lorde Lysle':

> Mine own good Cousin, In my most hearty mannere I recommend me unto you, and to my Lady, your wife, being glad to hear of your good health: praying you that where my friend Richard Baker is by your favour appointed to the King's service in Calais it [may] please you to be good lord unto him, and the rather for my sake, in all such things as ye may do him favour therein. For I do [*sic* ?doubt] not but that ye shall find him an honest man, and meet to do the King service. And thus I pray Jesu preserve you in good health, and prosperous, to his pleasure.
> At Bisham, the vith day of March,[3]
> Be yowr loyng cousin
> Margret Salysbery[4]

This shows that Arthur was recognised as her first cousin by Margaret, Countess of Salisbury, daughter of Edward IV's younger brother, George, Duke of Clarence. Incidentally, it also implies that Margaret and her cousin Arthur probably belonged to a fairly similar age group. And we know that Margaret was born on 14 August 1473.

The Complete Peerage states that Arthur was 'at first known as Arthur Waite'.[5] Unfortunately, it cites no source for this statement. Nevertheless, Arthur's connection with the Wayte family can certainly be proved. The many surviving letters from Antony Wayte [Waite] to Arthur's wife, Viscountess Lisle, do not hint at any family relationship between Antony and the viscountess. They refer to the writer by using such subservient terms as 'your humble orator and seuant'.[6] However, one surviving letter written to Antony Wayte by Arthur himself opens in a way which clearly shows the existence of a blood relationship between these two men, for Arthur addresses Antony as follows:

> Cousin Wayte, I commend me unto you, and have received the letter you sent to my wife.[7]

The relationship between Arthur and the Wayte family is also attested by his management of the property of the mentally defective John Wayte 'the Innocent'. In addition, the surviving Lisle letters include correspondence from Eleanor Wayte, from William Wayte of Titchfield, and from William Wayte of Wymering, together with references to the will of Leonard Wayte and references to other members of the Wayte family. Thus Arthur's blood relationship with the Waytes of Hampshire is established beyond doubt, and this connection can only have existed in respect of his mother. The logical conclusion is that his mother's surname was Wayte.

Superficially, this may appear initially to offer two possible interpretations. The first would be that the maiden name of Arthur's mother was Wayte. The second possible interpretation would be that Arthur's mother had some other maiden name, but had subsequently married into the Wayte family. However, the fact that, in the 1530s, Arthur had an acknowledged *blood* relationship with living (and dead) members of the Wayte family rules out the second possibility. The conclusion must therefore be that his mother had been born within the Wayte family of Hampshire.

The only questions then remaining are these: what was her Christian name, and what was her married surname (if she ever married)? As we have seen, George Buck, writing early in the seventeenth century, supplied an almost correct record of her *maiden* name, referring to her as 'Elizabeth *Wiatt* (alias Lucy)'.[8] Elsewhere, Buck specified that 'Elizabeth Lucy was the daughter of one Wyat of Southampton, a mean gentleman (if he were one) and the wife of one Lucy, as mean a man as Wyat'. He also states specifically that Edward IV 'had a childe by her, which was the bastard Arthur, called commonly (but unduly) Arthur Plantagenet, afterward made Viscount Lisle by H. 8'.[9]

Earlier in the present volume, the conclusion has been put forward that 'Elizabeth Lucy' was merely a 'Tudor' invention – a name created for political reasons – and that Buck's later attempt to identify her with Miss Wayte was a mistake on his part, to which he found himself pushed by the strength of the intervening 'Tudor' propaganda machine. A great deal of searching has been done by historians and genealogists in an attempt to identify the noble or knightly Lucy whom the Wayte girl allegedly married. But it has all been unsuccessful.

It is also worth noting that generally this quest seems to have completely ignored George Buck's very specific statement that the husband in question was 'as mean a man' as the maternal grandfather of Arthur, Viscount Lisle. That statement strongly suggests that, if he ever existed, the man in question held no kind of title, and certainly was never a knight. Another point worth noting is that Buck made a slight mistake in respect of the maiden name of Arthur's mother, referring to her as Wyat (or Wiatt) instead of Wayte. This suggests that, if she really did marry a man whose surname began with the letter L, Buck might also have made a slight mistake in respect of the spelling of her married name. Could it perhaps have been 'Lacy', or something similar, instead of 'Lucy'?

In this connection it might possibly be significant that, in respect of his office in Calais, Arthur, Viscount Lisle, had a colleague called Henry (or Harry) Lacy (or Lasy). Muriel St Clare Byrne makes the following statement about Lacy:

> Henry Lacy ... owes his survival as a personality to the preservation of the confiscated Lisle correspondence, and to a lesser degree to Cromwell's. He was not a member of the Retinue, but he was a man of property in England and Calais, a married man and a cousin of Thomas Scriven who introduces him to Lisle as his kinsman in No. 149 (Vol. 2). ... Lacy himself puts it on record in a 1539 letter to Cromwell that he had known Calais for thirty-four years. As he does not claim to be Calisien-born he was then presumably in his late fifties or early sixties.[10]

St Clare Byrne's statement is interesting in respect of Lacy's age and his ownership of property. The latter would appear to place him in the right social status as a potential relative of Viscount Lisle's mother's reportedly low-status husband, while the former suggests that he had been born in about 1479. He was therefore probably somewhat younger than Viscount Lisle, and could not possibly have been his late mother's husband. However, he could perhaps have been a relative (perhaps a nephew) of the husband in question.

As for St Clare Byrne's statement in respect of the letter of introduction to which she refers, that is actually somewhat misleading. In reality the letter of introduction had been addressed not to Viscount Lisle (who apparently already knew Henry Lacy) but to his wife:

> To the honorable and my synguler good Lady Lyle se ytt dd. at calles.

> Written at London, the xxv day of March 1533 [1534].
> Madame, I beseech you desire my lord to be a good lord unto my kinsman, Harry Lacy, in his suits now being afore my lord, and to help him to his right. For I know he hath many enemies and hath sustained much wrong a great while.[11]

This letter makes it clear that Lacy and his problems were already known to the Viscount himself. It is also clear from the surviving correspondence that Lacy later had problems with the Lisles – most particularly with the viscountess.[12]

There were undoubtedly families with the surname Lacy (Lacie) in Hampshire, and some of them had at times held parts of manors in the county,[13] which would suggest a family of the kind of social status implied by George Buck's statement. For example, the manor of Kilmeston had connections with the Skillyngs (and Elizabeth Skillyng was the wife of Thomas Wayte), but the manor was later held by a Lacie family.[14] Clearly, if Arthur Wayte's mother had married a Lacy / Lasy / Lacie of Hampshire that might possibly help to explain Buck's later assumption that she was to be identified with the 'Tudor' invented character known as 'Elizabeth Lucy'. But of course, it is equally possible that Miss Wayte never married, and that Buck's later account of her was simply swayed by the story that one of Edward IV's mistresses bore the fabricated name of 'Elizabeth Lucy'.

As for Arthur Wayte, the earliest surviving mention of him dates, not from the reign of his father, King Edward IV, but from 1501. It occurs in a letter written by Lady Margaret Beaufort to her son, King Henry VII. However, the letter does not actually mention Arthur's name. It merely refers to '[*blank*] the Bastard [*singular*] of King Edward's'.[15] From this point onwards the new royal dynasty seems to have accepted Arthur. In 1502 and 1503 he is named in the household expenses of his half-sister, Henry VII's consort, Elizabeth of York.[16]

The date of his first appearance is probably significant. A few years earlier Henry VII's government had been desperately trying to convince the Catholic Monarchs of Spain that the new English royal family's tenure of the throne of England was secure. The purpose of this was to ensure that the marriage of Arthur, Prince of Wales, to Catherine of Aragon should go ahead. As part of this attempt, Henry VII had 'Richard of England / Perkin Warbeck' executed, together with another Yorkist claimant known as Ralph Wilford, whom perhaps Henry VII and his own government had secretly promoted as a means of undermining the other Yorkist pretenders.[17] Henry VII also had the other allegedly royal prisoner executed, whom he held in the Tower of London under the name of the Duke of Clarence's son, the Earl of Warwick. At the same time, moves were also made to extract the de la Pole Yorkist claimants to the throne of England from their exile abroad.[18] In other words, Henry VII was trying very hard to make his throne tenure appear secure by exterminating all the potential Yorkist claimants. Given the possible source of 'Richard of England' which was put forward earlier in the present volume, the potential danger to Henry VII and his dynasty of royal bastards fathered by King Edward IV may have been very much in the sovereign's mind at this point in time. In this context, approaching Arthur Wayte and offering him formal recognition as a royal *bastard* would be one potential means of ensuring that he would never come forward as yet another Yorkist pretender.

The right to the title of Viscount Lisle was subsequently acquired by Arthur as the result of a curious coincidence, namely his marriage with the niece and heiress of Lady Eleanor Talbot's nephew and heir, Thomas Talbot, Viscount Lisle.[19] As for Henry VII's promotion of his illegitimate half-brother-in-law, and the fact that he allowed him to use the surname Plantagenet, that was probably another aspect of the careful policy of Henry's government. In this way the king effectively established that 'Plantagenet' was no longer the English royal surname. It had now become the surname of a royal bastard line.

As we have seen, there had undoubtedly been earlier medieval royal bastards in England. However, no contemporary evidence exists to show that any of them ever used the surname 'Plantagenet'. Of course, the fact that most of their fathers never used that surname makes it highly unlikely that the illegitimate children would have done so. Thus King Edward II's illegitimate son is known as 'Adam Fitzroy' – a surname which means 'King's-son', and which was certainly applied to royal bastards later in English history.[20] The evidence for Adam's tenure of that surname comprises contemporary documentation in Latin, which refers to him as *Ade filio domini Regis bastardo* ('Adam, bastard son of the lord king').[21] No one has ever claimed that Adam was called Plantagenet.

At the end of the fourteenth century, Edward II's grandson John of Gaunt produced bastard children by his mistress (and later third wife) Catherine de Roët. Like Adam, John's children were never referred to under the surname 'Plantagenet'. Instead they were given the newly invented surname of 'Beaufort', which they retained, even when the state and the Church acknowledged them as legitimate.

Later, Henry IV's son John of Lancaster, Duke of Bedford, produced two illegitimate children, Richard and Mary. They are usually referred to as 'Richard and Mary of Bedford', though no contemporary source appears to be cited to prove they used such a name, and it has been questioned what name they would have used if they were born before their father was given the title 'Duke of Bedford'.[22] Richard and Mary have also been referred to by modern writers of history under the name 'Plantagenet', but that appears to be mere mythology.

John's younger brother, Humphrey, Duke of Gloucester, also had two illegitimate children, Arthur and Antigone. They are usually referred to as 'Arthur and Antigone of Gloucester', but again, no contemporary source material is cited to prove that they used that appellation. Antigone has also been referred to in modern sources as 'Antigone Plantagenet',[23] but that just seems to be another example of modern mythology.

Finally, as we have seen, Richard of York, Duke of Gloucester (Richard III), also fathered two illegitimate children, John and Catherine. John's appointment by his father as Captain of Calais, on 11 March 1484/5, refers to him as 'John of Gloucester'.[24] Another contemporary record refers to him as 'John de Pountfreit Bastard'.[25] There is no evidence that John was ever called 'Plantagenet', even though his grandfather, Richard, Duke of York, seems to have (re)adopted that surname. However, Richard III's bastard daughter must have been hugely important in her father's eyes. An aristocratic marriage was arranged for her with William Herbert, Earl of Huntingdon, and in the surviving document in which Richard III set up this alliance, the girl is referred to as Lady Catherine Plantagenet.[26]

For an illegitimate royal son Henry VII's assignment of the surname Plantagenet to Arthur Wayte seems to have been unique. As was suggested earlier, his main object was probably political. But the action also proclaimed that Henry was kind to members of the house of York (so long as they were no threat to him). Henry VIII (always less subtle than his father) subsequently imprisoned Arthur, who eventually died in the Tower of London. However, he left three daughters, and he has living descendants.

Backing for the contention that Henry VII recognised Arthur Wayte as a royal bastard fathered by Edward IV as a move in his own interest is offered by the fact that it was also the 'Tudor' regime which reputedly recognised previously unknown bastard daughters of Edward IV and granted one of them arms which in some way reflected her royal paternity. As we saw earlier, Henry VII had Edward IV's bastard daughter, Grace, attend the Windsor funeral of Elizabeth Widville. The earliest surviving document referring to Lady Lumley (see above) as an illegitimate daughter of Edward IV dates from 1505.[27] Henry VII (or possibly his son) also appears to have granted royal recognition – together with arms showing her royal connection (see plate 35) – to Isabel Mylbery.[28] The colours of the arms represent 'the livery colours of the house of York, the white rose is of York and the demi lions are reminiscent of the lions of England'.[29] Finally, in 1574 the Kent Visitation posthumously recognised the unnamed wife of Henry Harman as a bastard daughter of Edward IV.[30]

29

CONCLUSIONS

The present account of the private life of King Edward IV has tried as far as possible to refer to contemporary evidence. Inevitably, some of its conclusions remain speculative. Nevertheless, what has emerged overall is a very different picture of the private life of Edward IV from the traditional one. Early marriage plans for the boy on the part of his father confirm that Edward really was the acknowledged son and heir of Richard, Duke of York, despite later myths which suggest that he may have been a bastard. Also, there is no proof that Edward produced numerous bastard children himself – unless, of course, one accepts the 1484 Act of Parliament which ruled that all his children by Elizabeth Widville were bastards!

There is also no proof that Edward IV ever had a mistress named 'Elizabeth Lucy', and no proof that he was the lover of Elizabeth Lambert ('Mistress Shore'). On the other hand, it is certainly the case that he had relationships with Eleanor Talbot, and with her first cousin Henry Beaufort, Duke of Somerset. It is also clear that he was later captivated by Elizabeth Widville. However, the contemporary fifteenth-century opinions which were critical of her and her family may well have been justified.

The prime source for some of the key stories which have come down to us regarding Edward IV's alleged liaisons is Thomas More's account of Richard III. Of course, Thomas More's written (but, in the author's lifetime, unpublished) account was essentially not about King Edward IV himself. It was focused upon his younger brother, Richard. And, almost certainly, Thomas More himself is not to be blamed for the inventions which his story contains. Indeed, he may well have been unaware of the fact that the 'history' he was propagating had been rewritten. Nevertheless, the account which he produced clearly formed part of the new regime's endeavours to blacken Richard III's reputation.

More is the earliest source in respect of Edward's claimed relationships both with 'Elizabeth Lucy' and with Elizabeth Lambert (Shore). In actual fact, as we have seen, no genuine evidence exists for either relationship. Indeed, there is no evidence to show that 'Elizabeth Lucy' ever really existed. As for More's claims to the effect that she had been put forward by Richard, Duke of Gloucester (Richard III), and other members of the house of York as the legal wife of Edward IV, that is patent rubbish.

On the other hand, More never mentions Eleanor Talbot, whose relationship with Edward IV was unquestionably real, and who had been named by Parliament as that king's legal wife. Of course, it is well known by any historian who takes a serious interest in authentic source material that More's account of Richard III is historically inaccurate and contains invented myths. It is also blatantly obvious that More was writing in a context in which those who held power were determined to manipulate accounts of the reign of Edward IV by completely eliminating from history the story of Eleanor Talbot and her relationship with the first Yorkist king.

The surviving evidence for that elimination is crystal clear. It comprises a key section of the earliest legislation of Henry VII, following his seizure of the English throne at the battle of Bosworth. As we have seen, in November 1485 the first 'Tudor' king decreed that all copies of the 1484 Act of Parliament were to be destroyed 'upon Peine of ymprisonment', explaining with amazing frankness that his purpose was 'that all thinges said and remembered in the said Bill and Acte maie be for ever out of remembraunce and allso forgot'.[1] Since the most important of those 'thinges' was the name of Eleanor, daughter of the Earl of Shrewsbury, and the existence of her valid marriage with Edward IV, it is clear that Henry VII wished to write Eleanor and her relationship with that king out of history.

It is as a follow-up to King Henry's manipulation of the Eleanor Talbot story that we then encounter the invention which refers to 'Elizabeth Lucy'. This claims that Richard III had asserted that Edward IV's first marriage had not been with the politically unmentionable Eleanor but with a woman who never really appears to have existed, and for whom the name of 'Elizabeth Lucy' is cited. This claim is set out in Thomas More's account. However, it is clearly an invention supplied to that young man by some other source – possibly by Cardinal John Morton, or by other leading members of the government of his day.

Presumably the aim behind this invented story was to muddle and confuse anyone who remembered the fact that the 1484 parliament had decreed that Edward IV had been bigamously married to Elizabeth Widville. Those who recalled that fact would also have been well aware that Parliament had cited the name of the king's legal consort. But since Eleanor had never been well known by the general public, those who preserved the Act of Parliament in their memories could easily have forgotten the name of the lady who had been mentioned in it. Thus, introducing the invented name of 'Elizabeth Lucy' could miraculously add to the general confusion in respect of the identity of the earlier – and valid – wife of Edward IV. At the same time, promotion of the story that Edward IV had fathered bastards – and indeed, having some of the alleged bastards recognised by the new government – may have seemed a good way of attempting to confuse anyone who remembered that the 1484 Act of Parliament had officially categorised all of Edward's children by Elizabeth Widville as bastards.

Of course, Thomas More's account of 'Elizabeth Lucy' never suggested that she was a member of the Wayte family. Nor did it refer to her as the alleged mother of Arthur, Viscount Lisle. *That* story only surfaced about a century later. Obviously it would have been difficult to put forward such a claim in the first quarter of the sixteenth century, when Thomas More was writing, because Arthur Wayte / Plantagenet was then alive, and in the service of his nephew, King Henry VIII. Moreover, it would have been a potentially very dangerous thing to do. The manipulated political propaganda was seeking to employ the invented character of 'Elizabeth Lucy' as a means of strengthening the 'Tudor' claim to the English throne. But if that story had become mixed up with a claim that the woman in question had borne King Edward a bastard son (who held a noble title, and who was still living), the outcome might well have proved to be the promotion of Viscount Lisle as a potential Yorkist pretender! That, of course, would not at all have been what the 'Tudor' government wanted.

It is therefore certain that the imagined connection between 'Elizabeth Lucy' and Miss Wayte was only formulated much later. It first appears in the seventeenth century. By that time, no living person could find any evidence in respect of the real name of Viscount Lisle's mother. Meanwhile, the family of King Henry VII had disappeared, having been succeeded on the English throne by the house of Stuart. The new dynasty, of Scottish origin, had nothing to fear from an imaginary connection between Arthur Wayte / Plantagenet and 'Elizabeth Lucy'.

Thomas More has nothing to say about Edward IV's relationship with the Duke of Somerset, despite the fact that contemporary source material for that did (and does) exist. Once again, there is probably a political reason behind this. After all, the story of that relationship was of no potential benefit to the new regime. Indeed, it might even have produced a harmful effect, given that Edward IV's daughter, Elizabeth of York, was the consort of the first king of the new dynasty and the mother of his successor. After all, as the fifteenth century ended and the sixteenth century began the official view of same-sex relationships was becoming more severely critical – a move which was subsequently reflected in the legislation of Edward IV's grandson, King Henry VIII.

The surviving contemporary source material matches later accounts in emphasising the importance of Edward IV's relationship with Elizabeth Widville. Both Elizabeth herself and her subsequent son-in-law, Henry VII, had strong motives for stressing the fact that she had been Edward's queen consort. However, some contemporary accounts also reveal a point which Elizabeth herself would have preferred to keep under wraps. This is the fact that, for many of the years during which she played the role of queen, she had been suffering from considerable anxiety regarding the validity of her marriage with Edward, and the future of her royal children. For her, the effect of the legislation of 1483 and 1484 was to demote her from royal status, in spite of the fact that she had been crowned as queen consort in Westminster Abbey.

As for Elizabeth Widville's reputation, although she did her best on that front, contemporary comments have survived which refer to the inappropriateness, not only of her family background but also of her conduct, once she found herself in a position of power. Although some later historians appear to have taken Elizabeth Widville's side, and have tried to undermine such criticisms, important sources remain which accuse her of having been the key person behind two political killings. These were the executions of the Duke of Clarence and of the Earl of Desmond. As Richard Neville, Earl of Warwick, and others were well aware at the time, Elizabeth was the power behind Edward IV's throne. Her later attempt to illegally seize regency powers in 1483 show how determined she was to remain in power, even after Edward IV had died. She must therefore have had some influence in having her own enemies put to death. And, as we have seen, significantly a surviving letter of King Richard III clearly shows that he was aware of this.

We also know that servants of the Duke of Clarence, and of John Mowbray and Elizabeth Talbot, were executed for political reasons. And it is intriguing to note that the contemporary view of the Duke of Clarence himself was clearly that his wife and younger son had been murdered, and that the life of his elder son and heir was also in potential danger. In this context, the premature and unexpected deaths of Eleanor Talbot and her brother-in-law the Duke of Norfolk may also be significant. Though no contemporary evidence survives which openly claims that they were murdered, both their deaths were beneficial in various ways to Elizabeth Widville, and to the future of her royal children. The intriguing suggestion has therefore now been put forward that these two unexpected deaths may also have been brought about by Elizabeth Widville for political reasons.

EDWARD IV'S PRIVATE TIMELINE

1445   Richard, Duke of York, proposes his son and heir's marriage to a French princess

1461   Edward IV's secret marriage with Eleanor Talbot

1462   Edward IV may perhaps have taken a mistress (name unknown)

1462/3   Possible birth of Edward IV's bastard daughter (later Lady Lumley)

1463   Edward IV's love affair with the Duke of Somerset
The Earl of Warwick's royal marriage negotiations (Scotland; France)

1464   Edward IV's secret marriage with Elizabeth Widville
Elizabeth Widville becomes (or claims to be) pregnant
The Widville marriage is acknowledged

1465   Elizabeth Widville is crowned queen

1466   Elizabeth Widville produces a daughter (Elizabeth of York)
Catherine de Clarington possibly becomes a royal mistress

1467   Elizabeth Widville becomes aware of Edward IV's earlier relationship with Eleanor Talbot

1468   Elizabeth Widville has two enemies killed (the Earl of Desmond and Eleanor Talbot)

1469   The Earl of Warwick and the Duke of Clarence attack the Widvilles

1470?   Miss Wayte becomes Edward IV's mistress
Edward IV, in exile, possibly takes a Flemish mistress

1471   Edward IV may have fathered three sons (Edward V, Arthur Wayte and a 'lord bastard' (who may have been 'Richard of England')

1472   Edward IV recognises his son, 'the lord bastard'

1474   Elizabeth Lambert (Shore) is claimed by later sources to have become Edward IV's mistress (but there is no contemporary evidence of this)

1475   Bishop Stillington is summoned to Rome to answer charges

1475/6   The Duke of Norfolk dies unexpectedly – possibly murdered by Elizabeth Widville

     The Duke of Clarence claims he should be the heir to the throne

1476   The Duchess of Clarence and her son Richard are both murdered

     The Duke of Clarence tries to smuggle his son and heir out of the country

1477   The Duke of Clarence is arrested

1477/8   Richard of Shrewsbury marries the late Duke of Norfolk's heiress

     The Duke of Clarence is executed

     Bishop Stillington is arrested (but later released)

1483   Edward IV dies

     Elizabeth Widville's attempted coup to seize regency power (prevented by Lord Hastings and the Duke of Buckingham)

     Edward IV is formally judged to have been legally married to Eleanor Talbot

     Edward IV's Widville children are formally declared bastards

     The throne is offered to Richard, Duke of Gloucester (Richard III)

1485   Henry 'Tudor' (Henry VII) seizes the crown

     Bishop Stillington is arrested and imprisoned for the rest of his life

     Eleanor Talbot is airbrushed out of history

     'Elizabeth Lucy' is invented

1486   Henry VII marries Elizabeth of York, who is declared to be the Yorkist heiress

1499   'Richard of England' is executed

1501   'Tudor' recognition of Arthur Wayte ('Plantagenet') as Edward IV's son

APPENDIX

THE mtDNA SEQUENCE OF THE 'PRINCES IN THE TOWER', BY GLEN MORAN

The discovery and subsequent identification of the remains of Edward IV's younger brother King Richard III in Leicester in 2012 has resulted in a renewed interest in another set of ancient remains. These are the bones currently housed in the Henry VII Chapel at Westminster, long thought to belong to the sons of Edward IV – Edward V and Richard, Duke of York, known commonly as the 'princes in the Tower'.

In 1674, workmen at the Tower of London discovered bones that appeared to be those of two infants, buried deep under a staircase. The location of the remains seemed superficially consistent with the account of the fate of the 'princes' given by Sir Thomas More.[1] It was therefore assumed that the workmen had found the final resting place of the sons of Edward IV. It appears that Charles II accepted the proposed identity of the bones and had them reinterred in an urn at Westminster, where they remain today. Unfortunately, as has already been seen, Thomas More's account is full of inconsistencies (see above, Introduction and elsewhere).

Greater weight was given to the identity claim when the bones were examined by Wright and Tanner in 1933, whose published findings seemed to support the view that the contents of the urn were indeed the remains of the sons of Edward IV and Elizabeth Widville.[2] Following the discovery of the body of Anne Mowbray in 1965, it was also claimed that evidence of hypodontia confirmed the alleged identity of the Tower of London bones.[3] However, these results have since been challenged and have led to renewed calls for the bones to be re-tested using modern methods and techniques.[4]

Given the importance of DNA testing in the identification of Richard III, the ability to test the contents of the Westminster urn (or indeed any other remains suspected of being those of the 'princes in the Tower'[5]), would be an essential step in any attempts to positively identify them. In the case of Richard III, mitochondrial DNA (mtDNA) was used to check whether or not an exact match could be found between the skeleton found at the Leicester Grey Friars site and known living relatives.[6] mtDNA is the DNA sequence passed exclusively along the female line and as such can only be checked against an all-female-line relative. In the case of Richard, the genealogical research of John Ashdown-Hill located an all-female-line descendant of Richard's sister Anne of York, from whom a sample could be extracted.[7] The use of mtDNA is considered in many ways more reliable than using the all-male Y-chromosome, due to the possibility of non-paternities.[8] Indeed this turned out to be the case when Richard's Y-chromosome was compared with supposed all-male-line relatives, demonstrating that a break in the line had occurred at an unknown point in history.[9] The discovery of Richard III's body means that any remains thought to be those of the 'princes in the Tower' could, at least in theory, be tested to see if a Y-chromosome match exists. The issue of non-paternity is a potential problem in this case, because doubts have been raised as to the paternity of Edward IV himself[10] (but see above, Introduction, Chapter 3 and Chapter 4). Thus a greater degree of certainty would be provided by checking the boys' mtDNA sequence. In order to achieve this, the identification of an all-female line relative of the boys' mother Elizabeth Widville is required.

Despite coming from a large family, all attempts to locate an all-female-line descendent of either Elizabeth Widville or one of her sisters have previously failed, with known all-female lines coming to an end in the early nineteenth century. This led researchers seeking to identify the mtDNA sequence of Elizabeth Widville to go to extraordinary lengths, including an attempt by John Ashdown-Hill to extract mtDNA from the hair of Elizabeth Widville's granddaughter Mary 'Tudor', Queen of France and Duchess of Suffolk. Unfortunately this proved difficult, meaning that the chances of identifying the mtDNA sequence of the 'princes in the Tower' seemed slim.[11]

I started my own research into the mtDNA sequence of the 'princes in the Tower' in early 2016, and, having failed to trace a line of descent from the sisters of Elizabeth Widville, I began to search for female-line relatives of her mother Jacquette of Luxembourg. Beyond the first few generations, information is not freely available for the relatives of Jacquette (at least not in English). On closer inspection of the Widville family tree, it became clear that many of the peerage collections that record the history of the noble families of England had made a significant mistake. Having identified the error in the historical records, a further female line was identified that opened up another possibility for the identification of an all-female line of descent, and with it the mtDNA sequence of the 'princes in the Tower'. After the discovery of this new all-female line, it was possible to identify a relative from whom mtDNA could be extracted and compared.

The newly discovered line starts with Margaret Widville (d. 1490), daughter of Jacquette of Luxembourg and her second husband, Richard Widville, Baron (later Earl) Rivers. Margaret was a younger sister of Elizabeth Widville. As the daughter of a relatively newly created baron, Margaret would most likely have been expected to marry a member of the landed gentry or at best a minor noble of similar rank to her father. But when her elder sister became Edward IV's consort, it was inevitable that a more advantageous marriage was sought for Margaret. Thus she was married to Thomas FitzAlan, 17th Earl of Arundel. This was one of the many advantageous marriages made for Elizabeth Widville's relatives that upset the English aristocracy.

The couple had two daughters: Margaret, who married John de la Pole, Earl of Lincoln, considered by many to have been the leading Yorkist heir to the throne following the death of Richard III; and Joan (d. 1508), who married George Neville (1469–1538), 5th Baron Bergavenny. Previous researchers have not been able to trace an all-female line from Joan FitzAlan and George Neville and this appears to be due to the previously mentioned error in many of the available sources. The couple had a daughter, Jane (d. 1539), who has often been misrepresented as the daughter of another George Neville, 4th Baron Bergavenny and father of the 5th baron by his wife Margaret Fenne. Were this to be accurate, it would make Jane the sister of George Neville, 5th Baron Bergavenny, and sister-in-law of Joan FitzAlan – and, therefore, of little interest to our search.

However, there are several pieces of evidence that prove that Jane Neville was in fact the daughter of Joan FitzAlan and the younger Baron Bergavenny, as Richardson rightly lists in his work *Magna Carta Ancestry: A Study in Colonial and Medieval Families.*[12]

ALLEGED PARENTAGE OF JANE NEVILLE

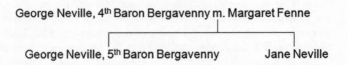

George Neville, 4th Baron Bergavenny m. Margaret Fenne

George Neville, 5th Baron Bergavenny   Jane Neville

TRUE ANCESTRY OF JANE NEVILLE

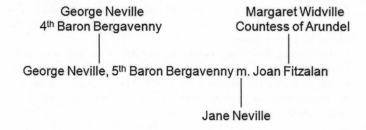

Although no record of Jane's birth survives, one would expect her to have been of similar age to her husband, Henry Pole, Lord Montague (1492–1539). It is thought that Margaret Fenne died in 1485, which would require Jane to have been at least seven years older than her husband and which, although possible, would not have been the norm. The younger George Neville would have been about twenty-three in 1492 and his wife Joan FitzAlan would have been nineteen. This would appear to support the idea the younger George Neville and his wife Joan FitzAlan are more likely candidates for the parents of Jane Neville.

While this cannot be taken as absolute evidence of the real parentage of Jane Neville, documentary evidence can be found in the will of George Neville, 5th Baron Bergavenny, in which he discusses 'Henry Lorde Montagewe and Jane the wife of the said Henry daughter to me, the said George Lorde Begavenney'.[13] This provides hard evidence that the Jane Neville married to Henry Pole, Lord Montague, was in fact the daughter of Joan FitzAlan (daughter of Margaret Widville), by her husband George Neville. More importantly, this would mean that Jane and any daughters would carry the mtDNA of the 'princes in the Tower', opening a further line of research previously missed by historians.

Jane Neville's husband, Henry Pole, was a man of historical significance as the son of Margaret, Countess of Salisbury (b. 1473), daughter of George, Duke of Clarence, the middle brother of Edward IV and Richard III.[14] George had a turbulent relationship with Edward, who eventually had him executed in 1477/8 (see above, chapter 25), although he first attainted him, removing his children from the royal succession.[15] Despite their removal from the Yorkist line of succession, Henry VII feared the threat posed by George's children. He imprisoned George's alleged son, Edward, and executed him in 1499,[16] and he married Margaret off to his own cousin Sir Richard Pole.[17] The marriage of Margaret and Richard has been seen as an attempt by Henry to control Margaret and ally any children she had to his own dynasty.[18]

Nonetheless, the threat posed by descendants of Clarence was felt by Henry VIII, who eventually had several members of the family executed, including the elderly Countess of Salisbury and her son Lord Montague.[19] Henry and Jane had a number of children, including a son called Henry born at some point in the 1520s. The younger Henry becomes important to the story as he was imprisoned in the Tower of London not long after the execution of his father and grandmother.[20] Nobody knows what happened to young Henry Pole, although it is feared he was murdered in the Tower. As the son of Jane Neville, the young Henry Pole would have inherited the same mtDNA sequence as the sons of Edward IV and Elizabeth Widville. As a result, any single remains found in the area of the Tower that are found to match the mtDNA sequence in question could be the remains of Henry Pole rather than of one of the 'princes'. The known age of Henry Pole at the point of disappearance is similar to that of the 'princes' in 1483, and radiocarbon dating might not be able to distinguish between remains from the 1480s and the time of Henry's disappearance. The Y-chromosome of the Pole family might be one of the few scientific ways to distinguish Henry Pole and the sons of Edward IV, although at present it is unclear if this is available in a living relative.

The mtDNA sequence of the 'princes' survived through Catherine Pole (b. 1520), the daughter of Henry Pole, Lord Montague, and Jane Neville. Catherine Pole survived the persecution of other members of the Pole family, perhaps due to her sex. She was married to Francis Hastings, 2nd Earl of Huntingdon, and among their many children was Henry Hastings, 3rd Earl of Huntingdon, who was considered as a possible heir to Elizabeth I due to his Yorkist blood.[21]

The marriage between Catherine and Francis Hastings also provides further evidence for the parentage of Jane Neville. For Catherine and Francis to marry, papal dispensation was sought as they were related within prohibited degrees. According to the dispensation, the couple were related within the third and fourth degree which matches the proposal of common ancestry from the Widville sisters, as Francis Hastings was the grandson of Katherine Widville, the sister of Margaret.

THE RELATIONSHIP OF CATHERINE POLE AND FRANCIS, EARL OF
HUNTINGDON

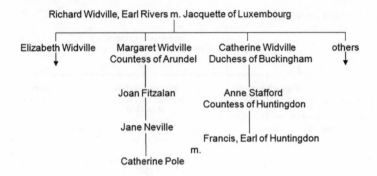

To our beloved in Christ, Francis Lord Hastings, the son and heir of
George, Earl of Huntingdon, and Katherine Mountegue alias Poole,
respectively of the diocese of London and of Winchester ... Recently
on your behalf it was explained to us that, out of eagerness to
confirm the mutual friendship between your families, and for certain
other just and reasonable causes moving your mind in this regard,
which have been explained to us and accepted by us, you desire to
contract a marriage between you, but because you are related to one
another in the third and fourth degrees of consanguinity you cannot
carry out your wish in this respect, without obtaining the above
canonical dispensation.[22]

Catherine and Francis Hastings had a daughter, Frances, born in 1545 at
the family seat of Ashby-de-la-Zouch in Leicestershire. Frances Hastings
married Henry Compton, 1st Baron Compton, whose mother Anne Talbot
was the daughter of George, 4th Earl of Shrewsbury, a distant relative of
Eleanor Talbot, the woman whose secret marriage to Edward IV led to the
illegitimacy of all the children of Edward IV by Elizabeth Widville. Frances
and Henry's daughter Margaret Compton (b. 1567) married Henry
Mordaunt, 4th Baron Mordaunt, who was suspected of being involved in
the Gunpowder Plot to assassinate King James I.[23] Margaret and Henry
had a daughter called Frances (b. 1604) who married twice, first to Sir
Thomas Neville and later in 1627 to the metallurgist Sir Basil Brooke, and

MtDNA Family Tree

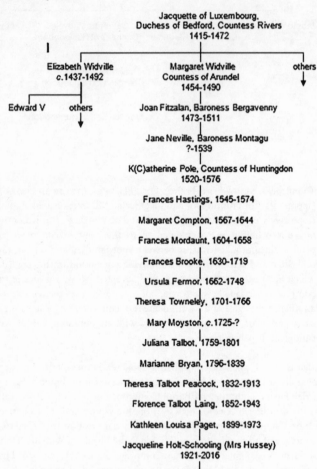

Jacquette of Luxembourg,
Duchess of Bedford, Countess Rivers
1415-1472

Elizabeth Widville
c.1437-1492

Margaret Widville
Countess of Arundel
1454-1490

others

Edward V   others

Joan Fitzalan, Baroness Bergavenny
1473-1511

Jane Neville, Baroness Montagu
?-1539

K(C)atherine Pole, Countess of Huntingdon
1520-1576

Frances Hastings, 1545-1574

Margaret Compton, 1567-1644

Frances Mordaunt, 1604-1658

Frances Brooke, 1630-1719

Ursula Fermor, 1662-1748

Theresa Towneley, 1701-1766

Mary Moyston, c.1725-?

Juliana Talbot, 1759-1801

Marianne Bryan, 1796-1839

Theresa Talbot Peacock, 1832-1913

Florence Talbot Laing, 1852-1943

Kathleen Louisa Paget, 1899-1973

Jacqueline Holt-Schooling (Mrs Hussey)
1921-2016

Second possible line of all female descent

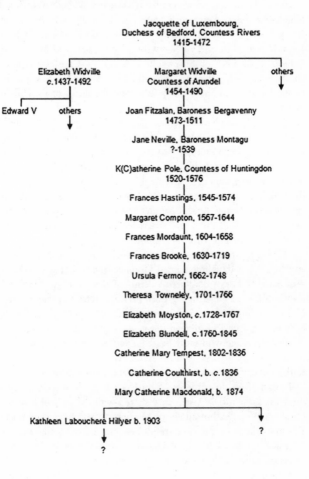

Jacquette of Luxembourg,
Duchess of Bedford, Countess Rivers
1415-1472

Elizabeth Widville
c.1437-1492

Margaret Widville
Countess of Arundel
1454-1490

others

Edward V   others

Joan Fitzalan, Baroness Bergavenny
1473-1511

Jane Neville, Baroness Montagu
?-1539

K(C)atherine Pole, Countess of Huntingdon
1520-1576

Frances Hastings, 1545-1574

Margaret Compton, 1567-1644

Frances Mordaunt, 1604-1658

Frances Brooke, 1630-1719

Ursula Fermor, 1662-1748

Theresa Towneley, 1701-1766

Elizabeth Moyston, c.1728-1767

Elizabeth Blundell, c.1760-1845

Catherine Mary Tempest, 1802-1836

Catherine Coulthirst, b. c.1836

Mary Catherine Macdonald, b. 1874

Kathleen Labouchere Hillyer b. 1903

?

?

had a daughter, also called Frances (b. 1630). Her daughter Ursula married Charles Towneley (b. 1658) and had a daughter named Theresa (b. 1701) who married Sir George Mostyn, 4th Baron of Talacre (b. 1700). Theresa and Sir George had two daughters, both of whom are of interest to this study as they both produce all-female lines of note.

Ironically, the line of descent from Margaret Widville to the modern-day female-line descendants once again continues through the Talbot family. Mary Mostyn married Charles Talbot (b. 1722), the great-grandson of John Talbot, 10th Earl of Shrewsbury (d. 1722), and brother of George Talbot, 14th Earl of Shrewsbury. Although Charles predeceased his childless brother, it was Charles and Mary's son Charles that succeeded to the Earldom of Shrewsbury following the death of his childless uncle in 1787.

The couple also had a daughter Juliana (b. 1759), who married Michael Bryan in 1784. Bryan was a noted art historian, most widely known for his multi-volume *Dictionary of Painters and Engravers*. A daughter Marianne was born in 1796 and although some sources indicate that she passed away in 1811, this appears to be another historical error.[24] Instead, it would seem that she lived on and married Thomas Peacock in 1818, with her correct year of death being 1871. A daughter named Theresa was born in Durham in 1832, adopting the double-barrelled name of Talbot-Peacock, further emphasising the link with the Talbot family.

Theresa married the Sunderland-based shipping magnate James Laing and in 1852 a daughter named Florence Talbot Laing was born. She in turn married Alwyn Blaquiere Valentine Paget (b. 1855), with a daughter, Kathleen Louisa Paget, being born in 1896. Kathleen Paget married John Holt-Schooling in 1919 and in 1928 married Alan Hughes. Three children have been traced to Kathleen Paget, a daughter Jaqueline (b. 1921) from her first marriage who sadly passed away in February 2016 and daughter Audrey (b. 1929) and son Alan Berkeley (b. 1933) from the second. Kathleen later married Leslie Cadman and passed away in 1973.

To date, four descendants of Kathleen Paget have been identified that carry the same mtDNA sequence shared with the sons of Edward IV and Elizabeth Widville, but all efforts to contact them have been unsuccessful. The individuals in question are all descended from Kathleen Paget's first marriage to John Holt-Schooling and attempts to identify living female-line descendants from Paget's second marriage are ongoing.

A further line of interest has also been discovered, extending from Theresa Towneley's other daughter Elizabeth. By the mid-nineteenth century the family line leads to Catherine Coulthirst (b. *c.* 1836), who married Archibald Keppel Macdonald, Baronet Macdonald. Catherine and Archibald Macdonald had a son, also named Archibald, who was the last to hold the title of Baronet Macdonald before dying childless in 1919. They also had a daughter, Mary Catherine (b. 1874), who married Leonard Ruthven Labouchere Hillyer in 1901. A daughter Kathleen followed in 1903, and Mary and Kathleen are listed on the 1911 census, living near the Macdonald family residence of Bramshott.

Following 1911, little information is available for either mother or daughter. Mary Catherine remarried in 1913 to Leonard Athelstan Latchford but no further records of the couple have been found. Whilst this branch of the all-female line of descent of Margaret Widville has not identified living individuals that carry the required mtDNA sequence, the potential discovery of further generations is a distinct possibility. Mary Macdonald may have had further children by her second husband Leonard Latchford. There is also the possibility that Kathleen Labouchere Hillyer had children of her own.

Whilst it has not proven possible as yet to extract the mtDNA sequence of living female relatives of the 'princes in the Tower', the research presented above demonstrates that it may be possible to do so in the future. It is hoped that the living relatives will one day consent to providing a DNA sample and in the meantime other lines of descent from Jane Neville are currently being explored. This certainly marks a significant breakthrough as previous research had been unable to identify any living female-line relatives.

Of course this is just one part of ongoing research to determine the fate of the 'princes'. At present, permission to test the Westminster bones seems unlikely to be granted, although this may change at some stage in the future. It is also possible that as research continues, other remains suspected of being those of the 'princes' may be discovered. It must be stressed that should the mtDNA be sequenced and successfully matched to any remains, this alone will by no means prove the identity of the remains. In the case of Richard III, the matching of the mtDNA of the bones with that of living all-female-line relatives of the king proved that the remains belonged to a member of the correct family line. But this had to be combined with other, circumstantial evidence to establish the identity of Richard's body.

Also, even if it ever becomes possible to identify remains of one or both of the sons of Edward IV and Elizabeth Widville, that by itself would in no way establish how or when they died.

NOTES

1 The Images and Royal Family Background of Edward IV

1. J. Gairdner, ed., *The historical collections of a citizen of London in the fifteenth century*, London (Camden Society, new ser., 17) 1876 [Lydgate, 'Verses on the Kings of England'], p. 54.

2. See below, chapter 22: reference to the *ODNB* account of Elizabeth Shore (*née* Lambert), written by Rosemary Horrox, where the author specifies that all the source material relating to the woman's alleged relationship with Edward IV is of 'Tudor' date.

3. Richard III and Henry VII.

4. https://finds.org.uk/database/artefacts/record/id/61806 (consulted April 2016).

5. J. Gough Nichols, 'Observations on the Heraldic Devices discovered on the Effigies of Richard the Second and his Queen in Westminster Abbey, and upon the Mode in which those Ornaments were executed; including some Remarks on the surname Plantagenet and on the Ostrich Feathers of the Prince of Wales', *Archaeologia*, vol. 29, part 1, 1841, pp. 32–59 (p. 42).

6. A. R. Myers, ed., G. Buck, *The History of the Life and reigne of Richard the Third*, London 1646, reprinted Wakefield 1973, pp. 4–7.

7. Gough Nichols, 'Observations on the Heraldic Devices discovered on the Effigies of Richard the Second and his Queen in Westminster Abbey ...', p. 44.

8. Gough Nichols, 'Observations on the Heraldic Devices discovered on the Effigies of Richard the Second and his Queen in Westminster Abbey ...', p. 44 (footnote), citing 'Rot. Pat. 17 Edw. IV. p. 2, m. 16, printed in Appendix V. to the Peerage Reports, p. 413'.

9. For more on this see J. Ashdown-Hill, *The Wars of the Roses*, Stroud 2015.

10. 'King Edward though his vices seemed not to adde vertues to the Condemned Prince, yet without question they doe, making all his

estimated ill actions of an other nature, he obtained his Crowne but rather
fortunatly then wisely ... for I thinke luste, or if you will terme it loue,
coulde not more haue preuailed with the moste licentious Creature, then
at once to breake the bandes of amitye, and discretion & pollicye, and
all to inioye a woman ... a widow & of his enimye, without bringing him
either alliance or riches props most pertinent to his new erected building,
(wherin besides his breach of regall discretion with his chifest frend the
Earle of Warwike, whom he had sent to ffrance to treate for a marriage
with a neece of the ffrench Kinges [Bona of Savoy]) wherein being deluded
he becamm his mortallest Enimy) his abuse to god was more abominable,
beinge before betrothed (as his owne mother constantly affirmed) to
the Lady Elizabeth Lucy ... how soone the wrath of god followed, his
irreligious inconstancy his being driuen from the seate roiall into exile the
birth of his sonne in a Sanctuary haueing no place els of freedome in all
his fathers kingdome) the misery of all his partakers, sufficiently testefyes,
in which his miserye whoe did more truely follow him? who more
faithfully ayded him then his now disgraced brother'. A. N. Kincaid, ed.,
W. Cornwallis, *The Encomium of Richard III*, London 1977, pp. 4–5.
Text dating from *circa* 1590–1600.

11. J. Tey, *The Daughter of Time*, Harmondsworth 1951, 1974, p. 82.

12. S. Penman, *The Sunne in Splendour*, London 1982, pp. 4–7; p. 9.

13. K. Dockray, *Edward IV, a source book*, Stroud 1999, p. 2.

14. Gairdner, ed., *The historical collections of a citizen of London in the
fifteenth century* [Gregory's Chronicle], p. 226.

15. N. Pronay and J. Cox, eds, *The Crowland Chronicle Continuations:
1459–1486*, London 1986, p. 150.

16. Pronay & Cox, *Crowland*, p. 151.

17. Pronay & Cox, *Crowland*, p. 153.

18. Pronay & Cox, *Crowland*, p. 161.

19. C. A. J. Armstrong, ed., D. Mancini, *The Usurpation* [sic] *of Richard the
Third*, Gloucester 1989, p. 67.

20. '*Eduardus ... cum Helisabettam duceret, aliam uxorem omni iure pactam
haberet*', Armstrong / Mancini, p. 96.

21. M. Jones, ed., Philippe de Commynes, *Memoirs*, Harmondsworth 1972,
p. 414.

22. Jones / Commynes, *Memoirs*, pp. 353–54.

23. Jones / Commynes, *Memoirs*, p. 354.

24. Dockray, *Edward IV a Source Book*, p. xxviii.

25. Myers / Buck, *Richard the Third*, p. 115.

26. The name 'Tudor' is employed here in inverted commas because a) there is
no more evidence that the royal family in question used this surname than

that the preceding royal family had used the surname 'Plantagenet', and b) because the present writer has argued that the alleged descent of King Henry VII from Owen Tudor is questionable (see J. Ashdown-Hill, *The Wars of the Roses*, Stroud 2015).

2 *1442–1458: Itinerary*

1. T. Hearne, *Liber Niger Scaccarii nec non Wilhelmi Worcestrii Annales Rerum Anglicarum*, vol. 2, London 1774, p. 525.

2. Hearne, *Wilhelmi Worcestrii Annales*, vol. 2, p. 525.

3. Hearne, *Wilhelmi Worcestrii Annales*, vol. 2, pp. 525–26.

4. J. Stevenson, ed., *Letters and papers illustrative of the Wars of the English in France during the reign of King Henry the Sixth, King of England*, vol. 1, London 1861, pp. 79–82.

5. Stevenson, *Letters and papers*, pp. 83–86.

6. http://en.wikipedia.org/wiki/Richard_of_York,_3rd_Duke_of_York#France_again_.281440.E2.80.931445.29 (consulted May 2015).

7. Hearne, *Wilhelmi Worcestrii Annales*, vol. 2, p. 526.

8. Hearne, *Wilhelmi Worcestrii Annales*, vol. 2, p. 526.

9. 'tydynges which dayly sprange, y syr Edwarde his sone, than erle of the March, was comynge towarde London with a strôge power of Welshemen & Marchmen'. Fabyan, *Chronicle*, p. 627.

10. J. Gairdner, ed., *The Paston Letters*, 1904, reprinted Gloucester 1983, vol. 2, p. 297.

11. Letter: M. Clive, *This Sun of York*, London 1973, p. xxxvi, citing BM Cotton MS, Vespasian f iii.f.16.

12. Letter: Clive, *Sun of York*, p. xxxvi; Gairdner, *Paston Letters*, vol. 1, p. 148, citing MS Cott., Vespasian F. xiii fol. 35.

13. 1455. *Hoc anno, feria quinta ante festum Pentecostes, id est, xxij° die mensis Majj, venit Dominus Ricardus Dux Eboracensis cum filio suo comite de Marche, Domino de Cromwell et alij plures cum magno exercitu, ac etiam Dux Northfolchiæ et Dominus Bowcer comes de Hyu cum eo et unanimi concensu, ad fortificandum predictum Ducem Eboracensem contra Ducem de Somershed, eorum capitalem adversarium, ad concilium domini Regis versus Leycester.* http://www.british-history.ac.uk/camden-record-soc/vol28/pp148-163 (consulted September 2015).

3 *1442: Parents, Siblings, Godparents, and Other Family Connections*

1. Clive, *Sun of York*, p. xxii.

2. 1442 *Natus est Edwardus, filius secundus Ricardi, Ducis Eboraci, & heres, Rex Angliae & Franciae, XXVIII° die Aprilis, hora II post mediam noctem in mane diei Lunae, apud Rothomagum, qui conceptus est in camera*

proxima capellas palacii de Hatfelde. Hearne, *Wilhelmi Worcestrii Annales,* vol. 2, p. 462.

3. *Natus est Dominus Edwardus, secundus filius illustrissimi principis Ricardi, &c. in civitate Rothomagensi, XXVII°. die mensis Aprilis, post meridiem, hora. XIIII. minut. XLV°. anno Domini M°. CCCCXLII. incompleto.* Hearne, *Wilhelmi Worcestrii Annales,* vol. 2, p. 525.

4. L. Stratford, *Edward the Fourth,* London 1910, p. 11, footnote 4.

5. Clive, *Sun of York,* p. xxi.

6. The relevant phrase, *conceptus est in camera proxima capellae palacii de Hatfield,* is quoted in J. A. Giles & J. Warkworth, *The Chronicles of the White Rose of York,* London 1845, p. 213, citing William Worcester, *Annals,* p. 462. See also *Rerum Britannicarum Medii Aevi Scriptores, or Chronicles and Memorials of Great Britain and Ireland during The Middle Ages,* London 1857, p. 763: '1442. *Natus est Edwardus, filius secundus Ricardi ducis Eboraci et heres, rex Anglia; et Franciae, xxviij. die Aprilis, hora ii. post mediam noctem in mane diei Luna;, apud Rothomagum, qui conceptus est in camera proxima capellai palatii de Hatfelde.* Footnote 2. [Qui ... Hatfelde] An addition in a later hand'.

7. J. Nicholls and J. Bruce, eds, *Wills from Doctors' Commons. A selection of Wills of eminent persons proved in the PCC 1495–1695,* Camden old series, vol. 83, London 1863, p. 1, my emphasis.

8. C. L. Scofield, *The Life and Reign of Edward the Fourth,* London 1923, 1967, vol. 1, p. 1.

9. Stratford, *Edward the Fourth,* pp. 11–12. The manuscript source cited by Stratford is listed by him as 'Addit. MS. 6113, folio 125b'.

10. Scofield, *Edward the Fourth,* 1, p. 1 and note 2.

11. For the dates of birth of Edmund and Elizabeth of York, see the list of York children, below.

12. '*Natus est Dominus Georgius, sextus filius praedicti principis, XXI die Octobris, apud castrum Debline in Hibernia, anno Domini M°CCCCXLIX, in meridie diei antedicti, & baptizatus in ecclesia Sancti Salvatoris*', Hearne, *Wilhelmi Worcestrii Annales,* vol. 2, p. 526; see also Giles, *The Chronicles of the White Rose of York,* p. 301.

13. This list is derived from the *Annals* of William Worcester (published in Hearne, *Wilhelmi Worcestrii Annales,* vol. 2, pp. 525–526), and from the Joan of Acre poem of Friar Osberne Bokenham OSA of Clare Priory (see below and note 37). William Worcester's earliest surviving list of the York children was obviously written in about 1450, because it ends with the birth of George. Worcester's list was later updated, but the updated versions contain some inaccuracies in respect of dates, and possibly of locations.

14. '*in quodam manerio Domini episcopi Eliensis nuccupato* [*sic* in MS] Hatfeld'.

15. In later copies of his list, Worcester says 9 August, or *Tuesday* 10 August.

16. In 1445 Edward was given the title 'Earl of March'. It is clear that he was then the Yorks' eldest son, because he is described as the heir, and his marriage with a French princess was being negotiated.

17. As has already been seen, in other versions of the list Worcester gives Edward's date of birth as *Monday* 28 April, which is impossible.

18. Elsewhere Worcester says *Monday* 17 May, which is impossible.

19. Elsewhere Worcester says Tuesday 22 *April*, but 22 April was not a Tuesday, and details of arrangements for Elizabeth's baptism show that she must have been born in September.

20. Later versions of the list (possibly confusing Margaret with William) incorrectly state that Margaret was born at Fotheringhay.

21. William and other children listed as dead by 1456 are named as dead in the Joan of Acre poem, which was written in that year.

22. William Worcester's original list (probably written down in about 1450) ends with George. Later versions of the list give brief details of Richard and Ursula, and include additional – and often erroneous – information regarding the births of the earlier children. But none of Worcester's lists mention Thomas.

23. For the relevant source material, see J. Ashdown-Hill, *Eleanor the Secret Queen*, Stroud 2009 / *The Secret Queen* (second edition), Stroud 2016, chapter 9.

24. They were married in 1449 or 1450, when Eleanor was still a minor. For this and other details of Thomas Boteler see Ashdown-Hill, *Eleanor / The Secret Queen*, chapter 8.

25. Ashdown-Hill, *The Secret Queen* (second edition), chapter 6, p. 1.

26. Scofield, *Edward the Fourth*, vol. 1, p. 2, citing Rolls of Parliament, V, 471.

27. *Et die Sabbati sequenti dictus dominus Scales, compater dicti comitis Marchiae* …, J. Stevenson, ed., *Letters and Papers Illustrative of the Wars of the English in France during the Reign of Henry the Sixth King of England*, Vol. 2, part 2, London 1864, p, 773 (William Worcester, Annales).

28. C. Ross, *Edward IV*, London 1974, p. 7, and citing *CPR*, 1467–77, p. 439.

29. *CPR*, 1476–85, p. 411.

30. Jones / Commynes, *Memoirs*, 1972, p. 258.

31. Jones / Commynes, p. 239.

32. Edmund never held the title Earl of March, which had been lost as a result of the execution of his father, Roger (i). The title was later restored to Edmund's son, Roger (ii).

33. King John was not Richard I's son, but his younger brother; thus the youngest legitimate son of Henry II.

34. Unidentified. The last two generations of the house of Anjou as recorded by Worcester seem to be an error. Fulk actually inherited the title Count of Anjou from his mother, Emmengarde of Anjou, and not from his father.

35. *Item iste Edwardus fuit filius praedicti Ricardi Plantaginett, qui fuit filius & heres Ricardi comes Cantebrigiae, qui fuit filius & heres Edmundi Langlei ducis Eboraci, & Isabellae uxoris eius, filiae et heredis Petri, vere et indubitati regis Castelliae et Legionum. Item iste Edwardus fuit filius praedicti Ricardi Plantaginett, filii Annae, filiae Rogeri Mortimer, filii et heredis Philippae et Edmundi comitis Marchiae, qui fuit Rogeri comitis, qui fuit Edmundi comitis, qui fuit Rogeri primi comitis Marchiae, qui fuit Gladesduy, quae fuit filia & heres Lewillini principis Walliae, et uxor Radulphi Mortimer militis, qui fuit Rogeri, qui fuit Hugonis de Mortimer et Matildae uxoris eius, filiae Willelmi filii Longespatae, qui fuit filius et heres Rollonis, primi ducis Normanorum. Item iste Edwardus est dux Andegaviae per patrem suum Ricardum Plantaginett, qui fuit filius Annae, quae fuit Rogeri, qui fuit Philippae, quae fuit Leonelli, qui fuit regis Edwardi tercii, qui fuit regis Ed[wardi] II*[di]. *qui fuit Ed[wardi] primi, qui fuit Henrici III*[cii]. *qui fuit Ioannis, qui fuit Ricardi, qui fuit Henrici IIdi. qui fuit Galfridi Plantaginett comitis Andegaviae, qui fuit Fulconis, qui fuit Galfridi, qui fuit Fulconis, qui fuit Rarisii, qui fuit Fulconis primi comitis Andegaviae.* Hearne, *Wilhelmi Worcestrii Annales*, vol. 2, p. 527.

36. See above: list of the York children and their dates and places of birth.

37. From *'The Dialogue at the Grave of Dame Johan of Acres'*, Friar Osberne Bokenham OSA, Clare Priory, Suffolk, 1456, K. W. Barnardiston, *Clare Priory*, Cambridge 1962, p. 69.

38. 'Sixteen was the normal age for the consummation of a marriage in which one (or both) of the contracting parties had been a minor'. B. J. Harris, *English Aristocratic Women, 1450–1550*, Oxford 2010, p. 45. On the other hand, in a personal communication to the present writer, Marie Barnfield suggested that 14 was an acceptable age for the bride. Possibly the *groom* was expected to be at least 16.

39. Personal communication from Marie Barnfield.

4 1445: *The Daughters of France*

1. C. Scofield, *The Life and Reign of Edward the Fourth*, two volumes, London 1967, vol. 1, p. 9.

2. Shown thus, with no explanation of whether a word is missing or illegible, in Stevenson's published translation (see below, note 4), and also in his published version of the original French text.

3. In the original French text of the letter, this verb is in the subjunctive mode ['*ait*']. That grammatical form, which is hard to represent in modern English, explains Stevenson's choice of the verb form 'have'.

4. Stevenson, *Letters and papers*, vol. 1, pp. 79–82. This is Stevenson's translation. The Duke of York's original letter is in French.

5. Actually Charles VII had FOUR available daughters at the time when this letter was written. But maybe the Duke of York was confused by the existence of two daughters called Jeanne (see below).

6. Stevenson, *Letters and papers*, vol. 1, pp. 83–86.

7. http://fr.wikipedia.org/wiki/Charles_VII_%28roi_de_France%29 (consulted April 2015).

5 *1445–1459: From France to England – and Ireland*

1. Henry Holland's father and grandfather were both dukes of Exeter. However, his grandfather was attainted and the ducal title was granted to Thomas Beaufort. Later, in 1444, the title was re-created for Henry's father.

2. See above: list of the York children and their dates and places of birth.

3. http://en.wikipedia.org/wiki/Page-boy (May 2015).

4. Clive, *Sun of York*, p. xxxvi, citing BM, Cotton MS, Vespasian F. iii, f. 16.

5. Clive, *Sun of York*, p. xxxvii.

6. Clive, *Sun of York*, p. xxxvii, citing O. G. S. Croft, *The House of Croft of Croft Castle*, privately printed 1949.

7. Gairdner, ed., *The Paston Letters*, vol. 1, p. 148, citing BM, Cotton MS, Vespasian F. xiii, fol. 35.

8. BL, Add. MS 46349, f. 9v; A. Crawford, ed., *Howard Household Books* (hereinafter *HHB*), Stroud 1992, part 1, p. 165.

9. No details of Catherine's symptoms are recorded, but it seems possible that she suffered from a persistent cough, since 'suger candy', 'wyne' and 'water of honysoclys' as well as unspecified 'medesyns' were supplied to her in 1465: BL, Add. MS 46349, ff. 86v, 87r; *HHB*, part 1, p. 304.

10. N. Davis, *Paston Letters and Papers of the fifteenth century*, 2 vols., Oxford 1971; 1976, vol. 1, p. 248.

11. Norwich & Norfolk Archaeological Society, shelf 2, no. 6, published in *HHB*, pp. xl–xlii.

12. On 30 April 1472 the Paston correspondence, mistaking the bride's family name, reported 'Dame Ely'beth Bowghcher is weddyd to þe Lorde Howardys soone and heyre': Davis, *Paston Letters*, vol. 1, p. 448.

13. On Gloucester's illegitimate children, see P. W. Hammond, 'The Illegitimate Children of Richard III', *Ric.* 5 (1979–81), pp. 92–96. Research by M. A. Marshall, published at second hand by Rose Skuse, 'Richard III's Children', *The Rose and Crown* (magazine of the Beds & Bucks Group of

the Richard III Society) no. 44, July 2008, pp. 6–7, suggests that John of Gloucester was born in June 1470, and Catherine Plantagenet in September 1471, but no evidence for those proposed dates is cited.

14. J. Ashdown-Hill, 'Yesterday my Lord of Gloucester came to Colchester', *Essex History*, vol. 36 (2005), pp. 212–17.

15. Gairdner, ed., *The historical collections of a citizen of London in the fifteenth century*, [Gregory's Chronicle], p. 226.

6 *1459–1461: Itinerary*

1. Clive, *Sun of York*, pp. xxxix, 3.

2. Pronay N., and Cox J., eds, *The Crowland Chronicle Continuations: 1459–1486*, London 1986, p. 109.

3. C. L. Scofield, *The Life and reign of Edward the Fourth*, London 1923, 1967, vol. 1, p. 41, citing *CPR*.

4. Gairdner, *Paston Letters*, vol. 1, p. 182.

5. Scofield, *Edward the Fourth*, vol. 1, p. 42.

6. Gairdner, *Paston Letters*, vol. 1, p. 182.

7. Gairdner, *Paston Letters*, vol. 3, p. 204.

8. W. & E. L. C. P. Hardy, eds, Wavrin, *Receuil des Chroniques*, vol. 5 Cambridge 1891, 2012, 6: 3, p. 293.

9. Gairdner, *Paston Letters*, vol. 1, p. 187.

10. Hardy / Wavrin, vol. 5, 6: 3, p. 296.

11. Gairdner, *Paston Letters*, vol. 3, pp. 221–22.

12. In company with the duke of Norfolk's cousin, John Howard, of Stoke-by-Nayland, Suffolk. (See L. J. F. Ashdown-Hill, *Thesis*, part 2). Suffolk Record Office, Ipswich, HA 246/B2/498.

13. He wrote a request for permission for his mother and siblings to stay at Fastolf's place.

14. Gairdner, *Paston Letters*, vol. 3, p. 233.

15. Pronay & Cox, *Crowland*, p. 111.

16. Hardy / Wavrin, vol. 5, 6: 3, p. 318.

17. http://www.british-history.ac.uk/camden-record-soc/vol28/pp58-78 (November 2015).

18. Gairdner, ed., *The Historical Collections of a Citizen of London in the Fifteenth Century*, p. 215.

19. TNA, C 81/782.

20. Hardy / Wavrin, vol. 5, 6: 3, pp. 335–36.

21. Both TNA, C 81/782.

22. Gairdner, *Paston Letters*, vol. 3, p. 267; TNA, C 81/782.

23. All three – TNA, C 81/782.

24. All TNA, C 81/782.

25. Both TNA, C 81/782.
26. All TNA, C 81/783.
27. TNA, C 81/783; TNA, C 81/784; TNA, C 81/785.
28. All TNA, C 81/785.
29. Both TNA, C 81/785.
30. All TNA, C 81/786.
31. All TNA, C 81/786.
32. TNA, PSO 1/21; TNA, C 81/786; TNA C 81/787.
33. TNA C 81/787; TNA C 81/788; TNA C 81/789.
34. TNA C 81/789.

7 1460–1462: *The Beautiful Eleanor*

1. See original source material published in J. Ashdown-Hill, *Eleanor the Secret Queen*, Stroud 2009 pp. 192, 195, 205–207.
2. J. Gairdner, *History of the Life and Reign of Richard the Third*, Cambridge 1898, p. 91.
3. *statim duxit in uxorem praeclaram dominam Elizabeth, filiam et* heredem *regis Edwardi IIII*. T. Hearne, ed., *Joannis Rossi Antiquarii Warwicensis Historia Regum Angliae*, London 1716, p. 218 (present author's emphasis).
4. Henry VII's Act of Parliament of 1485: J. Strachey, ed., *Rotuli Parliamentorum; ut et Petitiones, et Placita in Parliamento*, vol. 6, London 1777, p. 289.
5. J. Ashdown-Hill, *Eleanor the Secret Queen, the Woman who put Richard III on the Throne*, first edition published Stroud, 2009; updated second edition, *The Secret Queen*, 2016.
6. This information was corrected in the updated second edition: J. Ashdown-Hill, *The Secret Queen*, Stroud 2016.
7. The correct information in respect of date and location was also published in the appropriate chapter of J. Ashdown-Hill, *Royal Marriage Secrets*, Stroud 2012, p. 81.
8. See Ashdown-Hill, *Eleanor the Secret Queen*, p. 19.
9. The family tree of Eleanor's descent from Edward I published here is more accurate than the earlier version published in Ashdown-Hill, *Eleanor the Secret Queen* (first edition), plate 5.
10. M. Barnfield, 'Diriment Impediments, Dispensations and Divorce: Richard III and Matrimony', *Ricardian*, vol. 17 (2007), pp. 84–98 (p. 85).
11. More than 45 per cent of such women remarried: Harris, *English Aristocratic Women*, p. 10.
12. At the start of the fifteenth century Henry IV had married the widowed Joan of Navarre, while in the fourteenth century Edward III's heir, the 'Black Prince', had married the widowed Joan of Kent.

13. Ross, *Thesis*, vol. 1, p. 45; Pollard, *Thesis*, p. 8.

14. Ashdown-Hill, *Eleanor*, chapter 20.

15. H. Beaune and J. d'Arbaumont, eds, *Mémoires d'Olivier de la Marche*, 4 vols., vol. 3, Paris 1885, pp. 106–107.

16. A. Sutton and L. Visser-Fuchs, *The Royal Funerals of the House of York at Windsor*, London 2004, pp. 113–24.

17. Jones / Commynes, *Memoirs*, 1972, pp. 353–54. Present author's emphasis.

18. Jones / Commynes, *Memoirs*, p. 397.

19. E.g. *Muriel de Dunham* v. *John Burnoth* and Joan, his 'wife': N. Adams and C. Donahue, eds, *Select Cases from the Ecclesiastical Courts of the Province of Canterbury, c. 1200–1301*, London 1981, p. 337 and *passim*.

20. Curiously, it was almost exactly twenty-two years later – on Monday 9 June 1483 – that Bishop Stillington finally revealed Edward IV's marriage with Eleanor Talbot to the royal council, as grounds for ceasing to plan the coronation of Edward V, because he was illegitimate. (For the source for this information, see below, Chapter 27, note 11). Possibly the anniversary date was one of the factors which ultimately convinced the bishop that he then had to make the marriage public.

21. Myers / Buck, *Richard the Third*, pp. 116, 122.

22. Ashdown-Hill, *Eleanor* (first edition), p. 202, citing the petition of 26 June 1483 to Richard, Duke of Gloucester, as subsequently quoted in the Act of Parliament of January 1483/4 (*titulus regius*).

23. For a fuller discussion of the evidence in this matter, see J. Ashdown-Hill 'Lady Eleanor Talbot: New Evidence; New Answers; New Questions', *Ricardian* 16 (2006), pp. 113–32. It is also possible that Eleanor's Coldecot estate was part of Caldicot in Monmouthshire – a royal estate inherited by the Lancastrian kings from the de Bohun family: see O. Morgan and T. Wakeman, *Notes on the Architecture and History of Caldicot Castle, Monmouthshire*, Newport 1854. I am grateful to Mary Friend of the Richard III Society (Worcestershire Branch) for the suggestion regarding Caldecot, which, however, remains speculative.

24. Ashdown-Hill, *Eleanor*, p. 147 et seq.

25. *Calendar of Patent Rolls 1461–1467*, London 1897, p. 72.

26. *CPR, 1461–1467*, p. 191.

27. The patent rolls of Edward IV record commissions naming Lord Sudeley in July 1461, March 1461/2 and October 1462, June, October and December 1464, August 1466, February 1467/8 and November 1469.

28. '*aliam uxorem omni iure pactam haberet, quam dux Berbiciensium ei copulasset*' ('he was legally contracted to another wife to whom the Duke [*sic* = Earl] of Warwick had joined him'). Armstrong / Mancini, pp. 96–97.

29. 'and yt ... commonly is reportyd, that king Edward showld have assayed to do some unhonest act in the earle [of Warweke]'s howse; for as muche as the king was a man who wold readily cast an eye upon yowng ladyes'. Also a mariginal note: 'E. 4 is supposed to deflower some woman in the E., of Warwickes house'. H. Ellis, ed., *Three Bookes of Polydore Vergil's English History comprising the reigns of Henry VI, Edward IV and Richard III*, London 1844, p. 117.

8 *1461–1464: Itinerary*

1. All TNA C 81/789.
2. TNA C 81/789.
3. Both TNA, C 81/790.
4. Both TNA, PSO 1/21.
5. All TNA, PSO 1/21; TNA, C 81/790.
6. TNA, PSO 1/21.
7. Both TNA, C 81/790.
8. TNA, PSO 1/21; TNA, C 81/790.
9. TNA, PSO 1/21; TNA, C 81/790; TNA, C 81/791.
10. TNA, PSO 1/21.
11. TNA, POS 1/21; TNA, C 81/791.
12. TNA, PSO 1/21; TNA, PSO 1/22.
13. Both TNA, PSO 1/22.
14. Both TNA, PSO 1/22; TNA, C 81/791.
15. TNA, PSO 1/22; TNA, C 81/791.
16. TNA, PSO 1/22.
17. TNA, PSO 1/22; TNA, C 81/791.
18. TNA, C 81/791.
19. TNA, C 81/791.
20. TNA, C 81/791; TNA, C 81/792.
21. All TNA, C 81/792.
22. All TNA, C 81/792.
23. All TNA, C 81/792.
24. TNA, C 81/792; TNA, PSO 1/22.
25. Both TNA, C 81/792.
26. All TNA, C 81/792.
27. TNA, C 81/792; TNA, C 81/793.
28. Gairdner, *Paston Letters*, vol. 4, p. 142.
29. All TNA, C 81/793.
30. All TNA, C 81/793.
31. TNA, C 81/793.
32. TNA, PSO 1/22; TNA, PSO 1/23; TNA, C 81/793.

33. TNA, PSO 1/23; TNA, PSO 1/24; TNA, C 81/793.

34. TNA, PSO 1/24; TNA, C 81/793.

35. TNA, C 81/793.

36. Both TNA, PSO 1/24; TNA, C 81/793.

37. TNA, PSO 1/24; TNA, C 81/793; TNA, C 81/794; Red Paper Book of Colchester, f. 123v (published edition: W. Gurney Benham, ed. / trans. *The Red Paper Book of Colchester*, Colchester 1902, p. 60).

38. TNA, PSO 1/24; TNA, C 81/794; TNA, C 81/795.

39. Both TNA, PSO 1/24; TNA, C 81/795.

40. All TNA, C 81/795.

41. All TNA, C 81/795.

42. Both TNA, C 81/795.

43. TNA, C 81/795.

44. Both TNA, C 81/796.

45. TNA, PSO 1/24; TNA, PSO 1/25; TNA, C 81/796.

46. TNA, PSO 1/25; TNA PSO 1/27 (filed in the wrong chronological sequence – probably because year date is missing on the MS); TNA, C 81/796.

47. TNA, PSO 1/25; TNA, C 81/796; Gairdner, *Paston Letters*, vol. 4, p. 88.

48. TNA, PSO 1/25; TNA, C 81/796.

49. TNA, C 81/796; Gairdner, *Paston Letters*, vol. 4, p. 88.

50. TNA, C 81/796; Gairdner, *Paston Letters*, vol. 4, p. 92.

51. TNA, C 81/796.

52. Gairdner, *Paston Letters*, vol. 4, p. 94.

53. Gairdner, *Paston Letters*, vol. 4, pp. 92, 94–95.

54. TNA, PSO 1/25; TNA, C 81/796; TNA, PSO 1/26.

9 *1462–1463: 'The King Loved Him Well'*

1. R. Mazo Karras, *From Boys to Men*, Philadelphia 2003, pp. 50–51.

2. M. Cook, ed., *A Gay History of Britain*, Oxford 2007, p. 108.

3. Cook, ed., *A Gay History of Britain*, p. 107, citing Douglas, 'Two Loves', *Chameleon*, December 1894.

4. Cook, ed., *A Gay History of Britain*, p. 23, citing *Rotuli Parliamentorum*, vol. 2, p. 332.

5. Cook, ed., *A Gay History of Britain*, pp. 41–42.

6. Mazo Karro, *From Boys to Men*, p. 81.

7. R. Mills, 'Male-Male Love and Sex in the Middle Ages, 1000–1500'; Cook, ed., *A Gay History of Britain*, p. 1.

8. R. Tannahill, *Sex in History*, London 1980, p. 159.

9. L. Stone, *The Family, Sex and Marriage in England 1500–1800*, London 1979, 1990, pp. 309–10.

10. Mazo Karro, *From Boys to Men*, pp. 80–81.

11. Cook, ed., *A Gay History of Britain*, p. 22, citing E. M. Thompson, ed., *Chronicon Galfridi le Baker de Swynebroke*, Oxford 1889, pp. 33–34 and C. Babington & J. R. Lumby, eds, Ranulf Higden, *Polychronicon*, vol. 8, pp. 325–27.

12. J.-A Buchon, ed., G. Chastellain, *Chronique des Ducs de Bourgogne*, vol. 1, Paris 1827, p. 21.

13. '*un très grand seigneur et un des plus beaulx josnes chevaliers qui fust au royaume anglais*', quoted in A. F. Pollard, 'Beaufort, Henry (1436–1464)', in S. Lee, ed., *Dictionary of National Biography,* supplement 1, London 1901, p. 157–58 (p. 157).

14. Hearne's 'Fragment of an old chronicle from 1460 to 1470', in J. A. Giles, ed., *The Chronicles of the White Rose of York*, London 1845, p. 20.

15. This son, called Charles Somerset, is the reputed ancestor of the present Duke of Beaufort.

16. M. Jones, 'Beaufort, Henry, second Duke of Somerset', *ODNB*.

17. Alnwick Castle surrendered to Edward IV on Monday 10 January 1462/3 (see Itinerary).

18. 'Thenn Kyng Edward ... made hym redy towarde the Northe with any lordys, gentellys, and comyns with hym. And there he layde a sege to Anwyke Castelle, and to the castelle of Bamborowe, and to Dunsterborowe. Bamborowe and Dunsterborowe was kepte by Syr Raffe Persy and Syr Harry Bewforde, late Duke of Somersett, and the castelle of Anwyke with the Lorde Hungerforde. And Bamborowe and Dunsterborowe were yoldyn be Syr Raffe Percy and Syr Harry Beuford, late Duke of Somersett, to the Kyngys wylle, whythe the condyscyons that the sayde Raffe Percy schulde have the kepynge of the ij castellys, Bamborowe and Dunstarborowe. The sayde Syr Raffe Percy and Syr Harry Beuforde, late Duke of Somersett, were sworne to be trewe and faythefulle as trewe lege men unto owre kynge and soverayne lorde Edwarde the iiij[the]. And they com to Derham, and there they were sworne byfore owre kynge. And the kynge gaffe hem hys levery and grete rewardys.

'Ande thenn the for sayde Raffe Percys retornyde a-gayne in to Northehumberlond, and hadde the kepynge of the sayde ij castellys accordynge unto the poyntment. And the sayde Syr Harry Beuforde a-bode stylle whithe the kynge, and roode with hym to Lundon. And the Kynge made fulle moche of hym; in soo moche that he loggyd whythe the kynge in hys owne bedde many nyghtys, and sum tyme rode a huntynge be hynde the kynge, the kynge havynge a boute hym not passynge vj hors at the moste, and yet iij were of the Dukys men of Somersett. The kyng lovyd hym welle, but the duke thought treson undyr fayre chere and wordys, as hyt apperyd'. Gairdner, ed., *The Historical Collections of a Citizen of London in the Fifteenth Century* [Gregory's Chronicle], p. 219.

19. Jones, 'Beaufort, Henry', *ODNB*.

20. Jones, 'Beaufort, Henry', *ODNB*.

21. W. Stubbs, ed., Roger of Hovedon (Benedict of Peterborough), *Gesta regis Henrici Secundi Benedicti abbatis*, Rolls Series 49, London 1867, vol. 2, p. 7, as quoted in Mills, 'Male-Male Love and Sex in the Middle Ages, 1000–1500'; Cook, ed., *A Gay History of Britain*, p. 1.

22. Stone, *The Family, Sex and Marriage in England 1500–1800*, p. 322.

23. Jones, 'Beaufort, Henry', *ODNB*.

24. 'For a grete love the kyng made a grete justys at Westemyster, that he [Henry] shuld se sum maner sporte of chevalry aftyr hys grete labur and hevynys. And with grete instans the kynge made hym [Henry] to take harnys uppon hym, and rode in the place, but he wolde nevyr cope whithe no man and no man myght not cope whythe hym, tylle the kynge prayd hym to be mery and sende hym a tokyn, and thenn he ranne fulle justely and merely, and hys helme was a sory hatte of strawe. And thenn every man markyd hym welle'. Gairdner, ed., *The Historical Collections of a Citizen of London in the Fifteenth Century* [Gregory's Chronicle], p. 219.

25. Jones, 'Beaufort, Henry', *ODNB*.

26. The king actually arrived somewhat earlier in Northampton, since he was certainly there on 8, 18 and 19 July – see below, Appendix: Itinerary. However, it is possible that he did not remain continuously in Northampton itself, but had been travelling elsewhere in the region between 19 and 25 July, and then returned to Northampton on 25.

27. Gairdner, *The Historical Collections of a Citizen of London in the Fifteenth Century* [Gregory's Chronicle], pp. 221–22.

28. Gairdner, *The Historical Collections of a Citizen of London in the Fifteenth Century* [Gregory's Chronicle], p. 223.

29. Pollard, 'Beaufort, Henry (1436–1464)', *Dictionary of National Biography*, supplement 1, p. 157.

30. William Hay (de la Haye?) first Earl of Erroll ?

31. *Mense Martii dux Somersetiae reversus est de Flandria in una carvella in Scotia. Et regina Scotiae habuit ipsum in summo odio, eo quod discooperuit carnalem copulam eum ea regi Franciae et fecit dominum de Haylys sibi insidiari ad interficiendum.* Stevenson, *Letters and papers*, vol. 2, (citing William Worcester, Annales), London 1864, p. 779.

32. M. Jones, 'Beaufort, Henry second Duke of Somerset', *ODNB*.

33. R. Vaughan, *Charles the Bold*, second edition, Woodbridge 2002, p. 159.

34. Jones, 'Beaufort, Henry second Duke of Somerset', *ODNB*.

10 1460–1464: The First Royal Bastards?

1. https://en.wikipedia.org/wiki/Jane_Shore (consulted February 2016), citing P. M. Kendall, *Richard the Third*, London 1955, p. 173 (1973 edition, pp. 146–47). However, the evidence in question merely refers to Edward IV's sponsorship of *William* Shore on 4 December 1476, and does not mention Shore's ex-wife.

2. R. S. Sylvester, ed., St Thomas More, *The History of King Richard III and selections from the English and Latin Poems*, London 1976, p. xi.

3. Sylvester / More, *The History of King Richard III*, p. 57.

4. Sylvester / More, *The History of King Richard III*, p. 65.

5. Sylvester / More, *The History of King Richard III*, p. 67.

6. R. Edwards, *The Itinerary of King Richard III 1483–1485*, London 1983, p. 36.

7. Sylvester / More, *The History of King Richard III*, p. 65.

8. Myers / Buck, *Richard the Third*, p. 121.

9. Myers / Buck, *Richard the Third*, p. 121.

10. Myers / Buck, *Richard the Third*, p. 121.

11 1464–1465: Itinerary

1. TNA, C 81/796; TNA, C 81/797.

2. Both TNA, C 81/797.

3. TNA, C 81/797; TNA, C 81/798.

4. TNA, C 81/798.

5. Clive, *Sun of York*, p. 102.

6. Gairdner, *The Historical Collections of a Citizen of London in the Fifteenth Century* [Gregory's Chronicle], p. 226.

7. All TNA, C 81/798.

8. http://www.british-history.ac.uk/rymer-foedera/vol11/pp512-531

9. http://www.british-history.ac.uk/rymer-foedera/vol11/pp512-531

10. Both TNA, C 81/798.

11. All TNA, C 81/798.

12. TNA, C 81/798.

13. TNA, PSO 1/26; TNA, C 81/798.

14. Both TNA, C 81/799.

15. Chichester, in the south-west – or Chester, in the north? TNA, C 81/799.

16. http://www.british-history.ac.uk/rymer-foedera/vol11/pp531-538

17. TNA, C 81/799.

18. TNA, PSO 1/26.

19. TNA, PSO 1/26; TNA, C 81/799.

20. Gairdner, *Paston Letters*, vol. 4, p. 117; TNA, C 81/799.

21. http://www.british-history.ac.uk/rymer-foedera/vol11/pp531-538

22. TNA, C 81/799.
23. TNA, PSO 1/26; TNA, C 81/800.
24. TNA, C 81/800.
25. TNA, C 81/800; Gairdner, *Paston Letters*, vol. 4, p. 116.
26. Both TNA, C 81/800.
27. TNA, C 81/800.
28. TNA, PSO 1/26; TNA, C 81/800; TNA, C 81/801.
29. TNA, C 81/801.
30. TNA, C 81/801; TNA, C 81/802.
31. TNA, C 81/802; TNA, PSO 1/26.
32. All TNA, C 81/802.
33. TNA, PSO 1/26; TNA, C 81/802; TNA, C 81/803.
34. TNA, PSO 1/26; TNA, C 81/803.
35. All TNA, C 81/803.
36. TNA, C 81/803.
37. TNA, C 81/803; TNA, C 81/804.
38. All TNA, C 81/804.
39. TNA, C 81/804.
40. TNA, C 81/804; TNA, C 81/805.
41. All TNA, C 81/805.
42. TNA, C 81/805.
43. TNA, PSO 1/26.
44. TNA, PSO 1/26; TNA, PSO 1/27; TNA, C 81/805; TNA, C 81/806.
45. TNA, C 81/806.

12 1463–1464: Bona – Savoir faire

1. J. Ashdown-Hill, *Royal Marriage Secrets*, Stroud 2013, Appendix 1 (pp. 196–97).
2. *ODNB*, N. Macdougall, 'Mary of Gueldres'.
3. P. M. Kendall, *Warwick the Kingmaker*, London 1973, p. 104.
4. *ODNB*, Macdougall, 'Mary of Gueldres'.
5. Kendall, *Warwick*, pp. 143–44.

13 1463–1464: Deo devota

1. Gairdner, ed., *The Historical Collections of a Citizen of London in the Fifteenth Century* [Gregory's Chronicle], p. 226.
2. Kincaid, ed., Buck, *King Richard the Third*, p. 183.
3. N. Adams and C. Donahue, eds, *Select Cases from the Ecclesiastical Courts of the Province of Canterbury, c. 1200–1301*, London 1981, p. 337 and *passim*.
4. Ashdown-Hill, *Eleanor the Secret Queen*, pp. 110–11.
5. M. F. Serpell, *Kenninghall History and St Mary's Church*, Norwich 1982, p. 21.

6. Following Elizabeth Talbot's death, East Hall was demolished by the 3rd Howard Duke of Norfolk, who built a new residence, Kenninghall Place, a short distance to the east of the old site. This new house was habitable by 1526.

7. Serpell, *Kenninghall*, pp. 16, 21–27.

8. L. T. Smith, *The Itinerary of John Leland*, parts 6 and 7, London 1907–10, p. 120.

9. A. B. Emden, *A Biographical Register of the University of Oxford to A.D. 1500*, 3 vols, Oxford 1957–59, vol. 2, pp. 1035–36.

10. R. Masters, *The History of the College of Corpus Christi and the Blessed Virgin Mary*, Cambridge 1753, appendix, p. 53.

11. Masters, *The History of the College of Corpus Christi*, p. 46.

12. All Eleanor's siblings seemed to have shared a real and lively religious faith. This is evidenced in different ways by the wills of Sir Louis and Sir Humphrey Talbot, and by the lifestyle chosen by the dowager Duchess of Norfolk in her declining years.

13. H. Talbot, *The English Achilles: the life and campaigns of John Talbot, 1ˢᵗ Earl of Shrewsbury*, London 1981, p. 30.

14. W. E. Hampton, 'The Ladies of the Minories', *Ricardian* vol. 4, no. 62, September 1978, pp. 15–22.

15. Corpus Christi College, Cambridge, Parker Library, MS. XXXI. 121.

16. Personal communication from Sr. Gillian Leslie OCD.

17. J. Ward, *Women in Medieval Europe 1200–1500*, London 2002, p. 191.

18. C. Wolters, ed., *The Cloud of Unknowing*, Harmondsworth 1961, pp. 51–52.

19. R. Burrows, *Guidelines for Mystical Prayer*, London 1976, p. 105.

20. Ward, *Women in Medieval Europe*, pp. 193, 195.

21. Warwickshire Record Office, L1/81; Ashdown-Hill, *Eleanor*, plate 26.

22. WRO, L1/85.

23. WRO, L1/86; Ashdown-Hill, *Eleanor*, plates 36 & 37.

24. J. Ashdown-Hill, 'The Go-between', *Ricardian*, vol. 15, 2005, pp. 119–21.

25. HHB, part 1, pp. 153, 165, 180, 240, 332, 482, part 2, p. 116.

26. Ashdown-Hill, *Eleanor*, pp. 118–19.

27. HHB, part 1, p. 151. 'My lord' was Howard's cousin and Eleanor's brother-in-law, John Mowbray, fourth Duke of Norfolk.

28. HHB, part 1, p. 153.

14 1464: The Grey Mare

1. 'Although spelling of the family name is usually modernised to "Woodville", it was spelled "Wydeville" in contemporary publications by Caxton and the (later) inscription on her tomb at St George's Chapel, Windsor Castle is

"Edward IV and his Queen Elizabeth Widvile"'. https://en.wikipedia.org/wiki/Elizabeth_Woodville (consulted November 2015).

2. Clive, *Sun of York*, pp. 100–101.

3. Sylvester, ed., St Thomas More, *The History of King Richard III and Selections from the English and Latin Poems*, London 1976, p. 61.

4. J. Ashdown-Hill, *The Mythology of Richard III*, Stroud 2015, pp. 91–2, citing D. Enríquez del Castillo, *Crónica del Rey D. Enrique El Quarto De Este Nombre*, Madrid 1787, p. 252.

5. Sylvester / More, *The History of King Richard III*, pp. 61–2.

6. Sylvester / More, *The History of King Richard III*, p. 62.

7. Sylvester / More, *The History of King Richard III*, p. 62.

8. This date is also cited in Warkworth's Chronicle, Gregory's Chronicle and Hearne's Fragment, and is consistent with Edward IV's movements as published in the present volume's itinerary.

9. H. Ellis, ed., R. Fabyan, *The New Chronicles of England and France*, London 1811 (text of Fabyan's 1516 edition, collated with a manuscript of Fabyan's time), p. 654.

10. *ODNB*, M. Hicks, 'Elizabeth [*née* Elizabeth Woodville]'.

11. *ODNB*, M. Hicks, 'Elizabeth [*née* Elizabeth Woodville]'.

12. Dockray, *Edward IV a Source Book*, p. 46, citing *Great Chronicle of London*, pp. 202–03.

13. Ashdown-Hill, *Eleanor*, p. 202, citing *Rotuli Parliamentorum*, vol. 6, pp. 240–42.

14. 'Margaret was never crowned, being the first uncrowned queen since the Conquest.' http://en.wikipedia.org/wiki/Margaret_of_France,_Queen_of_England (consulted May 2015).

15. G. Smith, ed., *The Coronation of Elizabeth Wydeville, Queen Consort of Edward IV*, London 1935, reprinted Cliftonville 1975, p. 7.

16. Traditionally the bishops of Durham and of Bath and Wells escort English sovereigns to their coronations, but Edward IV was in the course of appointing to Bath and Wells Canon Robert Stillington – possibly as an encouragement to Stillington to keep his mouth shut in respect of Edward's earlier Talbot marriage. *Eleanor*, pp. 113–114.

17. J. L. Laynesmith, *The Last Medieval Queens*, Oxford 2004, p. 105, citing BL, MS, Cotton Julius B XII fos 30–1.

18. Smith, ed., *The Coronation of Elizabeth Wydeville*, p. 17.

19. Smith, ed., *The Coronation of Elizabeth Wydeville*, pp. 20–22.

20. Dockray, *Edward IV a Source Book*, pp. 46–7, citing *Great Chronicle of London*, pp. 202–03.

21. Ellis / Fabyan, *Chronicle*, p. 656–7.

22. Dockray, *Edward IV a Source Book*, p. 47, citing *Great Chronicle of London*, pp. 207–08.

23. He was confirmed in these posts early in the reign of Edward IV: H. C. Maxwell-Lyte, ed., *The Registers of Robert Stillington, Bishop of Bath and Wells 1466–1491 and Richard Fox, Bishop of Bath and Wells 1492–1494*, Somerset Record Society 1937, p. x, citing Patent Roll 1 Edward IV part v, m. 9.

24. A. J. Mowat, 'Robert Stillington', *Ricardian* vol. 4 (June 1976), p. 23.

25. Maxwell-Lyte, ed., *The Registers of Robert Stillington*, p. viii.

26. *CPR, 1461–1467*, p. 387.

27. Maxwell-Lyte, ed., *The Registers of Robert Stillington*, p. viii. Pope Paul II (Barbo) had succeeded Pius II (Piccolomini) at the end of August 1464.

28. Maxwell-Lyte, ed., *The Registers of Robert Stillington*, p. viii, citing Patent Roll 4 Edward IV, part 2, m. 2, nos. 37, 38, 51, 52.

29. *Calendar of Papal Registers*, vol. 12, *Papal Letters 1458–1471*, London 1933, p. 519. On Stillington's appointment, see also Mowat, 'Robert Stillington', p. 23, citing *CPR, 1461–67*, pp. 149–50, and Emden, *Oxford*, p. 1778.

15 1465–1469: Itinerary

1. TNA, C 81/806.

2. TNA, C 81/806; TNA, C 81/807.

3. TNA, C 81/807.

4. Both TNA, C 81/807.

5. TNA, C 81/807; TNA, C 81/808.

6. Both TNA, C 81/808.

7. All TNA, C 81/808.

8. Both TNA, C 81/808.

9. TNA, PSO 1/27; TNA, C 81/808; TNA, PSO 1/28; TNA, C 81/809.

10. TNA, C 81/809; Gairdner, *Paston Letters*, vol. 4, p. 247.

11. All TNA, C 81/809.

12. TNA, C 81/809.

13. Both TNA, C 81/809.

14. TNA, C 81/809; TNA, C 81/810.

15. TNA, C 81/810.

16. All TNA, C 81/810.

17. All TNA, C 81/810.

18. TNA, PSO 1/28; TNA, C 81/810.

19. TNA, PSO 1/28; TNA, C 81/810; TNA, C 81/811.

20. TNA, C 81/811.

21. TNA, PSO 1/28.

22. Both TNA, C 81/811.

23. TNA, PSO 1/28.

24. Both TNA, C 81/811.

25. All TNA, C 81/811.

26. TNA, PSO 1/28; TNA, C 81/811.

27. TNA, C 81/811.

28. TNA, C 81/812, 2113 (mis-filed under July, but it is definitely dated 1 June); TNA, C 81/811.

29. Clive, *Sun of York*, p. 121–24.

30. TNA, C 81/811.

31. TNA, C 81/811; TNA, C 81/812.

32. All TNA, C 81/813.

33. Both TNA, PSO 1/28; TNA, C 81/813.

34. TNA, PSO 1/28; TNA, PSO 1/29; TNA, C 81/813.

35. TNA, PSO 1/29; TNA, C 81/813.

36. TNA, PSO 1/29; TNA, C 81/814.

37. TNA, C 81/814.

38. TNA, PSO 1/29; TNA, C 81/814.

39. TNA, PSO 1/29; TNA, C 81/814.

40. TNA, PSO 1/29.

41. TNA, C 81/814.

42. All TNA, PSO 1/29; TNA, C 81/814.

43. A residence of the Bishop of Bath and Wells. http://www.british-history. ac.uk/rymer-foedera/vol11/pp576-601

44. Both TNA, PSO 1/29; TNA, C 81/814.

45. Both TNA, C 81/814.

46. TNA, PSO 1/29.

47. All TNA, C 81/815.

48. All TNA, PSO 1/30; TNA, C 81/815.

49. TNA, PSO 1/31; TNA, C 81/816.

50. Both TNA, C 81/816.

51. TNA, PSO 1/31; TNA, C 81/816; TNA, C 81/817.

52. TNA, C 81/817.

53. All TNA, C 81/817.

54. TNA, PSO 1/31; TNA 81/817; TNA, C 81/818.

55. TNA, C 81/818.

56. TNA, C 81/818.

57. Clive, *Sun of York*, p. 128.

58. TNA, C 81/818.

59. TNA, C 81/818.

60. J. Wilkinson, *Richard: The Young King to Be*, Stroud 2009, p. 145, citing *CCR 1461–1468*, pp. 456–7.

61. TNA, C 81/819.

62. C. Weightman, *Margaret of York Duchess of Burgundy 1446–1503*, Gloucester 1989, pp. 46–47.
63. TNA, C 81/819.
64. TNA, PSO 1/31; TNA, C 81/819.
65. TNA, C 81/819; TNA, C 81/820.
66. Both TNA, C 81/820.
67. TNA, PSO 1/31; TNA, C 81/820.
68. TNA, C 81/820.
69. TNA, PSO 1/31; TNA, C 81/820.
70. TNA, PSO 1/32; TNA, C 81/820; TNA, C 81/821.
71. TNA, PSO 1/31; TNA, C 81/821; TNA, PSO 1/32.
72. TNA, C 81/821; TNA, C 81/822; TNA, PSO 1/32; TNA, C 81/823.
73. TNA, PSO 1/32; TNA, C 81/823.
74. TNA, C 81/824.
75. All TNA, C 81/824.
76. Both TNA, C 81/824.
77. TNA, PSO 1/32; TNA, C 81/824.
78. TNA, C 81/825; TNA, PSO 1/32.
79. TNA, C 81/825.

16 1466?: *The Mysterious Catherine*

1. Myers / Buck, *Richard the Third*, p. 115.
2. Howell, *Eleanor of Provence*, pp. 72–3, as quoted in https://en.wikipedia.org/wiki/Clarendon_Palace (consulted December 2015).
3. *Calendar of Close Rolls, Edward IV, vol. 2, 1468-1476*, London 1953, pp. 148, 183 (nos. 573, 681).
4. *CPR, 1461–1467*, p. 25.
5. *CPR, 1461–1467*, p. 230.
6. *CPR, 1461–1467*, pp. 550–51.
7. *CPR, 1461–1467*, p. 550, see below.
8. 28 March 1482, *Calendar of Close Rolls, Edward IV, Edward V, Richard III, 1476–1485*, London 1954, p. 254 (no. 856).
9. http://powys.org/pl_tree/ps12/ps12_218.html (consulted December 2015), citing PRO [TNA] C/126/57.
10. 8 Feb 1483, *Calendar of Close Rolls, Edward IV, Edward V, Richard III, 1476–1485*, p. 262 (no. 879).
11. https://en.wikipedia.org/wiki/High_Sheriff_of_Surrey#1399.E2.80.931509; http://www.windowonwoking.org.uk/sites/goldsworthpark communityassociation/GPnews/sherrifs
(both consulted December 2015).
12. *CPR, 1461–1467*, p. 29.

13. *Calendar of Close Rolls, Edward IV, Edward V, Richard III, 1476–1485*, p. 209 (no. 719).

14. For example, a Katherine Melbury was married at St Mary's, Devizes, Wiltshire on 20 October 1694.

17 *1468: Disposing of the Rival*

1. Armstrong / Mancini, p. 63.

2. '*Circa festum Purificacionis beatae Mariae in Hibernia Comes Wigorniae fecit decollari Comitem Desmund, unde Rex in principio cepit displicenciam*'. Hearne, *Wilhelmi Worcestrii Annales*, vol. 2, p. 513; Stevenson, *Letters and papers*, vol. 2, p. 789. This was written in the second half of the fifteenth century, probably within twenty years of Desmond's execution.

3. *Calendar of the Carew Manuscripts at Lambeth*, vol. 2, 1575–88, London 1868, pp. cv–cvii.

4. J. Ashdown-Hill & A. Carson, 'The Execution of the Earl of Desmond', *Ricardian* vol. 15, 2005, pp. 70–93 (p. 85, fn. 41).

5. For the full details of the story, see Ashdown-Hill & Carson, 'The Execution of the Earl of Desmond'.

6. J. Gairdner, ed., *Letters and Papers illustrative of the Reigns of Richard III and Henry VII*, 2 vols., vol. 1, London 1861, p. 68.

7. Armstrong / Mancini, p. 63.

8. Weightman, *Margaret of York Duchess of Burgundy*, pp. 47–59.

9. L. T. Smith, *The Itinerary of John Leland*, parts 6 and 7, London 1907–10, p. 120.

18 *1469–1471: Itinerary*

1. TNA, C 81/825.

2. TNA, C 81/825; TNA, C 81/826.

3. Both TNA, C 81/826.

4. TNA, C 81/826.

5. Gairdner, *Paston Letters*, vol. 5, p. 28.

6. TNA, PSO 1/32; TNA, C 81/827.

7. TNA, C 81/827.

8. Both TNA, PSO 1/32; TNA, C 81/827.

9. TNA, C 81/827.

10. TNA, PSO 1/32; TNA, C 81/827.

11. Both TNA, C 81/827.

12. TNA, C 81/827.

13. H. T. Riley, ed., *Ingulph's Chronicle of the Abbey of Croyland*, London 1908, p. 445.

14. Clive, *Sun of York*, p. 141.

15. Riley, *Ingulph's Chronicle*, p. 445.

16. Riley, *Ingulph's Chronicle*, p. 445.

17. All TNA, C 81/827.

18. Clive, *Sun of York*, p. 144.

19. Pronay & Cox, *Crowland*, p. 117. But is this an error? – See below 'August'.

20. All TNA, C 81/827.

21. TNA, C 81/827.

22. TNA, PSO 1/33; TNA, C 81/827.

23. Pronay & Cox, *Crowland*, p. 117.

24. TNA, PSO 1/33; TNA, C 81/827.

25. TNA, PSO 1/33; TNA, C 81/827; TNA, C 81/828.

26. TNA, PSO 1/33; TNA, C 81/828; TNA, PSO 1/34; TNA, C 81/829.

27. TNA, C 81/829.

28. Pronay & Cox, *Crowland*, p. 117.

29. Pronay & Cox, *Crowland*, p. 117.

30. TNA, C 81/829; TNA, C 81/830.

31. Pronay & Cox, *Crowland*, p. 117.

32. TNA, PSO 1/34; TNA, C 81/830.

33. TNA, PSO 1/34; TNA, C 81/830.

34. TNA, PSO 1/34.

35. Clive, *Sun of York*, p. 151. Also http://www.british-history.ac.uk/rymer-foedera/vol11/pp650-660 (consulted September 2015).

36. Clive, *Sun of York*, p. 151.

37. Clive, *Sun of York*, p. 151; Pronay & Cox, *Crowland*, p. 121; TNA, C 81/830; TNA, C 81/831.

38. Both TNA, C 81/831.

39. Gairdner, *Paston Letters*, vol. 5, p. 70.

40. Clive, *Sun of York*, p. 151.

41. TNA, C 81/831.

42. All TNA, C 81/831.

43. All TNA, C 81/831.

44. All TNA, C 81/831.

45. TNA, C 81/832.

46. All TNA, C 81/832.

47. All TNA, PSO 1/34; TNA, C 81/832.

48. TNA, PSO 1/34.

49. All TNA, C 81/832.

50. TNA, C 81/832; Gairdner, *Paston Letters*, vol. 5, p. 83.

51. Clive, *Sun of York*, p. 155.

52. All M. Lulofs, 'King Edward IV in Exile', *Ricardian*, vol. 3, no 44, March 1974, pp. 9–11 (p. 10).

53. Lulofs, 'King Edward IV in Exile', p. 11.

54. Lulofs, 'King Edward IV in Exile', p. 11.

55. All Lulofs, 'King Edward IV in Exile', p. 11.

56. http://www.british-history.ac.uk/rymer-foedera/vol11/pp792-815 (consulted September 2015).

57. Lulofs, 'King Edward IV in Exile', p. 11.

58. Clive, *Sun of York*, p. 2.

59. L. Visser-Fuchs, 'Edward IV's Memoir on Paper to Charles, Duke of Burgundy', *Nottingham Medieval Studies XXXVI* (1992), pp. 167–227 (p. 210); Clive, Sun of York, p. 2.

60. Clive, *Sun of York*, p. 2.

61. Clive, *Sun of York*, pp. 2–3; p. 162–63.

62. Clive, *Sun of York*, p. 4.

63. Clive, *Sun of York*, pp. 4–5; Visser-Fuchs, 'Memoir on Paper', p. 210.

64. Clive, *Sun of York*, p. 5.

65. Clive, *Sun of York*, p. 6.

66. Clive, *Sun of York*, p. 7.

67. Clive, *Sun of York*, p. 8.

68. Visser-Fuchs, 'Memoir on Paper', p. 210.

69. Clive, *Sun of York*, p. 8.

70. Clive, *Sun of York*, p. 9; p. 165; Visser-Fuchs, 'Memoir on Paper', p. 211.

71. Clive, *Sun of York*, pp. 9–11; Visser-Fuchs, 'Memoir on Paper', p. 213. (Visser-Fuchs, 'Memoir on Paper', p. 211 implies that Edward stayed at Coventry for SIX days – but this seems unlikely. Possibly at some point the Latin numeral 'iij' was misread as 'uj'.)

72. Clive, *Sun of York*, p. 14.

73. Clive, *Sun of York*, p. 17; Visser-Fuchs, 'Memoir on Paper', p. 213.

74. Visser-Fuchs, 'Memoir on Paper', p. 213–14.

75. Pronay & Cox, *Crowland*, p. 125.

76. TNA, C 81/832.

77. Visser-Fuchs, 'Memoir on Paper', p. 213. (Clive, *Sun of York*, p. 175 claims Edward was at Windsor for the feast of St George but no source is cited.)

78. Visser-Fuchs, 'Memoir on Paper', p. 213.

79. TNA, C 81/832.

80. Clive, *Sun of York*, p. 28; p. 176.

81. Clive, *Sun of York*, pp. 28–29.

82. Clive, *Sun of York*, p. 31; Visser-Fuchs, 'Memoir on Paper', p. 216.

83. Clive, *Sun of York*, pp. 31, 32; TNA, C 81/832.

84. Clive, *Sun of York*, p. 38; Visser-Fuchs, 'Memoir on Paper', p. 213; TNA, C 81/832. NB. Pronay & Cox, *Crowland*, p. 129 says that Edward re-entered London on 23 May.

85. Clive, *Sun of York*, p. 38.

86. Clive, *Sun of York*, p. 38; Visser-Fuchs, 'Memoir on Paper', p. 218–219.

87. Clive, *Sun of York*, p. 39; p. 187; TNA, C 81/832; C. Scofield, *The Life and Reign of Edward the Fourth*, London 1967, vol. 2, pp. 8–9, citing letters.

88. TNA, PSO 1/34; TNA, C 81/832; TNA, C 81/833.

89. TNA, C 81/833.

90. TNA, C 81/833.

91. TNA, PSO 1/34; TNA, C 81/833.

92. TNA, PSO 1/35; TNA, C 81/833.

93. TNA, PSO 1/35; TNA, C 81/833.

94. TNA, C 81/833.

95. TNA, PSO 1/35; TNA, C 81/833; TNA, C 81/834.

96. TNA, PSO 1/35; TNA, C 81/834.

97. TNA, C 81/834.

98. TNA, C 81/834; TNA, C 81/835.

99. Both TNA, C 81/835.

100. TNA, C 81/835; TNA, C 81/836.

101. TNA, C 81/836.

102. TNA, PSO 1/35; TNA, C 81/836.

103. All TNA, C 81/836.

104. Gairdner, *Paston Letters*, vol. 5, p. 112; Scofield, *Edward the Fourth*, vol. 2, p. 20.

105. Both TNA, C 81/836.

106. TNA, PSO 1/35; TNA, C 81/836.

107. TNA, C 81/836.

108. TNA, C 81/836; TNA, PSO 1/35; TNA, C 81/837.

109. TNA, C 81/837.

110. TNA, C 81/837.

111. http://www.british-history.ac.uk/rymer-foedera/vol11/pp714-733 (consulted September 2015).

112. All TNA, C 81/837.

113. TNA, C 81/837.

19 1470?: The Light Wayte

1. *Complete Peerage*, vol. 8, p. 63.

2. See above, introduction.

3. https://en.wikipedia.org/wiki/Arthur_Plantagenet,_1st_Viscount_Lisle (consulted March 2016).

4. Victoria County History of *Hampshire*, vol. 4, London, 1911, pp. 403, 407, 408, 410, 501.

5. *List of Escheators for England and Wales*, List and Index Society, vol. 72, London 1971, p. 143: Richard le Wayte, Escheator for Southampton, Wiltshire, Bedfordshire, Buckinghamshire, Oxfordshire and Berkshire, 29 Nov. 1323 – 28 June 1326; p. 145: William Wayte, Escheator for Hampshire and Wiltshire, 16 Nov. 1420 – 19 May 1422, and 1 Oct. 1422 – 12 Nov. 1423; p. 147: John Wayte (first cousin of Edward IV's mistress?), Escheator 6 Nov. 1488 – 5 Nov. 1489. In addition John Wayte was Sheriff of the county of Hampshire in 1396–97. A number of Thomas Wayte's Popham ancestors also held the office of sheriff. A list of Hampshire sheriffs is published in W. Berry, *County Genealogies, Pedigrees of the Families of the County of Hampshire*, London 1833, p. viii.

6. As cited by St Clare Byrne, vol. 1, p. 140.

7. St Clare Byrne, vol. 1, p. 140, citing Anstis, *Register of the Garter*, 1724, vol. 2, p. 366, fn. 9.

8. Published in St Clare Byrne, vol. 1, p. 383.

9. See J. Ashdown-Hill, 'The Elusive Mistress', *The Ricardian*, vol. 11, no. 145, June 1999, pp. 490–505 (p. 495).

10. Victoria County History of *Hampshire*, vol. 3, London 1973, pp. 228–29, and St Clare Byrne, vol. 1, p. 218.

11. Sir John Popham the elder was still living in 1402, *CPR* 1401–1405, p. 93. Sir John Popham the younger was knighted before 1400 and married Isabel, daughter of William and Alice Romeseye, *CPR* 1399–1401, p. 372. For details of the family of Sir Philip Popham, *Calendar of Inquisitions Post Mortem*, vol. 17, p. 391, vol. 18, pp. 111–12, vol. 20, p. 53, and pp. 89–90, also *Calendar of Inquisitions, Edward III*, vol. 11, p. 95, together with *CPR* 1399–1401, p. 405, and *CPR* 1413–1416, p. 371.

12. Somerset Archaeological and Natural History Socierty, http://www.sanhs.org/Proc%20Extr/Proc%20Yatton.htm (consulted February 2015). See also appendices 1 and 2 below.

13. VCH, *Hampshire*, vol. 4, p. 374. John Skillyng was probably a relative (perhaps a brother, perhaps the son) of Michael Skyllyng, whose will was proved on 8 October 1463. John was named as an executor. First Register of Bishop William Wayneflete: probate of the will of Michael Skyllyng, Hampshire County Record Office, 21M65/A1/13, f. 79*. For details of the Skillyng's holdings in Wiltshire, see VCH, *Wiltshire*, vol. 11, London 1980, p. 110.

14. TNA (PRO) PROB 11/8, f. 52 r–v, published in Ashdown-Hill, 'The Elusive Mistress', *Ricardian*, vol. 11, no. 145 (June 1999), appendix, pp. 501–03 (p. 502).

15. VCH, *Hampshire,* vol. 4, p. 374.

16. N. Pevsner and D. Lloyd, *The Buildings of England: Hampshire and the Isle of Wight*, Harmondsworth 1967, p. 613.

17. A. Mee, *The King's England: Hampshire,* London 1939, pp. 348, 349.

18. TNA PROB 11/8, f. 52 r–v – published in Ashdown-Hill, 'The Elusive Mistress', pp. 501–03.

19. Scofield, *The Life and Reign of Edward the Fourth*, vol. 2, p. 161.

20. L. Toulmin Smith, ed., *The Itinerary of John Leland in or about the years 1535–1543*, parts 7 and 8, London 1909, p. 118: 'The advancment of Lumley to be lord was by mariage of a bastard doughter of King Edwarde 4.' As it stands, of course, this statement is clearly inaccurate, as the Lumleys already held the title of Lord.

21. J. Ashdown-Hill, 'The Wills of John Talbot, first Earl of Shrewsbury, and of his sons Lord Lisle and Sir Louis Talbot', *Transactions of the Shropshire Archaeological & Historical Society* 2010, pp. 31–37.

20 1470–1471: *Winter in Exile*

1. Jones / Commynes, *Memoirs*, pp. 188–89.

2. Clive, *Sun of York*, p. 155.

3. D. F. Sutton, ed., Bernard André, *De Vita atque Gestis Henrici Septimi Historia*, online 2010.

4. J. Gairdner, *History of the Life and Reign of Richard the Third to which is added The Story of Perkin Warbeck*, Cambridge 1898, p. 271, citing 'Speed' (?John Speede?) but with no source given.

5. Gairdner, *History of the Life and Reign of Richard the Third to which is added The Story of Perkin Warbeck*, p. 267.

6. Accounts Exchequer K. R. E. 101/412, no. 8, m.3, cited in M. St. Clare Byrne, *The Lisle Letters*, London 1981, vol. 1, p. 139.

21 1471–1476: *Itinerary*

1. The spelling of Brentford in Samuel Pepys' C17th diary was 'Brainford'.

2. All TNA, C 81/837.

3. TNA, PSO 1/35; TNA, C 81/837; TNA, C 81/838.

4. Both TNA, C 81/838.

5. TNA, C 81/838; TNA, C 81/839.

6. TNA, C 81/839.

7. All TNA, C 81/839.

8. All TNA, C 81/839.

9. Both TNA, C 81/840.

10. All TNA, C 81/840.

11. All TNA, C 81/840.

12. Both TNA, C 81/841.

13. Both TNA, C 81/841.

14. TNA, PSO 1/36; TNA, C 81/841.

15. Both TNA, C 81/841.

16. TNA, PSO 1/36; TNA, C 81/841.

17. TNA, PSO 1/36; TNA, C 81/841; TNA, C 81/842.

18. TNA, PSO 1/37; TNA, C 81/842.

19. TNA, PSO 1/37; TNA, C 81/842.

20. TNA, PSO 1/37.

21. TNA, PSO 1/37; TNA, C 81/842.

22. Both TNA, PSO 1/37; TNA, C 81/842.

23. TNA, PSO 1/37; TNA, C 81/842; TNA, C 81/843.

24. TNA, PSO 1/37; TNA, C 81/843.

25. All TNA, PSO 1/37.

26. TNA, C 81/843.

27. TNA, C 81/843.

28. TNA, PSO 1/37; TNA, C 81/843.

29. TNA, PSO 1/37; TNA, C 81/844.

30. TNA, C 81/844.

31. Gairdner, *Paston Letters*, vol. 5, p. 181.

32. Both TNA, C 81/844.

33. All TNA, C 81/844.

34. All TNA, C 81/845.

35. TNA, PSO 1/40/2056 – but NB the regnal year is missing from surviving MS.

36. All TNA, C 81/845.

37. All TNA, C 81/845.

38. All TNA, C 81/845.

39. Scofield, *Edward the Fourth*, vol. 2, p. 49.

40. TNA, C 81/845; TNA, C 81/846.

41. TNA, PSO 1/38; TNA, C 81/846.

42. TNA, PSO 1/38.

43. Both TNA, C 81/846.

44. All TNA, C 81/847; TNA, PSO 1/38.

45. All TNA, C 81/847.

46. Both TNA, C 81/847.

47. TNA, C 81/847.

48. TNA, PSO 1/38; TNA, C 81/847.

49. TNA, PSO 1/38; TNA, PSO 1/39.

50. TNA, PSO 1/39; TNA, C 81/848.

51. TNA, PSO 1/39; TNA, C 81/848.

52. TNA, C 81/848; TNA, C 81/849.

53. Both TNA, C 81/849.

54. http://www.british-history.ac.uk/rymer-foedera/vol11/pp815-820 (consulted September 2015).

55. All TNA, C 81/850.

56. All TNA, C 81/850.

57. All TNA, C 81/850.

58. Gairdner, *Paston Letters*, vol. 5, pp. 221–22. Letter of 29 Jan. 1474/5, referring to receipt of no letters from Sir John Paston since before the King came to Norwich.

59. Both TNA, C 81/850.

60. Gairdner, *Paston Letters*, vol. 5, p. 216; TNA, C 81/850.

61. TNA, C 81/850.

62. Both TNA, C 81/850.

63. http://www.british-history.ac.uk/rymer-foedera/vol11/pp820-842 (consulted September 2015).

64. TNA, C 81/850; TNA, C 81/851.

65. All TNA, PSO 1/40; TNA, C 81/851. Parliament was reopened at Westminster – Scofield, *Edward the Fourth*, vol. 2, p. 95.

66. TNA, PSO 1/40; TNA, C 81/851.

67. TNA, PSO 1/40; TNA, C 81/851.

68. TNA, PSO 1/40; TNA, C 81/851; TNA, C 81/852.

69. TNA, PSO 1/41; TNA, C 81/852.

70. TNA, PSO 1/41.

71. Both TNA, PSO 1/41; TNA, C 81/852.

72. TNA, PSO 1/41; TNA, C 81/852.

73. TNA, PSO 1/41; TNA, C 81/852.

74. TNA, PSO 1/41; TNA, C 81/852.

75. TNA, C 81/852.

76. All TNA, C 81/853.

77. Both TNA, C 81/854.

78. TNA, PSO 1/41; TNA, C 81/854.

79. Both TNA, C 81/854.

80. http://www.british-history.ac.uk/rymer-foedera/vol12/pp14-22 (consulted September 2015).

81. Clive, *Sun of York*, p. 222. Edward IV reportedly spoke good French.

82. TNA, PSO 1/41; TNA, C 81/854.

83. TNA, C 81/854.

84. Both TNA, PSO 1/41; TNA, C 81/854.

85. All TNA, C 81/855.

86. All TNA, C 81/855.

87. Both TNA, C 81/855.

88. TNA, PSO 1/41; TNA, C 81/855.

89. TNA, C 81/855.

90. TNA, C 81/855; TNA, C 81/856.

91. http://www.british-history.ac.uk/rymer-foedera/vol12/pp22-39 (consulted September 2015).

92. TNA, C 81/856.

22 The Confusing Third Elizabeth

1. A. F. Sutton, 'William Shore, merchant of London and Derby', *Derbyshire Archaeological Journal*, 106 (1986), pp. 127–39 (p. 127).

2. Sutton, 'William Shore', p. 130.

3. Sutton, 'William Shore', pp. 130–31.

4. See below, note 20. The reason for the relatively rare appearance of Shore's name in the surviving Howard accounts lies in the fact that, for the decade of the 1470s (during which time Shore's business relationship with Howard was developing) no Howard accounts survive.

5. F. Pedersen, *Marriage Disputes in Medieval England*, London, 2000, p. 117.

6. *Calendar of Entries in Papal Rgisters Relating to England*, xiii, pp. 487–8, cited in N. Barker, 'Jane Shore', *Etoniana*, no. 125, June 1972, pp. 383–91 (p. 388).

7. Scofield, *The Life and Reign of Edward the Fourth*, London 1923, 1967, vol. 2, p. 162, citing Tellers' Roll, Easter 14 Edw. IV.

8. Kendall, *Richard the Third*, p. 147; *CPR 1476–1485*, p. 9. For some curious reason Kendall assumes this shows that Elizabeth had then become the king's mistress. Obviously the evidence in question does not, in reality, prove anything of the sort.

9. ERO, D/B5 Cr76, m. 3r.

10. On the Hervys see L. J. F. Ashdown-Hill, *Thesis*, subsection 4.15.4.

11. ERO, D/B5 Cr 76, m. 17. Agard is not mentioned in the Howard accounts. More research is needed to identify him.

12. The quitclaim and grant are registered twice. Firstly on ERO, D/B5 Cr76, m 20v, where the entry is deleted, with the note that the insertion was out of sequence and a scribal error. It was then reinserted on m. 24.

13. Or possibly a relative of the apprentice, with the same name: Sutton, 'William Shore', p. 128, citing Mercers' Company: wardens' accounts 1463–64 and *Register of Freemen from 1347*.

14. Sutton, 'William Shore', p. 132.

15. ERO, D/B5 Cr76, m. 22v.

16. ERO, D/B5 Cr76, m. 25r.

17. ERO, D/B5 Cr76, m. 25r.

18. ERO, D/B5 Cr76, m. 26r.

19. ERO, D/B5 Cr76, m. 27r.

20. Soc. Ant., MS 76, f. 39r; *HHB*, part 2, p. 39. Sutton dates this to July, as part of Howard's provisions for the Scots campaign, but the entry in the Howard accounts is certainly under April. Although no first name is recorded, and although Howard also had dealings with a John Shore of Colchester, this entry clearly refers to William, for John Shore was merely a sailor, serving at this time as a member of the ship's company of Howard's vessel, the *Antony*: Soc. Ant., MS 76, p. 4 [f. 7r]; *HHB*, part 2, p. 7.

21. Soc. Ant., MS 76, f. 89r; *HHB*, part 2, p. 112.

22. Sutton, 'William Shore', p. 131.

23. Sutton, 'William Shore', p. 133.

24. Sutton, 'William Shore', p. 134.

25. Ashdown-Hill, *Thesis*.

26. See above: *Calendar of Entries in Papal Registers Relating to England*, xiii, 487–88.

27. C. L. Kingsford, ed., *The Stonor Letters and Papers*, Camden Soc. 3rd ser., 1919, vol. 30, p. 161, cited in Barker, 'Jane Shore', *Etoniana*, p. 388.

28. A. H. Thomas & I. D. Thornley, eds, *The Great Chronicle of London*, London 1938, p. 233.

29. *ODNB*, R. Horrox, 'Elizabeth Shore'; *CPR*, 1476–85, p. 371.

30. P. W. Hammond & A. F. Sutton, *Richard III: The Road to Bosworth*, London 1985, p. 194, citing Harleian MS, vol. 3, p. 259.

31. R. Edwards, *The Itinerary of King Richard III 1483–1485*, London 1983, pp. 10–15.

23 1475: *The Royal Will*

1. 'where we trust in God oure said Wiff bee now with childe'.

2. S. Bentley, ed, *Excerpta Historica*, London 1831, pp. 366–79, citing Rymer, BL, Add. MS 4615 (part of his miscellaneous collections for the *Foedera*).

24 1476–1479: *Itinerary*

1. TNA, C 81/856.

2. Both TNA, C 81/856.

3. TNA, PSO 1/41.
4. TNA, PSO 1/41; TNA, C 81/856.
5. All TNA, C 81/856.
6. TNA, PSO 1/42; TNA, C 81/856.
7. TNA, PSO 1/42; TNA, C 81/857.
8. All TNA, PSO 1/42; TNA, C 81/857.
9. All TNA, PSO 1/42; TNA, C 81/857.
10. TNA, C 81/857; TNA, C 81/858.
11. TNA, C 81/858.
12. TNA, PSO 1/42; TNA, C 81/858.
13. Both TNA, C 81/858.
14. TNA, PSO 1/42; TNA, C 81/858.
15. All TNA, PSO 1/43; TNA, C 81/858.
16. TNA, PSO 1/43; TNA, C 81/858.
17. TNA, PSO 1/43; TNA, C 81/859.
18. Both TNA, PSO 1/43; TNA, PSO 1/44; TNA, C 81/859.
19. TNA, PSO 1/44.
20. TNA, C 81/859.
21. Both TNA, C 81/859.
22. Both TNA, C 81/859.
23. TNA, C 81/860.
24. TNA, PSO 1/44; TNA, C 81/860.
25. TNA, PSO 1/44.
26. Both TNA, PSO 1/44; TNA, C 81/860.
27. TNA, C 81/860.
28. TNA, PSO 1/44; TNA, C 81/860.
29. Both TNA, C 81/860.
30. All TNA, C 81/860.
31. Both TNA, C 81/861.
32. TNA, PSO 1/44.
33. Both TNA, PSO 1/44; TNA, C 81/861.
34. Both TNA, PSO 1/44.
35. Both TNA, C 81/861.
36. TNA, C 81/861; TNA, PSO 1/44.
37. TNA, PSO 1/44; TNA, C 81/861.
38. TNA, PSO 1/44.
39. TNA, C 81/861.
40. Both TNA, C 81/861.
41. TNA, PSO 1/45; TNA, C 81/861.
42. TNA, PSO 1/45.
43. All TNA, C 81/861.

44. Both TNA, C 81/862.
45. TNA, PSO 1/45.
46. TNA, PSO 1/45; TNA, C 81/862.
47. TNA, C 81/862.
48. TNA, PSO 1/45; TNA, C 81/862.
49. TNA, PSO 1/45; TNA, C 81/862.
50. TNA, C 81/863.
51. Both TNA, C 81/863.
52. TNA, C 81/863.
53. TNA, C 81/863; TNA, C 81/864.
54. TNA, C 81/864.
55. TNA, PSO 1/45; TNA, C 81/864.
56. TNA, PSO 1/45; TNA, C 81/865.
57. All TNA, C 81/865.
58. TNA, C 81/865.
59. TNA, C 81/865; TNA, C 81/866.
60. All TNA, C 81/866.
61. Both TNA, PSO 1/45; TNA, C 81/866.
62. TNA, C 81/866.
63. TNA, PSO 1/45.
64. TNA, C 81/866.
65. Both TNA, PSO 1/45; TNA, C 81/866.
66. All TNA, PSO 1/46; TNA, C 81/866.
67. Both TNA, PSO 1/46.
68. Both TNA, C 81/866.
69. TNA, PSO 1/46; TNA, C 81/866.
70. TNA, C 81/866.
71. TNA, C 81/867.
72. All TNA, PSO 1/46.
73. TNA, C 81/867.
74. TNA, PSO 1/46; TNA, C 81/867.
75. All TNA, C 81/867.
76. TNA, PSO 1/46; TNA, C 81/867.
77. TNA, PSO 1/46.
78. All TNA, PSO 1/46; TNA, C 81/867.
79. TNA, C 81/867.
80. TNA, PSO 1/46; TNA, C 81/867.
81. Both TNA, PSO 1/46.
82. TNA, C 81/867.
83. TNA, PSO 1/46; TNA, C 81/867.
84. TNA, PSO 1/47; TNA, C 81/867.

85. TNA, C 81/867.
86. TNA, PSO 1/47.
87. All TNA, C 81/867.
88. TNA, C 81/867; TNA, C 81/868.
89. All TNA, C 81/868.
90. TNA, C 81/868.
91. TNA, C 81/868.
92. TNA, C 81/868.
93. TNA, C 81/868; C 81/869.
94. All TNA, C 81/869.
95. TNA, C 81/869.
96. TNA, PSO 1/47.
97. Both TNA, PSO 1/47; TNA, C 81/869.
98. TNA, PSO 1/47.
99. All TNA, C 81/869.
100. TNA, C 81/869.
101. TNA, C 81/869.
102. TNA, C 81/869; TNA, C 81/870.
103. TNA, C 81/870.
104. All TNA, C 81/870.
105. All TNA, C 81/870.
106. TNA, C 81/870; TNA, C 81/871.
107. All TNA, C 81/871.
108. TNA, C 81/871.
109. TNA, C 81/871; TNA, PSO 1/47.

25 1475–1478: *Gone but Not Forgotten*

1. Ashdown-Hill, *Eleanor*, Appendix 1 – repeal of *Titulus Regius*, November 1485. Also see above – Thomas More's invention of 'Elizabeth Lucy'.
2. Ashdown-Hill, *Eleanor*, Appendix 1 – letters of Chapuys. Since Chapuys was the Imperial ambassador to England, his source of information may have been in England or on the mainland of Europe.
3. N. Davis, ed., *Paston Letters and Papers of the Fifteenth Century*, 2 vols, Oxford 1976, vol. 1, p. 440: 'my lord of Norffolk and my lady wer on pylgrymage at Owre Ladye on foot'.
4. Davis, *Paston Letters*, vol. 1, p. 577.
5. Davis, *Paston Letters*, vol. 1, p. 586.
6. Davis, *Paston Letters*, vol. 1, p. 593.
7. Davis, *Paston Letters*, vol. 1, p. 594.
8. She may even, perhaps, have been pregnant on another occasion or occasions, not recorded, and have miscarried.

9. Scofield, *The Life and Reign of Edward IV*, vol. 2, p. 49, note 2, citing Martène & Durand, *Veterum Scriptorum Amplissa Collectio*, II, 1506.

10. Davis, *Paston Letters*, vol. 1, p. 489.

11. In 1468, when he was at war with the Paston family over Caister Castle, it was to the Duke of Clarence that John Mowbray appealed for help. Ashdown-Hill, *The Wars of the Roses*, p. 135.

12. H. Grimstone & T. Leach, eds, *Reports of Sir George Croke, Knight, of … Select Cases*, Dublin 1793, p. 122.

13. *Third Report of the Deputy Keeper of the Public Records* (February 28, 1842), London 1842, p. 213, citing *Baga de Secretis*, Bundle 1, MS. 9; present author's emphasis.

14. Davis, *Paston Letters*, volume 1, p. 492.

15. *Third Report of the Deputy Keeper of the Public Records* (February 28, 1842), p. 214, citing *Baga de Secretis*, Bundle 1, MSs. 58 & 59.

16. M. Hicks, *False, Fleeting, Perjur'd Clarence*, 2nd edition, Bangor 1992, p. 125.

17. I. S. Rogers, 'Tocotes, Sir Roger', *www.girders.net/To/Tocotes,%20Sir%20 Roger,%20(d.1492).doc* (consulted June 2013).

18. Jospeh Strutt, 1773, as quoted in A. Sutton & L. Visser-Fuchs, 'Richard III and the Knave of Cards: an illuminator's model in manuscript and print, 1440s to 1990s', *The Antiquaries Journal*, vol. 79 (1999), pp. 257–299 (p. 257).

19. J. E. Jackson, 'The Execution of Ankarette Twynyho', [published source unknown] 1890, [print-off in Wiltshire Archaeological and Natural History Society Library], p. 52.

20. *ibid.*

21. Armstrong / Mancini, p. 63.

22. Armstrong / Mancini, p. 63.

23. *CPR 1476–1485*, p. 572.

24. Gairdner, *History of the Life and Reign of Richard the Third*, p. 91, n. 1, citing the letter of that date from Elizabeth Stonor.

25. The precise date on which Stillington entered the Tower is not recorded, but Gairdner estimates that it was between 13 and 20 February.

26. *CPR 1476–1485*, p. 554.

27. Jones / Commynes, *Memoirs*, p. 397.

28. *CPR 1476–1485*, p. 102.

29. Ellis / Vergil, p. 167.

30. For the full text of the Act of Attainder, see J. Ashdown-Hill, *The Third Plantagenet*, Stroud 2014, chapter 13.

26 1480–1483: *Itinerary*

1. TNA, PSO 1/47; TNA, C 81/871; TNA, C 81/872.

2. TNA, PSO 1/47; TNA, PSO 1/48; TNA, C 81/872.

3. TNA, C 81/872; TNA, PSO 1/48.

4. TNA, PSO 1/48.

5. Both TNA, PSO 1/48; TNA, C 81/872.

6. TNA, PSO 1/48.

7. Both TNA, PSO 1/48; TNA, C 81/872.

8. TNA, PSO 1/48.

9. TNA, PSO 1/48; TNA, C 81/873.

10. All TNA, C 81/873.

11. TNA, PSO 1/48; TNA, C 81/873.

12. TNA, PSO 1/49; TNA, C 81/873.

13. TNA, PSO 1/49.

14. Both TNA, PSO 1/49; TNA, C 81/873.

15. TNA, C 81/873.

16. Both TNA, PSO 1/49.

17. Both TNA, C 81/873.

18. http://www.british-history.ac.uk/rymer-foedera/vol12/pp119-139 (consulted September 2015).

19. Both TNA, C 81/873.

20. Both TNA, C 81/873; TNA, C 81/874.

21. Both TNA, C 81/874.

22. All TNA, C 81/874.

23. TNA, PSO 1/49; TNA, C 81/874.

24. TNA, C 81/874.

25. All TNA, C 81/874.

26. TNA, C 81/874; TNA, C 81/875.

27. TNA, C 81/875.

28. Both TNA, C 81/875.

29. All TNA, C 81/875.

30. TNA, C 81/876.

31. TNA, C 81/876.

32. Both TNA, C 81/876.

33. TNA, C 81/876.

34. All TNA, PSO 1/49; TNA, C 81/876.

35. TNA, C 81/876.

36. TNA, C 81/876; TNA, C 81/877; TNA, PSO 1/49.

37. TNA, PSO 1/49.

38. TNA, PSO 1/49; TNA, C 81/877.

39. TNA, PSO 1/49; TNA, C 81/877.

40. TNA, PSO 1/49.

41. Both TNA, PSO 1/50; TNA, C 81/877.

42. TNA, PSO 1/49; TNA, C 81/877.

43. TNA, PSO 1/50; TNA, C 81/877.

44. Both TNA, PSO 1/50.

45. TNA, C 81/877.

46. TNA, PSO 1/50; TNA, C 81/877.

47. TNA, PSO 1/50.

48. TNA, PSO 1/50; TNA, C 81/877.

49. Both TNA, C 81/877; TNA, C 81/878.

50. TNA, PSO 1/50; TNA, C 81/877.

51. TNA, C 81/878.

52. All TNA, C 81/878.

53. Both TNA, C 81/878.

54. Both TNA, PSO 1/50; TNA, C 81/878.

55. All TNA, C 81/878.

56. TNA, C 81/878; TNA, C 81/879.

57. TNA, C 81/879.

58. TNA, C 81/879.

59. All TNA, C 81/880.

60. Both TNA, C 81/880.

61. All TNA, C 81/880.

62. http://www.british-history.ac.uk/rymer-foedera/vol12/pp145-158 (consulted September 2015).

63. TNA, PSO 1/50.

64. TNA, PSO 1/50; TNA, C 81/880; TNA, C 81/881.

65. All TNA, PSO 1/51; TNA, C 81/881.

66. All TNA, PSO 1/51; TNA, C 81/881.

67. TNA, PSO 1/51.

68. Both TNA, PSO 1/51; TNA, C 81/881.

69. TNA, PSO 1/52.

70. TNA, PSO 1/52; TNA, C 81/881.

71. TNA, PSO 1/52.

72. TNA, PSO 1/52; TNA, C 81/881.

73. TNA, PSO 1/52; TNA, C 81/881.

74. Both TNA, PSO 1/52; TNA, C 81/882.

75. TNA, PSO 1/52; TNA, PSO 1/53; TNA, C 81/882.

76. All TNA, PSO 1/53; TNA, C 81/882.

77. Both TNA, PSO 1/53; TNA, C 81/882.

78. All TNA, C 81/882.

79. http://www.british-history.ac.uk/rymer-foedera/vol12/pp159-172 (consulted September 2015).

80. Both TNA, C 81/883.

81. All TNA, C 81/883.

82. Soc. Ant., MS 77, f.6v; *HHB*, 2, p. 291.

83. All TNA, C 81/883.

84. TNA, PSO 1/53; TNA, C 81/883.

85. TNA, PSO 1/54; TNA, C 81/883; TNA, C 81/884.

86. TNA, PSO 1/54; TNA, C 81/884.

87. TNA, PSO 1/54.

88. TNA, PSO 1/54.

89. TNA, PSO 1/54; TNA, C 81/884.

90. All TNA, C 81/884.

91. TNA, PSO 1/54; TNA, PSO 1/55; TNA, C 81/884; TNA, C 81/885.

92. TNA, C 81/884.

93. TNA, PSO 1/55.

94. TNA, PSO 1/55; TNA, C 81/884.

95. TNA, PSO 1/55; TNA, C 81/884.

96. TNA, C 81/884; TNA, PSO 1/55.

97. TNA, C 81/884.

27 1483: *The Succession Problems*

1. R. Davies, *Extracts from the Municipal Records of the City of York*, London 1843 (reprinted Dursley, 1976) pp. 142,143, and footnote.

2. Armstrong / Mancini, p. 59.

3. Pronay & Cox, eds, *The Crowland Chronicle Continuations*, pp. 150–51. Later sources for this date include the Great Chronicle of London, Fabyan's Chronicle, and Hall's Chronicle.

4. *Obitus Edwardi V^ti xxij^o mens [sic for mensis] Junij regnavit ij menses et viij^o dies set non coronatus fuit occisus et nemo s[c]it ubi sepultus.* [The death of Edward V: 22 of the month of June, he reigned 2 months and 8 days but was not crowned, he was killed, and no one knows where he was buried.] Fitzwilliam Museum, Cambridge, MS. 329, f. 8r.

5. L. Lyell & F. D. Watney, eds, *Acts of Court of the Mercers' Company 1453–1527*, Cambridge 1936, p. 146.

6. The possibility that the Duke of Clarence's plot to save the Earl of Warwick had succeeded, by shipping his real son to safety abroad and replacing him with a substitute child, is explored in J. Ashdown-Hill, *The Dublin King*, Stroud 2015.

7. Pronay & Cox, eds, *The Crowland Chronicle Continuations*, pp. 154–55.

8. Pronay & Cox, eds, *The Crowland Chronicle Continuations*, pp. 156–57.

9. Armstrong / Mancini, pp. 76–79.

10. Pronay & Cox, eds, *Crowland Chronicle*, pp. 156–57.

11. Letter from Simon Stallworthe to Sir William Stonor, as explained in J. Ashdown-Hill, *Richard III's 'Beloved Cousyn'*, p. 93, citing *Facsimiles of National Manuscripts*, part 1, Southampton 1865, item 53.

12. J. Ashdown-Hill, 'Norfolk Requiem: the Passing of the House of Mowbray', *Ricardian* vol. 12 (March 2001), pp. 198–217 (p. 208).

13. Harl. 433, f. 308v; vol. 3, p. 190.

14. For references to Cecily's Scrope marriage see: Ellis / Vergil, p. 215, P. Sheppard Routh '"Lady Scroop Daughter of K. Edward": an Enquiry', *Ricardian* vol. 9 (1991–93), pp. 410–16 (pp. 412, 416, n. 12) and Laynesmith, *The Last Medieval Queens*, p. 199.

15. '*casamento da filha delRej Duarte de Inglaterra ... com o duque de Beja Dom Manuel ... o qual casamento antes fora a elRej apontado por Duarte Brandão sendo uindo por embaixador del Rej Richarte jrmão do ditto Rej Duarte a jurar as ligas e commeter casamento com a Iffante Dona Joana.*' A. Mestrinho Salgado and Salgado, *Álvaro Lopes de Chaves, Livro de Apontamentos (1438–1489)*, as cited in A. S. Marques, 'Álvaro Lopes de Cheves [*sic*]: A Portuguese Source', *Ricardian Bulletin*, Autumn 2008, pp. 25–27.

16. Maxwell-Lyte, ed., *The Registers of Robert Stillington, Bishop of Bath and Wells 1466–1491 and Richard Fox, Bishop of Bath and Wells 1492–1494*, p. xiii.

17. *Rotuli Parliamentorum*, vol. 6, p. 289.

18. Bernard André (who wrote for the Tudors, and esteemed the claimant an impostor) asserted that the first Yorkist pretender of Henry VII's reign impersonated Elizabeth Widville's second son by Edward IV, Richard of Shrewsbury, Duke of York: G. Smith, 'Lambert Simnel and the King from Dublin', *Ricardian* vol. 10 (December 1996), pp. 498–536, p. 499.

19. '... there [was] never a new torche but old torches', MS BL Arundel 26, f. 30, quoted in Sutton &. Visser-Fuchs, *The Royal Funerals of the House of York at Windsor*, p. 73.

28 1485–1574: Fates of the Royal Bastards

1. P. Beauclerk-Dewar and R. Powell, *Royal Bastards*, Stroud 2008, p. 18.

2. Incidentally, it is also claimed that the one recognised illegitimate son of Richard III was also executed by the government of Henry VII.

3. 1534?

4. M. St Clare Byrne, ed., *The Lisle Letters*, London 1981, vol. 2, p. 63, no. 136.

5. G. E. C., V. Gibbs, H. A. Doubleday &. Lord Howard de Walden, eds, *The Complete Peerage*, vol. 8, London 1932, p. 63.

6. St Clare Byrne, ed., *The Lisle Letters*, vol. 2, p. 271, no. 265.

7. St Clare Byrne, ed., *The Lisle Letters*, vol. 2, p. 619, no. 479.

8. Myers / Buck, *Richard the Third*, p. 115; (Kincaid / Buck, p. 175), present author's emphasis.

9. Myers / Buck, *Richard the Third*, p. 121; (Kincaid / Buck, p. 182).

10. *The Lisle Letters*, vol. 3, p. 465.

11. *The Lisle Letters*, vol. 2, p. 84, no. 149.

12. *The Lisle Letters*, vol. 3, pp. 466–67, no. 751.

13. http://www.british-history.ac.uk/search?query=Lacy&title=A%20 History%20of%20the%20County%20of%20Hampshire%3A%20 Volume%205 (consulted May 2015).

14. http://www.british-history.ac.uk/vch/hants/vol3/pp323-325 (consulted May 2015).

15. St Clare-Byrne, *Lisle Letters*, vol 1, p. 145; present author's notes.

16. St Clare-Byrne, *Lisle Letters*, vol 1, pp. 145; 148

17. See Ashdown-Hill, *The Dublin King*, chapter 17.

18. Ashdown-Hill, *The Wars of the Roses*, chapter 13.

19. Thomas Talbot, Viscount Lisle, was named as the heir of his aunt, Lady Eleanor, in her inquisition *post mortem*, PRO C 140/29: '... *Thomas Talbot miles dominus Lisle est heres eius propinquior*'. Arthur Plantagenet's first wife was Thomas Talbot's niece.

20. In the reigns of Henry VIII and Charles II. For example, 'in a correspondence from June 1525 the Cardinal [Wolsey] makes sure to ask for the King's son: *Your entirely beloved sonne, the Lord Henry FitzRoy*'. https:// en.wikipedia.org/wiki/Henry_FitzRoy,_1st_Duke_of_Richmond_and_ Somerset (consulted April 2016).

21. https://en.wikipedia.org/wiki/Adam_FitzRoy (consulted April 2016), quoting Edward II's Wardrobe account of 1322.

22. http://archiver.rootsweb.ancestry.com/th/read/GEN-MEDIEVAL/ 2003-03/1047357277 (consulted April 2016).

23. https://en.wikipedia.org/wiki/Antigone_Plantagenet,_Countess_of_ Tankerville (consulted April 2016).

24. P. W. Hammond & A. F. Sutton, *Richard III, the Road to Bosworth Field*, London 1985, p. 202, citing Foedera, vol. 12, p. 265. Rymer's *Foedera*, vol. 12 states 'Dilecti Filii nostri *Bastardi, Johannis de Gloucestria*', http://www. british-history.ac.uk/rymer-foedera/vol12/pp255-271 (consulted April 2016).

25. R. Horrox and P. W. Hammond, eds, *British Library Harleian Manuscript 433*, London, 1979, vol. I, p. 271.

26. C. A. Halstead, *Richard III*, vol. 2, London 1844, pp. 487–88 and pp. 569–70, citing Harl. MS 258, f. 11b.

27. P. Hammond, 'The Illegitimate Children of Edward IV', *The Ricardian*, vol. 13 (2003), pp. 229–233 (p. 231). The source for this document is not cited.

28. Hammond, *op. cit.*, p. 232.

29. Hammond, *op. cit.*, p. 232.

30. Hammond, *op. cit.*, p. 233.

29 Conclusions

1. November 1485: *RP*, vol. 6, p. 270.

Appendix

1. G. M. Logan, ed., Thomas More, *The History of King Richard the Third*, Indiana 2005, p. 100.

2. L. E. Tanner & W. Wright, 'Recent Investigations Regarding the Fate of the Princes in the Tower', *Archaeologia* 84 (1935), pp. 1–26.

3. E.g. by Dr Jean Ross; see R. Drewett and M. Redhead, *The Trial of Richard III*, Gloucester 1984, p. 66.

4. N. H. Bramwell and R. M. Byard, 'The Bones in the Abbey: Are They the Murdered Princes?: A Review of the Evidence', *American Journal of Forensic Medicine & Pathology:* 10, no. 1 (March 1989); Ashdown-Hill, *The Secret Queen* (2016 edition), pp. 249–50.

5. The assumption that the bones in the Westminster Abbey urn are those of the sons of Edward IV is little more than conjecture. Aside from some resemblance to the account of More, no other evidence exists to link the two. In fact, More did not claim that the bodies were permanently buried under the stairs, but that they were moved to an unknown location. Logan /More, *The History of King Richard the Third*, p. 101.

6. T. E. King *et al.*, 'Identification of the Remains of King Richard III', *Nature Communications* 5, no. Article 5631 (2014), http://www.nature.com/ncomms/2014/141202/ncomms6631/full/ncomms6631.html (consulted 12 July 2016).

7. J. Ashdown-Hill, 'Alive and Well in Canada – The Mitochondrial DNA of Richard III', *The Ricardian* 16 (2006) pp. 1–14 (p. 7).

8. T. E. King and M. A. Jobling, 'Founders, Drift, and Infidelity: The Relationship between Y Chromosome Diversity and Patrilineal Surnames', *Molecular Biology and Evolution* 26, no. 5 (2009), pp. 1093–1102.

9. King *et al.*, 'Identification of the Remains of King Richard III'.

10. M. Jones, *Bosworth: Psychology of a Battle*, London 2014, pp. 79–90; M. Jones, 'The Alleged Illegitimacy of Edward IV: a Window on a Scandal', *Foundations*, (2004) 1 (4), pp. 292–93 (http://fmg.ac/phocadownload/userupload/foundations1/issue4/292EdwardIV.pdf, consulted July 2016).

11. J. Ashdown-Hill, *The Last Days of Richard III and the Fate of His DNA: The Book That Inspired the Dig*, Stroud 2013, pp. 149–50.

12. K. G. Everingham, ed., D. Richardson, *Magna Carta Ancestry: A Study in Colonical And Medieval Families (Royal Ancestry)*, 2nd Edition, vol. 1, Salt Lake City 2011, p. 171.

13. The National Archives Website, 'Discovery: PROB 11/25/546. Will of Sir George Nevill or Lord Burgavenny' 4 July 1536, The National Archives, Kew, http://discovery.nationalarchives.gov.uk/details/r/D977212.

14. H. Pierce, *Margaret Pole Countess of Salisbury 1473–1541: Loyalty, Lineage and Leadership*, Cardiff 2003.

15. Strachey, ed., *Rotuli Parliamentorum; vol. 6, London 1777*, pp. 193–95.

16. D. Seward, *The Last White Rose*, London 2010, pp. 120–121.

17. A. Weir, *Britain's Royal Families: The Complete Genealogy*, London 1999, pp. 104–105.

18. Seward, *The Last White Rose*, p. 291.

19. *Op. cit.*, p. 302.

20. Pierce, *Margaret Pole Countess of Salisbury 1473–1541: Loyalty, Lineage and Leadership*.

21. Seward, *The Last White Rose*, p. 318.

22. '*Dilectis nobis in Christo Francisco domino Hastynges, filio et heredi Georgi comitis de Huntyngdonia, et Katherine Mountegue alias Poole, Londoniensis et Wintoniensis respectiue diocesium ... Nuper vero ex parte vestra nobis fuit expositum quod mutuam inter vtriusque vestrum familias amiciciam artiori vinculo confirmandi studio, ex certisque aliis iustis et racionabilibus causis coram nobis expositis et per nos approbatis animum vestrum in hac parte mouentibus, desideratis inter vos matrimonium contrahere, sed quia tercio at quarto consanguinitatis gradibus inuicem coniuncti estis, vestrum in hac parte desiderium adimplere non potestis, canonica dispensacione desuper non obtenta*'. H Chitty, ed., *Registra Stephani Gardiner et Johannis Poynet Episcoporum Wintoniensium*, vol. 37, Canterbury & York Society 1930, pp. 22–23 (translation J. A-H).

23. A. Fraser, *The Gunpowder Plot: Terror And Faith In 1605*, London 1996, pp. 170, 196, 274.

24. The obituary for Lady Laing published in *The Times*, Wednesday, 4 June 1913 includes the following text: 'Lady Laing, the widow of Sir James Laing, of Sunderland, died at Oxford on Monday, in her 81st Year. In the latter half of the last century Lady Laing took a leading part in the social life of Sunderland and was especially active in promoting charitable movements. Lady Laing was the second wife of Sir James and was the daughter of Mr. Thomas Peacock, of Bishop Auckland, and Marianne, his wife daughter of Michael Bryan, the author of "Dictionary of Painters and Engravers" and Juliana Talbot, his wife, sister of Charles, 15th Earl of Shrewsbury. Sir James Laing died in 1901.' 'Lady Laing', *Times* [London, England] 4 June 1913, p. 11. *The Times* Digital Archive (consulted 22 July 2016).

BIBLIOGRAPHY

Original Documents

Corpus Christi College, Cambridge, Parker Library, Ms. XXXI. 121

Essex Record Office (hereinafter ERO), D/B5 Cr76, m. 3r

ERO, D/B5 Cr76, m. 17

ERO, D/B5 Cr76, m. 20v

ERO, D/B5 Cr76, m. 22v

ERO, D/B5 Cr76, m. 25r

ERO, D/B5 Cr76, m. 25r

ERO, D/B5 Cr76, m. 26r

ERO, D/B5 Cr76, m. 27r

Essex Record Office, Red Paper Book of Colchester

Fitzwilliam Museum, Cambridge, MS 329, Anlaby Cartulary

Society of Antiquaries of London (hereinafter Soc. Ant.), MS 76

Soc. Ant., MS 77

Suffolk Record Office, Ipswich, HA 246/B2/498

The National Archives (hereinafter TNA), C 81/782

TNA, C 81/783

TNA, C 81/784

TNA, C 81/785

TNA, C 81/786

TNA, C 81/787

TNA, C 81/788

TNA, C 81/789

TNA, C 81/790

TNA, C 81/791

TNA, C 81/792

TNA, C 81/793

TNA, C 81/794

TNA, C 81/795

TNA, C 81/796

TNA, C 81/797

TNA, C 81/798

TNA, C 81/799

TNA, C 81/800

TNA, C 81/801

TNA, C 81/802

TNA, C 81/803

TNA, C 81/804

TNA, C 81/805

TNA, C 81/806

TNA, C 81/807

TNA, C 81/808

TNA, C 81/809

TNA, C 81/810

TNA, C 81/811

TNA, C 81/812

TNA, C 81/813

TNA, C 81/814

TNA, C 81/815

TNA, C 81/816

TNA, C 81/817

TNA, C 81/818

TNA, C 81/819

TNA, C 81/820

TNA, C 81/821

TNA, C 81/822

TNA, C 81/823

TNA, C 81/824

TNA, C 81/825

TNA, C 81/826

TNA, C 81/827

TNA, C 81/828

TNA, C 81/829

TNA, C 81/830

TNA, C 81/831

TNA, C 81/832

TNA, C 81/833

TNA, C 81/834

TNA, C 81/835

TNA, C 81/836

TNA, C 81/837

TNA, C 81/838

TNA, C 81/839

TNA, C 81/840

TNA, C 81/841

TNA, C 81/842

TNA, C 81/843

TNA, C 81/844

TNA, C 81/845

TNA, C 81/846

TNA, C 81/847

TNA, C 81/848

TNA, C 81/849

TNA, C 81/850

TNA, C 81/851

TNA, C 81/852

TNA, C 81/853

TNA, C 81/854

TNA, C 81/855

TNA, C 81/856

TNA, C 81/857

TNA, C 81/858

TNA, C 81/859

TNA, C 81/860

TNA, C 81/861

TNA, C 81/862

TNA, C 81/863

TNA, C 81/864

TNA, C 81/865

TNA, C 81/866

TNA, C 81/867

TNA, C 81/868

TNA, C 81/869

TNA, C 81/870

TNA, C 81/871

TNA, C 81/872

TNA, C 81/873

TNA, C 81/874

TNA, C 81/875

TNA, C 81/876

TNA, C 81/877

TNA, C 81/878

TNA, C 81/879

TNA, C 81/880

TNA, C 81/881

TNA, C 81/882

TNA, C 81/883

TNA, C 81/884

TNA, C 140/29, Inquisition post mortem of Eleanor Talbot, Lady Butler

TNA, PROB 11/8, f. 52, will of Dame Elizabeth Wayte (Skillyng)

TNA, PSO 1/21

TNA, PSO 1/22

TNA, PSO 1/23

TNA, PSO 1/24

TNA, PSO 1/25

TNA, PSO 1/26

TNA, PSO 1/27

TNA, PSO 1/28

TNA, PSO 1/29

TNA, PSO 1/30

TNA, PSO 1/31

TNA, PSO 1/32

TNA, PSO 1/33

TNA, PSO 1/34

TNA, PSO 1/35

TNA, PSO 1/36

TNA, PSO 1/37

TNA, PSO 1/38

TNA, PSO 1/39

TNA, PSO 1/40

TNA, PSO 1/41

TNA, PSO 1/42

TNA, PSO 1/43

TNA, PSO 1/44

TNA, PSO 1/45

TNA, PSO 1/46

TNA, PSO 1/47

TNA, PSO 1/48

TNA, PSO 1/49

TNA, PSO 1/50

TNA, PSO 1/51

TNA, PSO 1/52

TNA, PSO 1/53

TNA, PSO 1/54

TNA, PSO 1/55

Books

Adams N., and Donahue C., eds, *Select Cases from the Ecclesiastical Courts of the Province of Canterbury, c. 1200–1301*, London 1981

André B. – see Sutton D. F.

Armstrong C. A. J., ed., Mancini D., *The Usurpation [sic] of Richard III*, Gloucester 1989

Ashdown-Hill J., *Eleanor the Secret Queen*, Stroud 2009

Ashdown-Hill J., *Richard III's 'Beloved Cousyn'*, Stroud 2009

Ashdown-Hill J., *Royal Marriage Secrets*, Stroud 2012

Ashdown-Hill J., *The Last Days of Richard III and the Fate of His DNA*, Stroud 2013

Ashdown-Hill J., *The Third Plantagenet*, Stroud 2014

Ashdown-Hill J., *The Mythology of Richard III*, Stroud 2015

Ashdown-Hill J., *The Dublin King*, Stroud 2015

Ashdown-Hill J., *The Wars of the Roses*, Stroud 2015

Ashdown-Hill J., *The Secret Queen*, Stroud 2016

Baga de Secretis – see *Third Report of the Deputy Keeper of the Public Records*

Barnardiston K. W., *Clare Priory*, Cambridge 1962

Beauclerk-Dewar P. & Powell R., *Royal Bastards*, Stroud 2008

Beaune H., and d'Arbaumont J., eds, *Mémoires d'Olivier de la Marche*, 4 vols., vol. 3, Paris 1885

Bentley S., ed, *Excerpta Historica*, London 1831

Berry W., *County Genealogies, Pedigrees of the Families of the County of Hampshire*, London 1833

Bruce J., ed., *Historie of the Arrivall of Edward IV in England*, London 1838

Buchon J.-A., ed., G. Chastellain, *Chronique des Ducs de Bourgogne*, vol. 1, Paris 1827

Bibliography

Buck G. – *see* Kincaid; Myers

Burrows R., *Guidelines for Mystical Prayer*, London 1976

Calendar of Close Rolls, Edward IV, vol. 2, 1468–1476, London 1953

Calendar of Close Rolls, Edward IV, Edward V, Richard III, 1476–1485, London 1954

Calendar of Inquisitions, Edward III, vol. 11

Calendar of Inquisitions Post Mortem, vol. 17

Calendar of Papal Registers, vol. 12, *Papal Letters 1458–1471*, London 1933

Calendar of Patent Rolls 1399–1401, London 1903

Calendar of Patent Rolls 1413–1416, London 1910

Calendar of Patent Rolls 1461–1467, London 1897

Chitty H., ed., *Registra Stephani Gardiner et Johannis Poynet Episcoporum Wintoniensium*, vol. 37, Canterbury & York Society 1930

Chronicles of the White Rose of York – see Giles

Clive M., *This Sun of York*, London 1973

Commynes, P. de – *see* Jones

Complete Peerage, vol. 8 – see G. E. C.

Cook M., ed., *A Gay History of Britain*, Oxford 2007

Cornwallis – see Kincaid

Crawford A., ed., *Howard Household Books*, Stroud 1992

Crawford A., *The Yorkists: the History of a Dynasty*, London 2007

Crowland Chronicle – see Pronay

Davies R., ed. *Extracts from the Municipal Records of the City of York*, London 1843 (reprinted Dursley, 1976)

Davis N., ed., *Paston Letters and Papers of the fifteenth century*, 2 vols., Oxford 1971; 1976

Dictionary of National Biography, vol. 12, Oxford 1968

Dictionary of National Biography, vol. 46, London 1896

Dictionary of National Biography, supplement 1, London 1901 – see Lee, ed.

Dockray K., *Edward IV, a source book*, Stroud 1999

Drewett R. and Redhead M., *The Trial of Richard III*, Gloucester 1984

Edwards R., *The Itinerary of King Richard III 1483–1485*, London 1983

Ellis H., ed., Fabyan R., *The New Chronicles of England and France*, London 1811 Ellis H, ed., *Three Bookes of Polydore Vergil's English History comprising the reigns of Henry VI, Edward IV and Richard III*, London 1844

Emden A. B., *A Biographical Register of the University of Oxford to A.D. 1500*, 3 vols, Oxford 1957–59

Everingham K. G., ed., Richardson D., *Magna Carta Ancestry: A Study in Colonical And Medieval Families (Royal Ancestry)*, 2nd Edition, vol. 1, Salt Lake City 2011

Fabyan, Chronicle – see Ellis

Fraser A., *The Gunpowder Plot: Terror And Faith In 1605*, London 1996

Gairdner J., ed., *The Historical Collections of a Citizen of London in the Fifteenth Century*, London (Camden Society, new ser., 17) 1876

Gairdner J, *History of the Life and Reign of Richard the Third*, Cambridge 1898

Gairdner J., ed., *The Paston Letters*, 1904, Reprinted Gloucester 1983

G. E. C., Gibbs V., Doubleday H. A. & Lord Howard de Walden, eds, *The Complete Peerage*, vol. 8, London 1932

Giles J. A., & Warkworth J., *The Chronicles of the White Rose of York*, London 1845

Gregory's Chronicle – see Gairdner

Griffiths R. A., *The Reign of Henry VI*, London 1981

Grimstone H. & Leach T., eds, *Reports of Sir George Croke, Knight, of ... Select Cases*, Dublin 1793

Gurney Benham W., ed. / trans. *The Red Paper Book of Colchester*, Colchester 1902

Halstead C. A., *Richard III*, vol. 2, London 1844

Hammond P. W., & Sutton A. F., *Richard III: The Road to Bosworth*, London 1985

Hardy W. & E. L. C. P., eds, Wavrin, *Receuil des Chroniques*, vol. 5 Cambridge 1891, 2012.

Harris B. J., *English Aristocratic Women, 1450–1550*, Oxford 2010

Hearne T., ed., *Joannis Rossi Antiquarii Warwicensis Historia Regum Angliae*, London 1716

Hearne T., *Liber Niger Scaccarii nec non Wilhelmi Worcestrii Annales Rerum Anglicarum*, vol. 2, London 1774

Hearne's 'Fragment of an old chronicle from 1460 to 1470' – see Giles, ed., *The Chronicles of the White Rose of York*

Hicks M., *False, Fleeting, Perjur'd Clarence*, 2nd edition, Bangor 1992

Horrox R. and Hammond P. W., eds, *British Library Harleian Manuscript 433*, London, 1979, vol. I

Jones M., ed., *Philippe de Commynes Memoires*, Harmondsworth 1972

Jones M., *Bosworth: Psychology of a Battle*, London 2014

Kendall P. M., *Warwick the Kingmaker*, London 1973

Kincaid A. N., ed., W. Cornwallis, *The Encomium of Richard III*, London 1977

Kincaid A. N., ed., G. Buck, *The History of King Richard III (1619)*, Gloucester 1979

Kingsford C. L., ed., A Survey of London by John Stow, reprinted from the text of 1603, 2 vols, vol. 2, Oxford 1908

Kinney D., ed., *The Complete Works of St Thomas More*, 15 volumes, vol. 15, *Historia Richardi Tertii*, Yale University 1986

Laynesmith J. L., *The Last Medieval Queens*, Oxford 2004

Bibliography

Leland J. – see Toulmin Smith

Lee S., ed., *Dictionary of National Biography,* supplement 1, London 1901

List of Escheators for England and Wales, List and Index Society, vol. 72, London 1971

Lydgate – see Gairdner (1876)

Lyell L. & Watney F. D., eds, *Acts of Court of the Mercers' Company 1453–1527*, Cambridge 1936

Logan G. M., ed., Thomas More, *The History of King Richard the Third*, Indiana 2005

Mancini D., – *see* Armstrong

Masters R., *History of the College of Corpus Christi and the Blessed Virgin Mary*, Cambridge 1753

Maxwell-Lyte H. C., ed., *The Registers of Robert Stillington, Bishop of Bath and Wells 1466–1491 and Richard Fox, Bishop of Bath and Wells 1492–1494*, Somerset Record Society 1937

Mazo Karras R., *From Boys to Men*, Philadelphia 2003

Mee A., *The King's England: Hampshire*, London 1939

More T., *Richard III* – see published editions by Kinney; Logan; Rawson Lumby, and Sylvester

Morgan O., and Wakeman T., *Notes on the Architecture and History of Caldicot Castle*, Monmouthshire, Newport 1854

Myers A. R., ed., Buck G., *The History of the Life and Reigne of Richard the Third*, London 1646; Wakefield 1973

Nicholls J. and Bruce J., eds, *Wills from Doctors' Commons. A selection of Wills of eminent persons proved in the PCC 1495–1695*, Camden old series, vol. 83, London 1863

Paston Letters – see Davis; Gairdner

Pedersen F., *Marriage Disputes in Medieval England*, London, 2000

Penman S., *The Sunne in Splendour*, London 1982

Pevsner N. and Lloyd D., *The Buildings of England: Hampshire and the Isle of Wight*, Harmondsworth 1967

Pierce H., *Margaret Pole Countess of Salisbury 1473–1541: Loyalty, Lineage and Leadership*, Cardiff 2003

Pollard A. F., 'Beaufort, Henry (1436–1464)' – see Lee, ed., *Dictionary of National Biography,* supplement 1

Potter J., *Good King Richard?*, London 1983

Pronay N. & Cox J., *The Crowland Chronicle Continuations 1459–1486*, 1986

Rawson Lumby J., ed., Sir Thomas More, *History of King Richard III*, Cambridge 1883

Rerum Britannicarum Medii Aevi Scriptores, or *Chronicles and Memorials of Great Britain and Ireland during The Middle Ages*, London 1857

Riley H. T., ed., *Ingulph's Chronicle of the Abbey of Croyland*, London 1908

Ross C., *Edward IV*, London 1974

Rotuli Parliamentorum – see Strachey

St Clare Byrne M., ed., *The Lisle Letters*, 6 vols, Chicago 1981

Scofield C., *The Life and Reign of Edward the Fourth*, 2 vols, London 1923, 1967

Serpell M. F., *Kenninghall History and St Mary's Church*, Norwich 1982

Seward D., *The Last White Rose*, London 2010

Smith G., ed., *The Coronation of Elizabeth Wydeville, Queen Consort of Edward IV*, London 1935, reprinted Cliftonville 1975

Stevenson J., ed., *Letters and papers illustrative of the Wars of the English in France during the reign of King Henry the Sixth, King of England*, vol. 1, London 1861

Stone L., *The Family, Sex and Marriage in England 1500–1800*, London 1979

Strachey J., ed., *Rotuli Parliamentorum; ut et Petitiones, et Placita in Parliamento*, vol. 6, London 1777

Stratford L., *Edward the Fourth*, London 1910

Sutton A. F., and Visser-Fuchs L., *The Royal Funerals of the House of York at Windsor*, London 2004

Sutton D. F., ed., Bernard André, *De Vita atque Gestis Henrici Septimi Historia*, online 2010

Sylvester R. S., ed., St Thomas More, *The History of King Richard III and selections from the English and Latin Poems*, London 1976

Talbot H., *The English Achilles: the life and campaigns of John Talbot, 1ˢᵗ Earl of Shrewsbury*, London 1981

Tannahill R., *Sex in History*, London 1980

Tey J., *The Daughter of Time*, Harmondsworth 1951, 1974

The Visitation of Warwickshire, 1619, Harleian Society, vol. 12, 1877

Third Report of the Deputy Keeper of the Public Records (February 28, 1842), London 1842

Thomas A. H. & Thornley I. D., eds, *The Great Chronicle of London*, London: George W. Jones 1938

Thornbury W., *Old and New London*, 6 vols [n.d., 19th century] vols. 1 & 2

Toulmin Smith L., ed., *The Itinerary of John Leland in or about the years 1535–1543*, parts 7 and 8, London 1909

Vaughan R., *Charles the Bold*, second edition, Woodbridge 2002

VCH *Hampshire*, vol. 3, London 1973

VCH *Hampshire*, vol. 4, London, 1911

VCH, *Wiltshire*, vol. 11, London 1980

Vergil P., *English History* – see Ellis

Walford E., *Greater London*, 2 vols, London [n.d., 19th century] vol. 1

Bibliography

Ward J., *Women in Medieval Europe 1200–1500*, London 2002

Wavrin – see Hardy

Weightman C., Margaret of York Duchess of Burgundy 1446–1503, Gloucester 1989

Weir A., *Britain's Royal Families: The Complete Genealogy*, London 1999

Wilkinson J., *Richard, the Young King to Be*, Stroud 2009

Wolters C., ed., *The Cloud of Unknowing*, Harmondsworth 1961

Worcester, William – see Hearne; Stevenson.

Papers

Ashdown-Hill J., 'The Elusive Mistress: Elizabeth Lucy and her Family', *Ricardian*, vol. 11, June 1999, pp. 490–505

Ashdown-Hill J., 'Norfolk Requiem: the Passing of the House of Mowbray', *Ricardian* 12, March 2001, pp. 198–217

Ashdown-Hill J., 'Yesterday my Lord of Gloucester came to Colchester', *Essex History*, vol. 36, 2005, pp. 212–17

Ashdown-Hill J., 'The Go-between', *Ricardian* vol. 15, 2005, pp. 119–21

Ashdown-Hill J., & Carson A., 'The Execution of the Earl of Desmond', *Ricardian* vol. 15, 2005, pp. 70–93

Ashdown-Hill J., 'Alive and Well in Canada – The Mitochondrial DNA of Richard III', *Ricardian* vol. 16, 2006, pp. 1–14

Ashdown-Hill J., 'The Wills of John Talbot, first Earl of Shrewsbury, and of his sons Lord Lisle and Sir Louis Talbot', *Transactions of the Shropshire Archaeological & Historical Society* 2010, pp. 31–37

Barker N., 'Jane Shore', *Etoniana*, no. 125, June 1972, pp. 383–91

Barnfield M., 'Diriment Impediments, Dispensations and Divorce: Richard III and Matrimony', *Ricardian*, vol. 17 (2007), pp. 84–98

Bramwell N. H. and Byard R. M., 'The Bones in the Abbey: Are They the Murdered Princes?: A Review of the Evidence', *American Journal of Forensic Medicine & Pathology:* 10, no. 1, March 1989

Hammond P., 'The Illegitimate Children of Edward IV', *Ricardian*, vol. 13, 2003, pp. 229–233

Hampton W. E., 'The Ladies of the Minories', *Ricardian*, vol. 4, no. 62, September 1978, pp. 15–22

Gough Nichols J., 'Observations on the Heraldic Devices discovered on the Effigies of Richard the Second and his Queen in Westminster Abbey, and upon the Mode in which those Ornaments were executed; including some Remarks on the surname Plantagenet and on the Ostrich Feathers of the Prince of Wales', *Archaeologia*, vol. 29, part 1, 1841, pp. 32–59

Jackson J. E., 'The Execution of Ankarette Twynyho', [published source unknown] 1890, [print-off in Wiltshire Archaeological and Natural History Society Library]

King T. E. and Jobling M. A., 'Founders, Drift, and Infidelity: The Relationship between Y Chromosome Diversity and Patrilineal Surnames', *Molecular Biology and Evolution* 26, no. 5 (2009), pp. 1093–1102

Lulofs M., 'King Edward IV in Exile', *Ricardian* vol. 3, no 44, March 1974, pp. 9–11

Marques A. S., 'Álvaro Lopes de Cheves [*sic*]: A Portuguese Source', *Ricardian Bulletin*, Autumn 2008, pp. 25–27

Mowat A. J., 'Robert Stillington', *Ricardian* vol. 4 (June 1976), p. 23

Sheppard Routh P. '"Lady Scroop Daughter of K. Edward": an Enquiry', *Ricardian* 9 (1991–93), pp. 410–16

Skuse R., 'Richard III's Children', *The Rose and Crown* (magazine of the Beds & Bucks Group of the Richard III Society) no. 44, July 2008, pp. 6–7

Smith G., 'Lambert Simnel and the King from Dublin', *Ricardian* vol. 10, December 1996, pp. 498–536

Sutton A. F., 'William Shore, merchant of London and Derby', *Derbyshire Archaeological Journal*, 106 (1986), pp. 127–39

Visser-Fuchs L., 'Edward IV's Memoir on Paper to Charles, Duke of Burgundy', *Nottingham Medieval Studies XXXVI* (1992), pp. 167–227

Internet

Calendar of *IPM* 20 – part 2 (consulted February 2015)

Calendar of *IPM* 20 – Part 3 (consulted February 2015)

http://archiver.rootsweb.ancestry.com/th/read/GEN-MEDIEVAL/2003-03/1047357277 (consulted April 2016)

https://en.wikipedia.org/wiki/Adam_FitzRoy (consulted April 2016)

https://en.wikipedia.org/wiki/Antigone_Plantagenet,_Countess_of_Tankerville (consulted April 2016)

https://en.wikipedia.org/wiki/Arthur_Plantagenet,_1st_Viscount_Lisle (consulted March 2016)

https://en.wikipedia.org/wiki/Clarendon_Palace (consulted December 2015)

https://en.wikipedia.org/wiki/Elizabeth_Woodville (consulted November 2015) (consulted June 2015)

https://en.wikipedia.org/wiki/Henry_FitzRoy,_1st_Duke_of_Richmond_and_Somerset (consulted April 2016)

https://en.wikipedia.org/wiki/High_Sheriff_of_Surrey (consulted December 2015)

https://en.wikipedia.org/wiki/Jane_Shore (consulted February 2016)

http://en.wikipedia.org/wiki/Margaret_of_France,_Queen_of_England (consulted May 2015)

http://en.wikipedia.org/wiki/Page-boy (consulted May 2015)

http://en.wikipedia.org/wiki/Richard_of_York,_3rd_Duke_of_York (consulted May 2015)

Bibliography

http://fr.wikipedia.org/wiki/Charles_VII_%28roi_de_France%29 (consulted April 2015)

http://records.ancestry.co.uk/jane_greene_records.ashx?pid=41442247 (consulted February 2015)

https://finds.org.uk/database/artefacts/record/id/61806 (consulted April 2016)

http://www.windowonwoking.org.uk/sites/goldsworthparkcommunityassociation/ GPnews/sherrifs (consulted December 2015)

http://powys.org/pl_tree/ps12/ps12_218.html (consulted December 2015)

http://www.british-history.ac.uk/search?query=Lacy&title=A%20History%20 of%20the%20County%20of%20Hampshire%3A%20Volume%205 (consulted May 2015)

http://www.british-history.ac.uk/vch/hants/vol3/pp323-325 (consulted May 2015)

http://www.british-history.ac.uk/vch/hants/vol4/pp417-422 (consulted February 2015)

http://familytreemaker.genealogy.com/users/d/u/n/Sandra-J-Duncan/WEBSITE-0001/UHP-0183.html (consulted February 2015)

http://www.mytrees.com/ancestry/United-Kingdom/Married-1444/Wa/Wayte-family/Thomas-Wayte-el000623-38908.html (consulted February 2015)

http://www.sanhs.org/Proc%20Extr/Proc%20Yatton.htm (consulted February 2015) http://wc.rootsweb.ancestry.com/cgi-bin/igm.cgi?op=GET&db=ancesto rsearch&id=I41336 (consulted February 2015)

Jones M., 'The Alleged Illegitimacy of Edward IV: a Window on a Scandal', *Foundations*, (2004) 1 (4), pp. 292-93, http://fmg.ac/phocadownload/ userupload/foundations1/issue4/292EdwardIV.pdf (consulted July 2016)

King T. E. et *al.*, 'Identification of the Remains of King Richard III', *Nature Communications* 5, no. Article 5631 (2014), http://www.nature.com/ ncomms/2014/141202/ncomms6631/full/ncomms6631.html (consulted 12 July 2016)

Rogers I. S., 'Tocotes, Sir Roger', *www.girders.net/To/Tocotes,%20Sir%20 Roger,%20(d.1492).doc* (consulted June 2013)

Rymer T., *Foedera*:

http://www.british-history.ac.uk/rymer-foedera/vol11/pp512-531 (consulted September 2015)

http://www.british-history.ac.uk/rymer-foedera/vol11/pp531-538 (consulted September 2015)

http://www.british-history.ac.uk/rymer-foedera/vol11/pp650-660 (consulted September 2015)

http://www.british-history.ac.uk/rymer-foedera/vol11/pp714-733 (consulted September 2015)

http://www.british-history.ac.uk/rymer-foedera/vol11/pp792-815 (consulted September 2015)

http://www.british-history.ac.uk/rymer-foedera/vol11/pp815-820
   (consulted September 2015)
http://www.british-history.ac.uk/rymer-foedera/vol11/pp820-842
   (consulted September 2015)
http://www.british-history.ac.uk/rymer-foedera/vol12/pp14-22
   (consulted September 2015)
http://www.british-history.ac.uk/rymer-foedera/vol12/pp22-39
   (consulted September 2015)
http://www.british-history.ac.uk/rymer-foedera/vol12/pp119-139
   (consulted September 2015)
http://www.british-history.ac.uk/rymer-foedera/vol12/pp145-158
   (consulted September 2015)
http://www.british-history.ac.uk/rymer-foedera/vol12/pp159-172
   (consulted September 2015)
http://www.british-history.ac.uk/rymer-foedera/vol12/pp255-271
   (consulted April 2016)
Three Fifteenth-Century Chronicles: http://www.british-history.ac.uk/camden-record-soc/vol28/ (consulted May 2015)
Times [London, England] 4 June 1913, p. 11. *The Times* Digital Archive http://find.galegroup.com.ezproxy.library.yorku.ca/ttda/infomark.do?&source=gale&prodId=TTDA&userGroupName=yorku_main&tabID=T003&docPage=article&searchType=AdvancedSearchForm&docId=CS186712260&type=multipage&contentSet=LTO&version=1.0 (consulted 22 July 2016)

Oxford Dictionary of National Biography
Hicks M., 'Elizabeth [*née* Elizabeth Woodville]'
Horrox R., 'Shore (*née* Lambert), Elizabeth'
Jones M., 'Beaufort, Henry, second Duke of Somerset'
Macdougall N., 'Mary of Gueldres'

Unpublished Sources
Ashdown-Hill L. J. F., *The client network and connections of Sir John Howard (Lord Howard, first Duke of Norfolk) in north east Essex and south Suffolk*, unpublished PhD Thesis, 2 vols., University of Essex 2008
Pollard A. J., *The Family of Talbot, Lords Talbot and Earls of Shrewsbury in the Fifteenth Century*, unpublished PhD thesis, University of Bristol 1968
Ross B., *An account of the Talbot Household at Blakemere in the County of Shropshire, 1394–1425*, unpublished M.A. thesis, 2 vols., University of Canberra 1970

ACKNOWLEDGEMENTS

I am very grateful to my publishers at Amberley for asking me to write this book. The initial inspiration for it came from them!

I should also like to thank Glen Moran for very kindly allowing me – and helping me – to include his research regarding the mtDNA of Elizabeth Widville and her descendants in an appendix.

Once again I have to thank Dave Perry for proofreading my text for me, and ironing out my typos. In addition, I am grateful to him for helping me in a number of ways with my research on, and publication of, the itinerary of Edward IV.

I should also like to thank all those at The National Archives who assisted me in various ways with my research on Edward IV's movements.

ABOUT THE AUTHOR

John Ashdown-Hill is a historian, a Fellow of the Society of Antiquaries, a Fellow of the Royal Historical Society, and a member of the Society of Genealogists, the Richard III Society and the Centre Européen d'Études Bourguignonnes. He was Leader of Genealogical Research and Historical Advisor for the Looking for Richard Project and is the author of The Last Days of Richard III, the book that inspired the dig. John lives near Colchester in Essex.

INDEX